Contemplative Intimacy

By the same author:
Exploration into Contemplative Prayer
A Work Begun
Meeting Schools of Oriental Meditation

Contemplative Intimacy

HERBERT SLADE SSJE

DARTON LONGMAN AND TODD

First published in Great Britain in 1977
by Darton, Longman and Todd Ltd
85 Gloucester Road, London SW7 4SU

© 1977 Herbert Slade

ISBN 0 232 51367 8

Printed in Great Britain by The Anchor Press Ltd
and bound by Wm. Brendon & Son Ltd, both of Tiptree, Essex

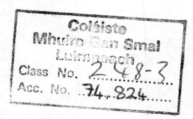

Contents

Preface

It is dangerous to generalise about the state of theological thought but some risks must be taken and already have been taken by others of great authority and theological skill. To take two examples: the Fathers of Vatican II and more recently members of the Doctrine Commission of the Church of England. Both have shared certain theological conclusions which we may take as representing important trends in theological thought.

They have rejected a great deal of traditional theological material. They have questioned the conclusions of many of their predecessors from the manicheistically biased teaching of much of St Augustine's moral theology to the fundamental approach to Holy Scripture. They have cut great swathes through much that until recently has been accepted by the Church without question.

Again they have moved into an open attitude towards many problems that once were accepted as solved. A pluriformity of faith is now commonly recognised as the best way of formulating truth about God. Similar liberty is allowed with regard to liturgy and the great debate about sexuality has moved into much more open ground. The accepted conclusion that sexuality was for the procreation of children and that other ways of using this energy were dangerous perversions is now being once more seriously examined. Vladimir Solovyev's courageous exploration of this subject in his great book *The Meaning of Love* is once more being re-examined.

With this openness to the Christian tradition has grown an interest and flexibility towards others. No longer is there to be found among Christian theologians that exclusive confidence that all truth is to be found in the teaching of the Church. With St John, theologians are now ready to find and recognise the true light in other traditions. This does not seem likely to lead to serious syncretism; there are already signs that open contact with other traditions wonderfully illuminates one's own.

As a result of these theological changes traditional church structures are now under severe critical scrutiny. This applies both to the organisation of the Church and ministry and to the religious life in its many forms. Once more the doors are open and the adventure of faith in terms of exploration has begun.

All these theological trends must have their repercussions on the life of thoughtful Christians and especially on those engaged in the living experiences of contemplative prayer. This prayer leads to God and to mankind in increasing degrees of intimacy and this intimacy presents problems which insist on being faced by those who would grow in prayer. They are the great theological and moral problems of contemporary theology; faith, inter-relationships, especially sexuality in all its forms, and life structures. All who would explore contemplative prayer in depth must meet them on the way.

This book is offered as a contribution of some discoveries in a venture of contemplative prayer which has now been lived out the hard way through more than seven years of shared exploration. It does not attempt to give final solutions but the sharing of what has been found on the way may well reassure and encourage others and it is hoped that it will contribute towards the great task of the Christian Church to achieve and share its life in God.

1
The Anchorhold family

When the senator, Arsenius, lived in a palace, he prayed God to lead him in the way of salvation and a voice said to him: 'Arsenius, flee from men and you will be saved'. Having been trained in the greatest civil service in the world and being accustomed to understand orders literally Arsenius left his palace and his companions and joined the desert fathers to seek salvation through the lonely disciplines of the solitary life. Before and since his time many believers in many religions have chosen this path, some to find his peace and others to be frustrated by ego-fantasies of terrifying proportions.

The New Testament makes it quite clear that this was not the way taken by the incarnate Lord during his pre-resurrection ministry nor the path mapped out by Him for his Church when He sent her forth to every part of the world with orders to proclaim the good news to the whole creation. Nor is it the way of the Society of St John the Evangelist as received through the father founder. At an early stage it seemed that it might be the inescapable vocation of a small offshoot of the Society, but mercifully events led to another course.

NO HERMIT VOCATION

The small offshoot started to grow in January, 1969 with two members, but by the end of February this family was reduced to one. To that one member it might well have seemed that his vocation was to be a flight from men, and in those early days of loneliness in a small house and garden the horror of this possible situation was painfully realised. Then events which changed this future began to happen.

Slowly the nucleus of a family was formed as one by one men were sent to share the adventure. Gradually visitors joined this nucleus for short periods, and then came invitations to go to a few parts of the whole creation to share the good news. It became clear that whatever life was going to grow it would not take the solitary form of the desert fathers and that so far from this vocation being a withdrawal from men it was to be an ever-deepening intimacy with the whole creation. For not only was the family increased by the coming of friends, it grew with the incorporation of other creatures: bees, two tortoises who stayed only a short time, hens and, later, a pair of loyal and sin-bearing goats.

SOME FAMILY MODELS

Natural and religious

There were two family experiences to draw on: the natural family and the religious family. Both of these had valuable contributions to make towards our own building, but we soon found that neither could give us all we needed. From the natural family we had the memories of firm parental guidance, a deep happiness and the need to withdraw at the growing point of adolescence in order to find a mature response to the Father's business. From the religious family there were experiences of a novitiate which had powerfully eradicated one form of egotism leaving the possibility of immature dependence on traditional ways and rules. There were also memories of the deepest joy, which helped to obliterate the fears of going out into the world and coming into intimate relationships with the whole creation. These family experiences seemed to have prepared us for the attainment of the threshold of our adventure. Now other models were needed.

The new models of family life which were at hand and which have proved of the greatest value were found in the description of Scott's Antarctic family and Wilfred Owen's record of the community life he found during the first world war, supplemented by experiences which confirmed his picture and had been shared by some of our contemporaries in the second.

Scott at Hut Point

Scott's Antarctic family was a remarkable and original achievement, especially when considered against the background of his times. It has been described by an artistic genius who, in the objective prose of his journal, left behind the materials needed to reconstruct its life with all the vividness of emotion recollected in tranquillity. Its founder had already failed in the natural family and part of his quest was to find an environment in which he could work out the frustrations of a complicated personality. In founding and guiding this family, Scott created a unique pattern of community life and through it led a mixed group of men to an intimacy which transformed his expedition from a failure into one of the supreme triumphs of the human spirit. A glimpse of this achievement shines through these concluding words:

'We are in a desperate state, feet frozen, etc. No fuel and a long way from food, but it would do your heart good to be in our tent, to hear our songs and the cheery conversation as to what we will do when we get to Hut Point. . . .'

(Scott's Last Expedition: Extracts from the personal journals of Capt. R.F. Scott, R.N.)

Having decided not to kill themselves these men found 'that in fighting there is a painless end' and Scott's certainty that pain would be transcended came true as he left the world 'fresh from harness and full of good health and vigour'. Such an end proved the soundness of his family structure and encouraged us to examine it more carefully as a model for our own.

Scott's family was made up of the most varied ingredients. When the Terra Nova left Port Lyttelton it was loaded like a Noah's ark. There were men from almost every background: scientists, professional soldiers and sailors, photographers and men of every kind of skill. There were also the animals, the ponies and the dogs. When this family landed at Hut Point the variety was increased by the addition of penguins, seals and birds. Scott played these different components with the skill of a trained naval officer who had commanded battleships.

The family life designed by Scott worked because he never forgot that he was handling intelligent human beings who required appropriate work as well as food and shelter for their wellbeing. At Hut Point he organised the life so that this work was available for everyone. The scientists had space and equipment for their researches, those in charge of the animals were given special quarters: so it was with all the rest. No one was forgotten. Scott also displayed a lively interest in all that was going on and, to relieve the boredom of the long evenings, there were lectures, music and the occasional guest evening. Games were organised and on Sundays Scott read divine service. The hut, fifty feet long by twenty-five feet wide and nine feet to the eaves was both a home and a training ground for the supreme achievement which Scott always kept before the family as its inspiration and unifying force.

Scott used, as the controlling purpose of his family the goal of being the first to reach the South Pole. This was an objective big enough to unite these different and strong-willed individuals into a common thrust of achievement. When it was withdrawn by the discovery that Amunsden had arrived first, it has been rightly said: 'their spirits began to droop and there is little doubt that this disappointment had its effect on the rate of progress back to their base'. So long as it lasted their purpose had channelled an energy of spirit and depth of courage which carried five men to the South Pole and created a saga which will always stir the heart of the world.

Some of the basic structures of Scott's family have been transferred to the Anchorhold. It has rejected the over-detailed and protective features of the natural family and the more rigid and legalistic structures of the religious community and in their place it has used the variety of ingredients which distinguished Scott's creation. The Anchorhold may be less varied in membership than the Terra Nova and the inhabitants of Hut Point, still less of Noah's ark, but there is still a considerable variation, ranging from goats and bees and hens to men and women from all kinds of backgrounds, education, religions and interests. And for their needs some activity, apart from the practice of contemplative prayer, is always provided. Life at the Anchorhold may not have the full richness of life at Hut Point, but any evening in our family after supper would provide activity to compare favourably with the activities of Scott's family.

But it is in having a large and inspiring purpose, capable of uniting its varied elements into a single whole that the Anchorhold most nearly reproduces the Scott pattern. This purpose is not the achievement of an external goal, but the realisation of an inner goal, the loving contemplation of God. It is a more subtle purpose than Scott put before his family, but it is even more effective. Of Scott's sixteen companions at Hut Point no more than five could reach the South Pole. All can reach the Anchorhold goal and there is no question of a first or last. 'We shall be like him, because we shall see him as he is'. (I Jn 3:2) This purpose has proved strong enough to raise our spirits in times of disappointment, and has given sufficient glimpses of the vision and intimacy stored up for the future to make any present hardship bearable.

Owen and the Army

The second family model which has influenced the Anchorhold was created during the two world wars, an experience interpreted and deepened by the poetry of Wilfred Owen and his life. Here is another pattern of family intimacy, centred around a focus of even more profound meaning than that discovered by Scott and his companions.

Wilfred Owen gives this picture of the family intimacy in what he describes as 'The Smoky Cellar in the Forester's House':

'So thick is the smoke in this cellar that I hardly see by a candle 12 ins. away, and so thick are the inmates that I can hardly write for pokes, nudges & jolts. On my left the Coy. Commander snores on a bench, other officers repose on wire beds behind me. At my right hand, Kellett, a delightful servant of A Coy. in The Old Days radiates joy and contentment from pink cheeks and baby eyes. He laughs with a signaller, whose left ear is glued to the Receiver; but whose eyes rolling with gaiety show that he is listening with his right ear to a merry corporal, who appears at this distance away (some three feet) nothing but a gleam of white teeth & a wheeze of jokes. . . .

It is a great life. I am more oblivious than alas yourself, dear Mother, of the ghastly glimmering of the guns outside, and the hollow crashing of the shells.' (Jon Stallworthy, *Wilfred Owen*, p. 283).

This authentic picture of family life under war conditions evokes many similar memories drawn from experiences in the Second World War. Christmas in a barn in Holland with carols being sung with Dutch civilians and men resting; cottages where smaller families of this kind formed and dissolved many times during the evenings in the Ardennes; spontaneous discussions of great matters shared by men who had come in from the cold and were to go out to die.

On this flexible model the Anchorhold family forms and re-forms. It is Barth's conception of the visible Church in miniature: something always in movement and change. In his own words: 'The Church *is* when it takes place, and it takes place in the form of a sequence and nexus of definite human activities.' (*Church Dogmatics,* vol. IV, part 1, p. 652). The Anchorhold family, like this vision of the Church, is continually gathered in a fellowship which can only be made out of varying degrees of strictness or looseness in organisation and constitution. How different this is from the religious family, and how close to the family of war.

Wilfred Owen's other picture of the family under war conditions occurs in this description of his work as an officer. He penetrates more deeply in this image, reaching an insight of mystical awareness.

'For 14 hours yesterday I was at work – teaching Christ to lift his cross by numbers, and how to adjust his crown; and not to imagine he thirst till after the last halt; I attended his supper to see that there were no complaints; and inspected his feet to see that they should be worthy of the nails. I see to it that he is dumb and stands to attention before his accusers. With a piece of silver I buy him every day, and with maps I make him familiar with the topography of Golgotha.' (*Wilfred Owen*, p. 265)

Owen saw that the essence of the war family was not merely Christ in you but Christ manifest and suffering in you. It was a conviction that often came to others in the Second World War and it was not only Christ suffering which was felt. Christ was also in the laughter and in the worship and in the conversation of men who journeyed together across Europe and shared each others' lives at the deepest level. True, Christ outraged appeared in the face of the young, dead and mutilated German youth who sat like a broken *kouros* in the Normandy cottage. But even more completely was He present in the village church of Sébécourt at eight o'clock in the evening when the regiment halted at the end of its advance towards the Seine and met in the church to share evensong with the returning French peasants. It was a moment when men heard the great Bible story of Samuel called by night and listened breathlessly for the God who always speaks when men's ears are open to hear Him. And then there were the early mornings in the church tent where the eucharist was shared by the Christian leaven of many units and the Lord was present in triumphal glory to renew His own. All of it echoed what Wilfred Owen had seen of the Christ-presence, and yet there seemed something even more complete as the Christ of the resurrection and the ascension added these mysteries of Himself to the passion experiences of an earlier generation.

Christ in us in this wider meaning is what the war experiences have given to our family life at the Anchorhold, Christ made more richly manifest because He is revealed in such a variety of people, the sick, the lame, the blind, the failures and also in the laughing confidence of those who have not yet reached Golgotha and rejoice in a simple and spontaneous Galilee experience.

THE FAMILY CHRIST

It is the recognised presence of this complete Christ which has given to the members of the Anchorhold their unafraid intimacy. All experiences are received, shared and communicated. There is a cultivated intimacy of physical life in which people matter so much more than buildings and where secrecy and concealment are no longer necessary. It is not the self-conscious openness of the nudist colony but the transcended physical relationship in God which enabled Simon Peter to fish naked and feel no embarrassment. There is a sharing of emotions, the peaceful and the aggressive, the discovery that well-used anger is a way to deepened understanding: that joy and sorrow are always available in the Lord and in His great gifts. In such firmly centred life the slow building up of a common mind, formed by the Spirit and sharing the mind of God becomes a growing fact. The family learns not only to think His thoughts but to receive them. And the presence is shared and transmitted as others, like the returning French peasants, find themselves come home.

Scott gave his family a unifying objective in the form of the conquest of the South Pole. War gave us the objective of victory. It is true that almost before the fighting was over the objective of victory was seen as a hollow and deceptive sham, but it did its work in the earlier days, giving men hope and courage for their task.

Father Benson, founder of the author's religious order, in the early days of the formation of his religious family set this image before his sons in this remarkable way;

'We must see varied manifestations of the divine goodness. That essence, which we cannot approach in itself, is manifested completely in the Person of Christ, and the perfect manifestation which is in the incarnate Son of God makes its rays shine in what belongs to the economy of the Incarnation. All the varied surroundings glow with traces of the divine glory.' (*The Religious Vocation*, p. 201.)

The image was uncompromisingly that of the glorified Christ, but it was a Christ not merely manifested in sacraments and the affairs of Christian worship but shining through varied manifestation and included in all the activities of life. Such an omnipresent Christ is the centre of the Anchorhold family, giving adventure to its most humdrum activities in house, workshop and garden and making the rays of His presence illuminate every form of contemplative prayer. Here is an objective stronger than any which inspired Scott or those who made war-families, and its power has already been tested to the full. The image we create is capable of meeting everything that belongs to the economy of the incarnation, and it goes beyond death into eternal life. Such a centre and goal is the secret of stability in the Anchorhold family; it provides a bond stronger and more elastic than any written constitution or nicely formed plan of government. Around this centre revolve the varied experiences of our family life: the joy and sorrow, the anger and forgiveness, love and resentment, the many failures and also the glow of an intimacy deeper than anything its members have ever before been asked to bear. The cosmic Christ in the centre and His Spirit are enough to keep us in living balance and tension.

THE LANGUAGE OF INTIMACY

Every family shapes a language for communicating both within and outside itself. Scott's family, under his skilled direction, used the restrained idiom of naval language, inspired as they were by the imagery of great surroundings and the imagination of a poet. Scott's journal is a model of the way the deepest experiences should be communicated. This record made of Captain Oates by Cherry-Garrard and a companion shows how far the style of communications used by Scott had become the style of the family:

'Hereabouts died a very gallant gentleman, Captain L.E.G. Oates of the Inniskilling Dragoons. In March 1912, returning from the Pole, he walked willingly to his death in a blizzard, to try and save his comrades, beset by hardships. This note is left by the Relief Expedition of 1912.'

(The Worst Journey in the World)

Here is nothing emotional. There is a scientific precision about the facts. But it is the expression of a love which goes beyond the words and yet is adequately conveyed through the extreme economy with which they are used. Not what is said so much as the silence which is communicated is the secret; the reader waits in that silence and finds his imagination making an anamnesis of the event and giving him a share in this noble fellowship.

The army family had a language of its own, too, which is in part conveyed by such writers as Wilfred Owen. The basis of that language was an irrationality which came from constant swearing and obscenity. This should not be condemned but understood. This family was asked to live in chaos, with reason overthrown, and it preserved its balance by a continuous undercurrent of meaningless words. Again, emotion was rigidly avoided in speech lest men's courage should be overwhelmed. But there was much laughter and gaiety, and the poets infused beauty into the ugliness of their world. Whenever one attempts to recall this past family the language returns with the faces and it brings with it a glory and clarity which held the members together and still communicates their life. It was far removed from the language of today or of any other time. Much of it could not be used outside the family in which it was made without giving offence and misunderstanding, but for those who shared the life and used that tongue it had the message of the Word within the words and brought men into an intimacy with God.

Today, under different conditions, we must forge a language with which to communicate and express ourselves. Man must speak, since he is indwelt by the Word of God, and he must speak of those things he experiences now. New thoughts are being formed, and old experiences are being brought out of secret cellars into the light of day.

In our Anchorhold family we have been conscious of this growth in verbal and other forms of communication. The experiences of contemplative prayer and intimacy insist on being expressed. Many of the old words are still adequate, and we use them, but new ones are needed and this is where, as Thomas Merton saw, another tradition such as that of the East with its precise Sanscrit terms helps us to find the words we need. So it is with the deepened experiences of family intimacy. The present-day openness has encouraged us to use the permitted words and to uncover areas of experience which have not been described before. But words are no more than one form of expression. The whole body is an instrument of thought and communication. We use stillness and movement and symbols and silence, and out of this variety of instruments grows a language of increased power to express some of the experiences of the intimacy to which contemplative prayer leads. The truths of theology and prayer cannot be enclosed in mere words, however carefully chosen. They need a new language, and in that language the body and movement and image must take their share.

In helping to make this language many materials are at hand. They may be roughly considered in two groups: the raw materials of old traditions and the materials developed by present-day scientific discovery.

In the Doctrine Commission of the Church of England Report, *Christian Believing* (S.P.C.K., 1976), there is a section headed 'The Pastness of the Past'. It is not a very fortunate phrase, but it contains valuable observations on our inherited traditions. The Commission admitted to the difficulty of making the words of the past our own and of entering into an understanding of a past which has so little to do with our own present experience. It concluded that 'the only form in which the past is relevant to life here and now is in its end-product, the present situation'. (p. 10) This is true and, with the general abandonment of Latin and Greek as the basis of a sound education, we are rapidly being deprived of important language material which in the past has formed the main structure of theological definition. This is a great loss and one which will have to be faced practically by means of new translations and, if necessary, paraphrases.

But whilst sensitive to change, the Commission emphasised that other disciplines besides theology are required to adjust 'the accumulated knowledge of the past as a basis' for present work. This applies to language as well as to ideas. There are many inherited words and concepts for which there are no satisfactory modern counterparts and when this is recognised they will continue to be used. Such words as *hypostasis, physis* and the other technical words of Chalcedonian thinking enshrine and communicate ideas of fundamental importance. This part of our inheritance needs to continue as part of the old Christian tradition which will live with the new.

In a lecture on 'The Symbolic Life' given in 1939 Jung expresses the hope that a new generation of priests will appear who will try to 'translate the language of the unconscious, even the language of dreams, into proper language'. He believed that much of his work would come to fruition when accepted by the Church as a new vehicle for communicating the Christian truth. It would be difficult for this to come completely true, but there is a vast amount of language material in present-day psychology which might well be considered by the clergy as a help in their heavy task of proclaiming the Gospel and which could be incorporated into a contemporary translation of the Christian tradition. The words are already at hand and, when used with accuracy, they provide a valuable amount of raw material for the remaking of the language of Christian contemplative prayer. It is only necessary to select a few to encourage others to make their own list: ego, self, unconscious, consciousness, supraconscious, projection, transference, psyche, centre, archetype. Philosophy is another language source; so is poetry and even good journalism.

In making her borrowings from other disciplines, as the Church has always done, the principle of incarnation must be observed: she must also transfigure borrowed words into a genuine growth within her own tradition. As the Lord, who borrowed from all creation for His own purposes, taught us, the process is one of grafting the new on to the old so that both grow from the one sustaining root.

Language and its changes are some of the most important parts of this adventure of discovery which Christian believing imposes on us all.

2
Intimacy

We have described a family based on contemplative intimacy: we have now to explain in more detail what we mean by this experience. We face something of the same difficulty Dr Johnson faced in compiling his dictionary.

In the dictionary preface Dr Johnson begins by admitting failure. Words, he writes, can never be adequately defined. As living things, they refuse to be embalmed. The most that can be achieved is a description of contemporary use and meaning. Even in this undertaking there are insuperable difficulties, for the number of available authorities far exceeds the capacity of the writer's time and power to consult them. Should he attempt to do this his work would never be done. Dr Johnson found himself forced to this compromise:

'It was too late to look for instruments when the work called for execution and whatever abilities I had brought to my task with those I must finally perform it.' (Samuel Johnson, *Selected Writings*, p. 236)

In other words, he decided to depend upon his own experience rather than on the written authorities. But this brought another difficulty: his experience must necessarily be limited.

We share something of Dr Johnson's predicament when it comes to defining the meaning of intimacy. Like him we must use words, quote living examples, use our experience, but we cannot consult all the authorities nor can we have all the experiences. We must select from a few of the greatest authorities and look inwards to our own deepest family experiences. Then we must prepare for failure before we begin, but we must hope for a failure which may encourage others to take the task further and develop the experience. The authority and experience we have chosen as our main guide is the author of the greatest exposition of intimacy within the Christian tradition, the author of the Song of Songs.

THE SONG OF SONGS

The 'Song of Songs' is the strangest book of the Bible. It seems out of place, especially in its Old Testament context where so much of the writing is concerned with God and his people and the legal relationship between them. This frank love-poem has embarrassed many a commentator and many a reader. They have often tried to conceal its meaning under the veil of allegory and spiritual interpretation, but although this is a legitimate extension of its meanings it is literally a love poem of the most physical and outspoken proportions. It erupts into the Old Testament with a shock and originality which parallels our own permissive revolution. Uncompromisingly it declares that God loves man and uses as the analogy of that love the love between the lover and the beloved. It is a saga of intimacy which surpasses anything achieved in the literature of other religions. It has been used as a source of deepest spiritual teaching by some of the greatest mystics. Much of their teaching on prayer has been based on this song of love.

Hippolytus used it to develop his teaching on the relationship between God and His Church and the individual soul. Origen followed his example.

Led by Dionysius the Pseudo-Areopagite, a succession of commentators used the 'Song of Songs' as the basic source of mystical teaching. This came to fruition in St Bernard's eighty-six Homilies on Canticles. He was followed by Richard Rolle, St Teresa and St John of the Cross, who used the 'Song' as the inspiration of his own *Spiritual Canticle*.

In our own time, and to the astonishment of many, Karl Barth puts this work in the first place as the greatest writing of the Old Testament: he justifies his conclusion by the fact that it most clearly describes the intimacy between Yahweh and his people in its frankly erotic terms. In this quotation there is some of his main teaching. He writes:

'The 'Song of Songs' is one long description of the rapture, the unquenchable yearning and the restless willingness and readiness

with which both partners of this covenant hasten towards an encounter.' (Karl Barth, *Church Dogmatics,* vol. III, part 1, p. 313)

This is the *eros* side of the relationship which he frankly recognises but
always against the deeper meaning, the union between Yahweh and
his people. Again he writes:

'Love and marriage between man and woman become . . . in some
sense irresistibly a parable and sign of the link which Yahweh has
established between himself and his people, which in his eternal
faithfulness he has determined to keep and which he for his part has
continually renewed. In this way they irresistibly see even this most
dangerous sphere of human existence in its old and new glory.'
(ibid, p. 315)

Barth insists that Yahweh is always the lover, bridegroom and husband. And His lost people is always His beloved, His bride and His
wife. He sees the 'Song of Songs' as a statement that the Old Testament gives finally a proper meaning and seriousness to the sexual
relationship as such, that is an outward sign of the union between God
and man. He finds a connection between the teaching of St Paul on
marriage in Ephesians and the 'Song of Songs': it is the great mystery
of the union between Christ and His Church. In spite of the disruption
of the relationship by man's sin he is sure that eventually the mercy of
God will heal the division and the love between God and man will be
restored to its predestined glory. He claims that the 'Song of Songs' is
about *eros* but it is 'the eros for which there is no such thing as
shame.' (ibid, p. 313).

The danger of bringing God and *eros* into this close relationship,
according to Barth, must have been recognised by the Old Testament
writers, but he says:

'An inner necessity breaks through every reservation. God the
Lord and sexual eros, well known in Israel especially as a
dangerous daemon, are brought into close relationship. The 'flame
of the Lord' and the very different flame of love (Song of Songs,
8:6) are necessarily mentioned together and openly and distinctly
compared and related. (ibid, p. 314)

This produced no contradiction between the righteous and holy God
revealed in other parts of the Old Testament. The holy and righteous
God was also the great lover of the 'Song of Songs', and the purpose
of the trials and disciplines of His people was not merely to bring them

to repentance but, like the testing of Gomer in the prophecies of Hosea, to bring God's people to the capacity to respond to His love. Barth sums it up when he writes: 'What lies at the back of the creation saga is the thought of the beginning of the covenant, and what lies at the back of the Solomonic love song is the thought of its goal.' (ibid, p. 314)

These are some of Karl Barth's interpretations of the 'Song of Songs': we must now venture to add some of our own.

The structure of the Song of Songs has been well brought out in the New English Bible translation. This shows that it is not a straight forward narrative or poem, but nearer to a play. The bride and the bridegroom are the main characters, but they share the stage with many others of almost equal importance: the chorus, the natural wonders and a variety of creatures.

In describing the chief characters as bride and bridegroom the translators follow Barth in trying to fit the poem into the framework of a marriage song. It may be this, but it is also much more. It is a poem about love in its eros form and the chief characters are much more than bridegroom and bride: they are the lover and the beloved. This is an important distinction, for marriage is not the only form of love and the author writes of intimacy in all its loving forms. This is one of the main themes of this song.

In this drama the beloved often takes the initiative. She invites her lover and the lover comes like the eastern bridegroom in all his splendour to claim his beloved. He knocks and she opens to him. It is she who searches for him in the garden when he disappears and finds him. It is a strange reversal of roles and one that would still scandalise an eastern audience.

The action is simple: the imagery and the emotional content superb. All creation shares in this love. It is a cosmic intimacy of contemplative proportions in which the physical relationship is an introduction rather than a climax. The lover and the beloved achieve an intimacy far beyond the orgasm and yet one in which the orgasm shares. It is a complete intimacy of ecstatic indwelling.

Barth notes that in the Song there is no reference to the child, which supports the theory that it is not concerned with the family in its relationship to marriage but with intimacy of profound proportions between the woman and the man. This is not the only omission. There is no direct reference to God either. God of course is implied in the love between lover and beloved, but not as a separate entity: He is included in the love. This inclusive greatness of love was understood by Shakespeare when he made Juliet say:

'My bounty is as boundless as the sea,
My love as deep; the more I give to thee,
The more I have, for both are infinite.'
(Romeo and Juliet, act II, sc. 2)

This is a divinisation through love. The lover becomes identified with God through his love and this is the message of the Song, conveyed by the very absence of a specific reference to God. He is everywhere assumed: intimacy with the beloved and creation is intimacy with God Himself.

We may go further and say that God and the lover are identical. This is a mystery expressed in all the great love poems of the world: Krishna is more than a shepherd in love with Radha, he is the incarnate Lord. The lover of the 'Song' is a being of many forms but behind them all is the Lord Himself.

He is Solomon the king. He 'wears the crown with which his mother crowned him on his wedding day, on his day of joy'. (Song 4:11) He is also like a gazelle or a young wild goat. He is, in this lovely passage, the universe itself in its perfection:

'My beloved is fair and ruddy,
A paragon among ten thousand.
His head is gold, finest gold;
His locks are like palm fronds. . . .
His cheeks are like beds of spices or chests full of perfumes,
His lips are lilies, and drop liquid myrrh;
His hands are golden rods set in topaz;
His belly a plaque of ivory overlaid with lapis lazuli. (ibid, 5:10–11:13–14)

How reminiscent this picture is of the account of the furnishings of the temple. How close to the Johannine description of the risen Lord in the Revelation, 'the seven standing lamps of God, and among the lamps one like a son of man'. (Rev 1:13) And the unambiguous declaration: 'I am the first and the Last, I am the living one'. (ibid, 1:18) Rightly, the Church has identified the Lord with the lover in the 'Song of Songs' and has used readings from this poem, as did her predecessor, the Jewish Church, after Passover to celebrate her own Easter.

The way to the present Lord in the other is through love. This is the message of the 'Song of Songs' and of the Johannine writings. 'Only the man who loves his brother dwells in the light.' (I Jn 2:10) It is a love which leads not only to the Lord but to intimacy with the whole of His creation. Simile after simile is used in the 'Song' to describe it. 'Your love is more fragrant than wine.' (1:2) 'Your name is like perfume poured out.' (1:3) 'My beloved is like a gazelle or a wild goat.' (2:9) The intimacy is with nature in all her forms. It penetrates to the deep places of the city at night. It is at home with the human form and rises to the glories of the court of Solomon. The love of these two beings unites the whole creation and centres it in God.

This relationship between human love and the rest of creation was understood by Shakespeare. In *Romeo and Juliet* their union is with the darkness of 'civil night' and all nature shares their love. Juliet is able to see this in an eternal form when she sees Romeo for ever inscribed in the face of heaven.

'. . . And when he shall die,
Take him and cut him out in little stars,
And he will make the face of heaven so fine
That all the world will be in love with night,
And pay no worship to the garish sun.' (ibid, act II, sc.2)

True love is no mere ingrown intimacy between two possessive lovers. It swells out into cosmic proportions and takes to itself all consciousness. The love of the 'Song of Songs' is both *eros* and *agape,* it is physical and leads through the physical to a total union in which all the faculties play their part. The physical comes first in order and there is no concealment of the beauty of erotic love. The poem begins by making it clear that this love shall have its place. 'I will sing the song of all songs to Solomon that he may smother me with kisses.' (1:1) Figure is piled on figure to emphasise the delight of this love. But the emotions are also given full play, and they lead to an awakening of total consciousness in which state the act of love is fulfilled.

The two main characters share the emotions of this poem with the other creatures. The emotions arise from the free play of the senses and are felt rather than verbalised. They are corporately experienced and therefore rightly expressed through the chorus.

'Let us rejoice and be glad for you;
Let us praise your love more than wine,
And your caresses more than any song.' (1:4)

Joy is the dominant emotion, a joy which harmonises the other emotions. It is the climax of hope, the transformation of fear and itself the way to love.

In a much-needed introduction to Jewish spirituality Rabbi Lionel Blue writes:

> 'How loving, how tender is the creator of this vastness, with what love he feels for us. The language is more startling than a Christian would at first realise, for 'love' in Hebrew includes not only 'agape' but also 'eros'. ('To know' in Hebrew also includes 'to love.') (*To Heaven with Scribes and Pharisees*, p. 59)

Love leads to knowledge, intimacy to contemplation: this seems to be one of the constantly repeated messages of the 'Song of Songs' and indeed of all great love poetry.

Love in the 'Song of Songs' is not a static achievement but a voyage of unlimited exploration and discovery;

> 'My dove, that hides in holes and cliffs
> Or in crannies on the high ledges,
> Let me see your face, let me hear your voice;
> For your voice is pleasant, your face is lovely.' (ibid, 2:14)

This love reaches a climax of discovery when the lover attains the essence of beauty in the beloved and she in him.

> 'How beautiful you are, my dearest, how beautiful.' (4:1)

> 'My beloved is fair and ruddy,
> A paragon among ten thousand.' (ibid, 5:10)

The contemplative form of this intimacy is worth studying and comparing with other traditions. It is far from the apophatic *nirvāna* of Buddhism or the monistic absorption of *vedanta* Hinduism. It has none of the negative withdrawal from physical experience which marks so much evangelical Christianity. It is frankly dualistic. The contemplation is shared by two persons made intensely alive and transparent through love. And what is it they contemplate in each other? Not God invisible and incomprehensible. It is God manifesting Himself in beauty, which is also truth and love. The 'Song of Songs' turns away from the Jewish belief that God is without form and can only be represented by a cube of emptiness. Here He fills all things and it is with His beauty that they are filled.

From the 'Song of Songs' we can find much to enlarge our concept of intimacy and to sharpen the outline of our own experiences. Certain aspects of this concept stand out clearly. These are the preeminence of a relationship with God, with each other and with the whole creation, expressed most completely in contemplative prayer.

The Old Testament predicted a time when God would be one with His people and they one with Him. But it is only in the 'Song of Songs' that this intimacy is realised in a developed way. In the New Testament the total meaning of this intimacy is revealed in terms of a complete indwelling: the Word becomes flesh and dwells in our manhood. He offers Himself as food and drink. He is experienced as the glory of man infused through the Spirit into the centre of His life. By divine intimacy we mean the active, communicating presence of God, which is given to man as a free gift for each of us to appropriate by faith and prayer. This divine presence and action give the fullest meaning to intimacy and raise it to the greatest of all experiences. It is the end of life and is offered through every human experience. Intimacy with any other object is a shadow of perfect intimacy. Every other relationship points towards this as its final goal.

A reduced form of this intimacy occurs in every human relationship. It can exist between man and man, but it reaches greater proportions when it occurs between man and woman. In that relationship the deficiencies of each are made good by the contributions of the other. As in the Song of Songs, the lover and the beloved are fulfilled in their mutual intimacy. There is no rivalry. In the act of mutual giving each finds the other completed. In human intimacy all experiences contribute. *Eros* has a part, so have *philia* and *agape*. The body, the emotions and the will have each contributions to make. There is no term, no carefully graded measurement in this mutual self-giving and as it reaches completion so the intimacy becomes a reciprocal indwelling. Perfect intimacy involves divine immanence: it involves a human immanence as well.

Human nature has a capacity for divine and human intimacy, but this does not exhaust all its faculties. The human ego can identify in deep intimacy with every part of creation. In identifying with creatures and nature the power of human nature for intimacy is not dissipated or reduced. Creation intensifies the relationship between the lover and the beloved in the 'Song', and it is so in all human experience. The whole of creation is an instrument for growth in intimacy and the more deeply the life of creation is shared the greater becomes man's power to identify with it.

Intimacy expresses itself in many forms. All the degrees of love play their part. There is a place for movement, for emotional interplay. Above all there is a place for contemplation, that development of consciousness by which the object of intimacy is fully known. Like the other faculties for intimacy, this faculty for consciousness grows with use. No act of intimacy is complete unless it culminates in an act of knowing between the subject and object of the relationship. This is the message of the 'Song of Songs'; the depth of the knowledge each partner had of the other. The understanding is the most sensitive and complete of all the faculties in the achievement of intimacy and, when used to the fullest extent in contemplative prayer, it leads to the heart of God.

All this and more is told us about intimacy in the 'Song of Songs'.

OTHER SONGS OF SONGS

Every person and every generation, as it struggles to realise the self in some form of intimacy, writes its own 'Song of Songs'. We cannot do better than take note of any attempts to do this in literature. We cannot of course, any more than Dr Johnson, read and master all the instruments and authorities, but there are other forms of the 'Song of Songs' which have opened ways into intimacy. They are a book by a contemporary writer which emphasises aspects of divine intimacy, an exposition of human intimacy, and Dante's masterpiece, *The Divine Comedy*.

Fynn and Anna

The first book is by a friend who conceals his delightful character under the pseudonym, Fynn. His book is entitled *Mr God, this is Anna*. Since publication, besides having a considerable impact on general readers it has been welcomed as a piece of profound theological writing.

The book is ostensibly about a brief friendship between Fynn and a small child, Anna. It tells us a great deal about each partner in this intimate experience, but especially about the problems and growth of its author.

Anna, like the Christ of the gospels, does not fit into the accepted categories of scientific history. Memory has touched the facts: 'the light that never was on land or sea' has shone upon her. She is an imaginative figure, a work of anamnesis, based on unmistakable fact, who supplied what Fynn, with his vast expanse of unexplored territory, needed, and in his loving intimacy with her he found God.

It is in the conclusion that the heart of Fynn's discovery is found. Anna has died and Fynn is frozen with grief. In this state he comes across a book by Coleridge in which he reads that poetry deals with the ideal world and that the poetic imagination takes from individual experiences the universal states they reveal and infuses them in symbol form into our minds. This is a difficult concept, but when he applies it to his life with Anna he realises that her life has not been cut short. It has been completely fulfilled. On visiting the cemetery he sees why. The grave is marked by a little cross leaning drunkenly. Around it is a carpet of red poppies with a family of mice scurrying backwards and forwards. Suddenly the total meaning of his experience hits him. Fynn must put this in his own words.

> 'A finger of thrill went down my spine and I thought I heard her voice saying, "What's that the answer to, Fynn?" "That's easy. The question is 'Where's Anna?'" I had found her again – found her in my middle. I felt sure that somewhere Anna and Mister God were laughing.' (ibid, p. 189)

So ends a great twentieth-century 'Song of Songs' in the contemplative discovery that God and His creatures exist in a perfect immanence, that all things coinhere each other. This was where his exploration of intimacy led Fynn and he may well prove a forerunner to many in a permissive society who are wondering how to use their recently gained freedom.

Steppenwolf

Another 'Song of Songs' is Hermann Hesse's strange novel, *Steppenwolf*. It was written between the two world wars and published in 1927. It is a book which has caught the attention of many young people and shown a remarkable power to speak to their needs.

Hesse achieved the unusual distinction of reaching fame twice. During his lifetime he was recognised as an important novelist and his *Das Glasperlenspiel* received the Nobel prize immediately after the Second World War: but he became a world best-seller only after his death. This may reassure us that we are not wasting our time in trying to master some of his teaching nor using unimportant instruments and authorities in our search for the meaning of intimacy.

Hesse was a man of outstanding courage and prophetic insight. His analysis of the German situation before the war was proved true by events, and forced him into exile. He diagnosed the sickness of his time in terms of an inner conflict, a quest for the true self, and accurately revealed the fallacy of trying to solve it by reviving community life in terms of herd development without leading men to an authentic and personal renewal. For the same reason he condemned the nostalgic search into the past for freedom and happiness as a manifestation of what he called 'the spirit of indolence' among us. He summed up the way forward in his novel *Demian* in these words:

'There was but one duty for a grown man; it was to seek the way to himself, to become resolute within, to grope his way forward wherever that might lead him. There was only one true vocation for everybody – to find the way to himself. (*Demian*, p. 120)

This was the theme of most of Hesse's writing, especially of *Steppenwolf.*

Hesse's greatness does not lie in the answers he gives to his own questions. This is the least adequate part of his achievement, for he leaves nothing resolved. *Steppenwolf* ends with all the questions about the self asked and Haller, the hero, about to start all over again in quest of an answer. The same thing happens with Magister Knecht, the hero of *The Glass Bead Game:* he dies on the verge of a solution. This is the great weakness of Hesse: he asks questions which he leaves unanswered.

But at least the right questions have been asked and some readers will find themselves roused to embark on their own voyage of discovery. What is the self? How is it realised? What are the materials and experiences for the work? Here are questions of fundamental importance in the search for contemplative intimacy. We can learn from Hesse's failures, and take the problem nearer a solution by other means.

Though Hesse gives no final answers, he gives clues which are of vital importance to our own discovery. Some of them need to be frequently recalled: the relationship of God to the self; the hostile elements in the self; the shape of the integrated self; its relationship to other selves both in the conscious and unconscious states of being.

Hesse was brought up in a Lutheran environment and he eventually rejected much of the limited and legal teaching of this form of Christianity. But he never lost his hold on the reality of God and the mystery of the incarnation. Rather, he developed the dogmatic formulae of his inherited faith into the living situations of his novels. For him God was at the centre of the self, even though the presence was hidden. The incarnation was not God taking the body of a man, as is suggested in so many simplified forms of Christianity, but God clothing Himself in the whole of creation. He saw God present and working everywhere with a clarity which equalled St Paul's vision in the captivity epistles. God and the self, God and creation were for Hesse not separate beings but one living, communicating whole. He had glimpses of this though he never achieved a permanent synthesis.

His certainty did not blind Hesse to the presence of evil in the self. He was very sensitive to the presence of demonic powers, to the unsubdued animal in man. This was the main theme of *Steppenwolf*. But

this recognition did not make Hesse into a Manichee, setting up evil as
a rival power to God. In the mysterious conception of God under the
name of Abraxas in *Demian* he shows evil related to God, but also
subordinate to Him and serving His purposes in developing and
transforming the self. In all his novels this transformation of evil into
co-operating good is a major theme.

Hesse wisely does no more than give hints of the shape of the integrated self. He comes near a full portrait in *Demian* where we read
this description of the essence of love between man and woman:

> 'She stood before him and surrendered herself to him and the sky,
> forest and stream all moved back towards him in new and resplen-
> dent colours and spoke to him in his own language. And instead of
> winning a woman he had the whole world in his heart and every
> star in heaven glowed in him and joy coursed through his being. He
> had loved and by so doing had found himself.' (*Demian*, p. 141)

This is no more than a hint – but it opens up a universe.

Our present selves give a different picture. It is fragmented. We see
with St Paul no more than puzzling reflections in a mirror, when we
hope to see a complete face. But there is another conclusion to live
and wait for: the 'face to face' vision. The mystery of life is a bringing
together of the fragments of the picture into a single whole, which shall
be a perfect harmony. Hesse points towards this, but he never
achieves the final image. Both Dante and St John achieved this: Dante
in the image of the rose, St John in the image of the city, the new
Jerusalem gave us the great images of the completed self.

Hesse's great contribution towards the understanding of intimacy
seems to lie along the paths of the mystery of the self and the way to
the realisation of the self. He states the problem and the way to the
solution, although none of his characters achieve the complete
journey. When we try to understand the real meaning of intimacy we
must look for it in its most complete form in the self, and when we try
to experience it, love is the guide we must take. It may be love between
mother and son, as in *Demian*; man and woman, as in *Steppenwolf*;
man and God, as in *Narziss and Goldmund*. In saying this Hesse
speaks clearly to our generation.

Dante and Beatrice

Psychologists very often use as research models people recognised
as imbalanced and in need of some kind of treatment. Few psychiatrists have taken normal people for their models and still fewer
have used the great imaginative characters of literature. Another ar-

tistic achievement is in the many characterisations in Dante's *Divine Comedy* and it is to this we now turn for those instruments and experiences to help us in our exploration of true intimacy.

Dante and his *Divine Comedy* bring together and expand the insights into intimacy we have already discovered in the 'Song of Songs', Fynn and Hesse. In himself he offers a biography of growth in intimacy, and this he projects with artistic emphasis in his literary creation. Both his life and work give us an expanded and detailed model. In them we find the human, physical and divine aspects of intimacy which are brought out in the 'Song of Songs', the interaction of the feminine mind on the masculine revealed in Fynn's story, the mystery of the self described by Hesse: and all this brought to a climax in the final section of the poem. We may receive our most complete image of contemplative intimacy from it.

Dante was born in Florence in 1265 and married in 1293. He first met Beatrice, the inspiration of his greatest work, in 1274. She was then about a year younger than himself. Like Dante, Beatrice lived her own separate life. She married the banker, Simone dei Bardi, in 1287 and died in 1290.

Dante began the *Divine Comedy* with a rich background of experience in all the preliminary forms of intimacy. He knew the experiences of physical love and family life. His marriage was satisfactory and fruitful. His children remained faithful to him up to his death. He also had the rare experience of seeing in Beatrice the feminine image which was to control his imaginative life. Added to this, he had passed through many of the mental struggles which precede the harmonising of the fragmented self. He also knew the divinely-given thirst for the vision of God which was the primary theme of his life's work.

When he came to write the *Divine Comedy* Dante was a complete man, enriched by the experiences of life and suffering, and in his description of the way to divine intimacy he insists on an affirmation in which all the human faculties and every experience should be involved. Charles Williams saw this clearly when he wrote:

'Eros need not for ever be on his knees to agape; he has a right to his delights; they are a part of the Way. The division is not between the eros of the flesh and the agape of the soul; it is between the moment of love which sinks into hell and the moment which rises to the in-Godding.' (*Religion and Love in Dante*, p. 40, Dacre Press)

Dante saw that the vital condition is the direction of the soul. If it is turned towards God then love in all its forms contributes to intimacy. This he illustrates in every part of the *Divine Comedy*. He moves towards God through love for the poet, Virgil; more deeply through his love for Beatrice and St John; most deeply through his love for the incarnate Lord. This is Dante's great interpretation of the mystery of divine intimacy. In these days when love is so often rejected, misunderstood or misused under the dangerous pseudonyms of permission or liberation, he has a message of adventurous exploration for all. The Paradise of Dante is a door through which all genuine explorers may pass and learn the art of love.

We shall follow the path made by Dante most closely in the concluding part of this book when we consider the mystery of divine intimacy. Here he enriches our understanding of intimacy and helps to bring us to the situation where we may attempt to focus our definition.

CONTEMPLATIVE INTIMACY

With our chosen guides to help us we are now in a position to make some tentative outline of the meaning we intend to apply to the title of our theme, contemplative intimacy. We can divide our task into two parts, beginning first with contemplation.

Contemplation

Charles Williams sums up the contemplative aspect of Dante's work in these words:

> 'The general maxim of the whole way in Dante is attention; 'Look', 'look well'. At the beginning he is compelled to look by the shock of the vision, later his attention is enforced by command and he obeys by choice.' (Charles Williams. *The Figure of Beatrice*, p. 16).

Here we have one of the essential meanings of contemplation, which is illustrated in all the authorities we have chosen. It is an act of looking, of looking well, with a total concentration of all the faculties.

But contemplative looking has a special object. It is not just looking at anything and being content to see it as a physical object. Contemplative looking goes deeper. Dante did not merely look at a beautiful woman or a series of inner visions. The two lovers in the 'Song of Songs' were looking at something more than each other reflected in each other's eyes. Fynn and Anna fascinated each other because as they looked well they found something more than themselves. The frustration which so often occurs in a reading of

Hesse, is because his characters do not look well for they see no more than each others' unsolved problems.

Who is it that those who look well seek and find? The answer is God. Dante finds Him as a radiantly bright point in the eye of Beatrice and in that point is contained His glory. The lovers in the 'Song of Songs' find the divine beauty in each other and in the whole creation. Fynn ends his faithful looking at Anna on the convincing note that somewhere she and Mister God were laughing. Because Hesse did not achieve the contemplation of God he was frustrated. Contemplation is not just looking, looking well: it is looking towards God.

But God, as the first article of religion in the Church of England says, 'is one living and true, everlasting, without body, parts or passions; of infinite power, wisdom and goodness; the maker and preserver of all things both visible and invisible'. This poses a profound problem for the contemplative. If God is the object of his looking, what is there to look at in a being who is without body, parts or passions?

Our contemplative authorities are not bewildered by this apparent contradiction. For them contemplation does mean looking towards God who in His essential being is invisible: but it also means looking towards God who looks towards our human selves and who has manifested Himself in forms capable of contemplation. The invisible has become visible in Christ and energises the contemplative through the gift of His Spirit. How this has happened each of our authorities describes in his own way.

Take the lovers in the 'Song of Songs'. They proclaim that the earth is 'crammed with heaven'. In every part of nature and above all in themselves they see the flames of God's presence. In a less exalted but no less convincing way Fynn and Anna make the same discovery. Dante, steeped in the theology of St Thomas, writes with greater detail and precision about God making Himself visible through the incarnation, the Church, Beatrice and the saints. He goes still further and analyses the way in which this many-splendoured manifestation can be assimilated through the senses, the imagination, the reason and the understanding and the discipline of meditation, leading to the ecstasy of vision. For all of them contemplation was looking, looking towards God and finding Him in the things that He has made. Their witness is a commentary on St Paul's answer to the problem of how it is possible to contemplate an essentially invisible God.

'For all that may be known of God by men lies plain before their eyes; indeed God Himself has disclosed it to them. His invisible attributes, that is to say His everlasting power and deity, have been visible, ever since the world began, to the eye of reason, in the things he has made.' (Rom 1:20)

A further insight into the meaning of contemplation is given by these witnesses. For them it was looking towards God with a growing vision. This growth was due to two things: growth in the clarity of the divine manifestation, and growth in the power of human assimilation.

Dante was especially insistent that God manifested Himself in stages. In the 'Inferno', the 'Purgatorio' and the 'Paradiso' he described them under the traditional images of purgation, illumination and union. He thought of God concealing Himself under the conditions of the 'Inferno', gradually making Himself known under the conditions of the 'Purgatorio' and unveiling Himself in the final ecstasy of the 'Paradiso'. The lovers of the 'Song of Songs' found this growing revelation in terms of beauty, and Fynn and Anna came to it most simply of all as they groped their way through doors God gradually opened. This is an important aspect of contemplation that over-eager contemplatives sometimes tend to forget; contemplation is not reached in its fullness in a single leap, because God reveals Himself gradually and in varying degrees.

Equally is this true of our contemplative response. We look towards God with increasing intensity as our faculties for this work and our skill in using them grow. Here Hesse and Steppenwolf are a help. When Haller is first introduced he is almost totally introverted and depressive, unable to look at anything beyond his own tragic predicament. Gradually he develops the faculties he needs for contemplation: the dance, an awareness of beauty, a sense of humour. He never fully masters them all but at the end of the story he is able to admit:

'I understood it all. I understood Pablo. I understood Mozart, and somewhere behind me I heard his ghastly laughter. I knew that all the hundred thousand pieces of life's game were in my pocket. A glimpse of its meaning had stirred my reason and I was determined to begin the game afresh.' (*Steppenwolf*, p. 252)

This was not fully developed contemplation, but he had come a long way. The others − Dante, Fynn and Anna, the lovers − went much further.

The contemplative grows in contemplation as he develops certain faculties. These are faculties of stillness, tension and flexibility in the physical body, clarity of imagination in the mental body, and capacity for loving union in the spiritual body. All this is clearly described in

Dante's great journey but it is in the 'Song of Songs' that we find this
state summed up in a single phrase:

'I sleep but my heart is awake.
Listen. My beloved is knocking.' (Song, 5:2)

Contemplation, then, is a looking towards God, who looks towards
us, with a growing vision as the faculties of body, heart and will expand under the influence of His grace.

Intimacy

Our next task is to form the clearest idea we can of intimacy and in
doing this we shall have to follow Dr Johnson's determination 'to con-
fide in myself and no longer to solicit auxiliaries'. For intimacy is
about the innermost part of being, the centre of ourselves. We shall
not entirely dispense with auxiliaries, for their guidance helps us to
make our own journey inwards: and some of them have already
reached a stage of intimacy which is still far beyond our own experience.

Intimacy is the relationship which occurs at the centre of ourselves.
Anna saw that when she taught Fynn that: 'Mr God was, He was the
king-pin, the centre, the very heart of things.' (*Mister God, this is Anna,* p. 178) And again that 'We had to recognize that He was all these
things and that meant that we were at our own centre, not God. God
is our centre and yet it is we who acknowledge that He is the centre.'
(ibid, p. 179) He is the secret of the deepest intimacy. It is at our centre, a centre occupied by ourselves and God. Intimacy of this kind
begins when God knocks and we open.

Because God is the centre He is potentially the centre of all creation. Here our own experience and the witness of our auxiliaries are
unanimous that in many parts of creation this integration with the
Centre at the centre has not yet been achieved. This causes the present
imperfection of so many forms of intimacy. It is true of creation as a
whole which 'groans in all its parts as if in the pangs of childbirth'.
(Rom 8:22) It is true of most of us most of the time.

Although creation groans in all its parts and is fallen, nevertheless it
is more open to the divine centre than man and therefore more capable
of complete intimacy. This is one of the messages of the 'Song of
Songs'. The lovers find a profound level of intimacy reflected in
nature. In their relationship with her they share an already achieved
intimacy which they still strive to realise in each other. In nature they
find God revealed in His beauty, and, as they share in this beauty, so
they move more intimately towards each other. This leads us to the es-

sence of developed intimacy. It is a relationship with another at the deepest level. Ultimately this Other is God but He uses creation as a ladder of ascent to Himself.

Because God is love, intimacy with the centre is always a relationship of love. This love is of many degrees, depending on the nearness to God and the capacity to respond to His love. Dante shows this at its least and its greatest. In the 'Inferno' he describes men who have lost the good of intellect and as a result achieve the slightest degree of intimacy with each other and God. In the 'Paradiso' he describes, under the image of the celestial rose, men who have achieved the deepest intimacy with each other and 'the love that moves the sun and other stars'. Hesse less adequately shows the same growth as Haller moves from a state of infernal lovelessness to a purgatory of renewal. Fynn and Anna make a happier pilgrimage, since from the beginning of their intimacy they recognize God as its centre. All of these auxiliaries confirm our own experience: however dim our intimacy, if it exists at all, God is its centre and His love demands a growing response.

In spite of his many mistakes, St Augustine reached the heart of intimacy when he wrote: '*Ama et fac quod vis*' – Love and do what you will. This advice is ambiguous and has been variously interpreted. We may take it to mean that provided love is the motive intimacy can be expressed in whatever way we will. This does not open the door to an unrestricted permissiveness as might at first appear. Intimacy which injures the object of love is not permitted and this injury is caused whenever there is exploitation for self-satisfaction. This is the root of every unloving and immoral act. Such intimacy is not love at all: love makes all such acts impossible, and it is a sufficient safeguard in all acts of intimacy. With love as the rule no other rules are needed, for where love is God is, on His throne.

Loving intimacy has not one but innumerable forms. Each form is right which attempts to express love in terms of the degree of intimacy reached at that time. The lovers in the 'Song of Songs' knew this and embarked on an inexhaustible variety of loving intimacy. So did Fynn and Anna, and Dante most of all. Even Haller experimented cautiously in variations of the theme of love and came alive.

One of Blake's most devastating poems is a condemnation of the Church's attempt to limit the forms of love to the narrow limits of a code of moral laws. It is a solemn warning, not only to the Church but to the work of those who attempt by legislation and propaganda to interfere with man's freedom to express his love. Blake writes with devastating simplicity and prophetic judgement.

'I went to the Garden of Love,
And saw what I never had seen;
A chapel was built in the midst,
Where I used to play on the green.

And the gates of the chapel were shut,
And 'Thou shalt not' writ over the door;
So I turn'd to the Garden of Love
That so many sweet flowers bore;

And I saw it was filled with graves,
And tomb-stones where flowers should be;
And Priests in black gowns were walking their rounds,
And binding with briars my joys and desires.'

(The Garden of Love)

The love of true intimacy cannot be legalised. It is of the Spirit. Not even the traditional categories of *eros, agape, philadelphia* and *sterge* are wide enough to include its infinite variety. Each must make his own exploration and the only condition is to be faithful in love. This will always lead to the appropriate intimacy, that loving relationship with God at the centre of the self expressed with an absolute freedom of spirit.

Contemplation as understood in this enquiry is inseparable from intimacy, and the two activities reach full development in the state of ecstasy. This we shall consider in greater detail later on, but our authorities already give us many examples of this truth. The lovers of the 'Song of Songs' come together in contemplative love which lifts them to a state of ecstatic union. So for a brief moment do Fynn and Anna, and Dante's work progresses towards this climax.

Fully developed contemplative intimacy is a corporate experience. It takes place with nature, with creatures, with mankind and above all with God in the richness of His triune life. This is witnessed in all traditions. We find it in the 'Song of Songs' and in all the great Christian mystics. It lies behind the profound experiences of our eastern brothers with their love of nature and their insights into the creative and loving being of God. We can watch its corporate growth in the New Testament where God reveals Himself to His mother, then to the shepherds and to His creatures and on through His life to an ever-increasing congregation of people, finally dying and ascending to the glory of the Father and the heavenly host. Whatever contemplative intimacy means it is not less than this family experience. A lonely isolation may be a beginning, but a starved beginning at that. In its fully developed form it is the life of the one communion and fellowship in the mystical body of Christ Himself.

We are called to share in this multiple intimacy now and in the following chapters an attempt will be made to describe some of the experiences of this fellowship and the ways to prepare for a full share in its joys.

3
The Doors of Perception

When Blake described the senses as 'doors of perception' he was revealing his own interpretation of the world. It was not a lifeless lump of matter, a series of Newtonian laws, but a living organism capable of stimulating the senses. He saw it as an instrument of contemplative intimacy and the senses as organs communicating with this instrument and capable of being raised to a state of intimate awareness. For him the universe had a personality which could evoke a sympathetic response from man.

MOTHER EARTH

This view of the universe contrasts with the impersonal interpretation of science and belongs to an ancient tradition. It appears in the Indian idea of Shakti, in the Greek myth of Gaia as the original source of creation, in the Roman myth of Tellus. This attitude towards creation is not so clear in much of the Old Testament because of the prevailing fear of idolatry, but it pervades the Song of Songs. There what is called the pathetic fallacy, the crediting of nature with human emotions, is everywhere present. It appears again with much greater emphasis in the New Testament, and especially in the accounts of our Lord's relationship with the creation.

There is an incident in the Gospel which brings this into special prominence. Our Lord is with the disciples in a boat on the lake and a sudden storm descends from the hills. He is asleep, and the disciples wake Him since there is a danger of the boat being swamped. St Mark describes what followed in this way: 'He stood up, rebuked the wind, and said to the sea, "Hush, Be still". The wind dropped and there was a dead calm.' (Mk 4:39) From this the disciples drew their logical conclusion: 'Who can this be whom the wind and the sea obey?'

Here we have the creation addressed personally, but also we have the Son of God claiming an absolute control and relationship over it. He speaks as its Lord and master.

The creation as a living and growing organism is what St Paul believed it to be, and he developed the insight that the Lord was its centre and controlling force. In the Epistle to the Colossians where he describes the cosmic Christ he writes:

> 'He is the primacy over all created things. . . . Through Him God chose to reconcile the whole universe to Himself.' (Col 1:15)

The meaning of creation as a living whole presented in the Gospels takes us much further than the interpretations of the Old Testament and the old mythology. They give us the picture of a living and sympathetic structure: the New Testament enlarges this to the concept of the universe as the house and throne of God. 'Heaven and earth are full of thy glory' is the confession of the Christian Church, and in St John's Gospel there is the clear-cut statement that the Lord entered into his own realm, that He indwells His world and, though unrecognized, He uses creation for Himself. (John 1:10)

We have already seen one way in which the Lord commanded His world. In the parables and sacraments we can see others. Through the parables He communicates His thoughts and the secrets of His working. In the sacraments He communicates His life. The world is indeed full of His glory and is the instrument through which He offers intimacy with men.

The poets are the masters who respond to the world in this way. Wordsworth used all nature as a mother-presence to heal and inspire his imagination. Almost within our own times we have this example of a man, like ourselves, reacting with contemplative awareness to the impact of a creative experience upon his senses. Fynn writes this about his first meeting with Anna:

> 'I put my hands on her shoulders and held her off at arm's length, and then came that look that is entirely Anna's – mouth wide open, eyes popping out of her head, like a whippet straining at the leash. Every fibre of that little body was vibrating and making a delicious sound. Legs and arms, toes and fingers, the whole of that little body shook and trembled like Mother Earth giving birth to a volcano.'
> (*Mister God this is Anna,* p. 17)

All this took place in an east London street on a cold night. Mother Earth was not at her best, at her most beautiful: but she was Mother Earth and that was the essential insight of her being which Fynn and Anna were about to explore for the next few years.

Mother Earth is an instrument of contemplative intimacy in whatever form she appears. In the glory of the 'Song of Songs', in the majesty of the incarnate Lord or in the homely warmth of a London grating on a cold night. She has the power to adjust her stimulation to the needs of her children and even her imperfections are part of her gifts. St Thomas Aquinas said: 'The universe is for the best considering the present postulates, but not considering what God could have done.' (*Disputationes, III* de Potentia, 16, ad 17) And so in the Christian tradition there is the Mother in the form of the slave-girl of the Lord and the Mother as the Queen of heaven and the Lord engaged on the task of renewing His creation and making it reflect His own glory. But nature now is reduced to man's capacity to respond. She is much more like Fynn's mother than the garden of Eden described in the Song of Songs.

Fynn, who saw nature so clearly as a mother giving birth, had no illusions about her. His life in the East End of London was an experience of fallen nature, and yet nature was still able to supply him with the stimulation to thought and love he needed. She was like his own mother, misshapen and illiterate, but a cauldron of love. She is so much the background of his life with Anna that his own description must be given:

> 'Mum had a unique anatomical structure which still puzzles me, for she had a fourteen-stone heart in a twelve-stone body. Mum was a real lady and wherever she may be now she'll still be a lady.'
> (*Mister God this is Anna*, p. 21)

How splendidly she understood her family, and how adequately she met their needs, overflowing in compassion to everyone outside. Such is our experience of nature as she adapts herself to the needs and inadequacies of us all.

Wordsworth, in 'Tintern Abbey', has given us his experience, recollected in the tranquillity of many years of growth. In this great poem he analyses how nature ministered to him and how he responded to her ministrations. She came to him in two ways: in his youth and in the maturer days of his middle years.

In youth nature matched his need for 'coarser pleasures' and 'glad animal movements'. Then she haunted him like a passion with sounding cataracts, tall rocks, colours and forms. She stirred his senses and awakened his capacity to love so that he was lifted to aching joys and dizzy raptures. As she had acted on Anna she acted on him: she brought him to birth with the energy of a volcano. All he needed she physically and emotionally supplied. She brought him to vision and intimacy with herself. The rough pleasures she gave then, the wild ecstasies, the energies of thoughtless youth were raw materials which brought depth and joy to his later years.

In the later years nature continued her ministrations, but now in different ways to meet new needs. With the growth of thought and insight other appetites had to be satisfied: memory and imagination now predominated. These required material for pictures in the mind, rhythms to stir deeper emotions, and above all guidance into the divine presence 'whose dwelling is the light of setting suns'. Nature did not fail him. She led him by new paths and with familiar materials into the experiences he now required.

Nature succeeded with Wordsworth. He made the response she needed to achieve her end. He brought to her a life uncluttered with overmuch academic training. His senses and emotions were largely unspoilt: so when she called to him he heard and answered. Fynn was not such an apt pupil. His huge body was prematurely hardened by slave work under harsh conditions. He needed the ministry of Anna to recover some of the sensitivity to nature he had lost. Yet he did regain it, and with her to guide him, learnt to respond with all his senses and emotions to nature. The opening up of his life to the influence of Mother Earth took place and, as with Wordsworth, the record of this experience is there to reassure us as we try to open out to the same mother. We have to make our own pilgrimage of intimacy and to this we now turn. It is a journey which involves the opening of the doors of perception, the development of all the senses, the imagination, the emotions.

THE SENSES

The senses are not self-stimulating. They require an external and internal source of stimulation. Nature provides the external stimulation and the imagination, working on recollections of nature, provides the internal. Like nature herself the senses are imperfect. In the child they are embryonic but very acute: as the child becomes the man they develop, but lose much of their accuracy and are confused by a host of indoctrinated forms of association. But in whatever state of disorder, the senses communicate with nature and nature communicates with us through them.

Much of the story of Fynn and Anna is a saga of this sense exploration of nature. They do it in nature's least perfect manifestation, the East End of London and with the fewest pieces of scientific equipment, in a small back garden with Bossy the cat and a few neighbours, with a few bits of coloured glass and a mirror book, and yet this sense stimulation was enough for them to probe the whole purpose of creation. They came to a contemplative intimacy with God, which was in harmony with the economy of the incarnation: God emptying Himself and in the form of a servant with a minimum of pressure manifesting His glory without overwhelming His people. It was a merciful dilution in which both the earth and the senses shared.

Our senses may be imperfect and some of the doors of perception almost closed, but in the process of communication with the God incarnate in the earth they are destined to grow to the point where they can sustain the glory of God manifested in a new creation. So the smallest and the greatest sense stimulation is available in proportion to each man's capacity. In the East this truth is put in this way: the creature has the power to become infinitely small (*manimā*) and infinitely great (*mahimā*). He is both a macrocosm and a microcosm. He shares in the greatness and the smallness of created life.

Anna started small in her exploration but in the few years she shared with Fynn she grew very large indeed. 'Anna,' wrote Fynn, with perhaps a touch of exaggeration, 'at six was a theologian, mathematician, philosopher, poet and gardener'. She was in the Lord's words the little child who enters the kingdom and she did so, not by taking the complicated path of the academic theologian with his traditions and criticism and text books: she followed the path of the Bible, starting with life in a garden and learning God's ways by living in the deepest intimacy with the life and history of His least conditioned people. She ascended to God by the simplest road provided by Himself, the ladder stretching from the East End to heaven.

Mercifully Fynn and Anna were spared the obstacles which so often insulate the senses from direct contact with the rungs of this ladder. They were protected from much modern technology. They lived just before the days of television. When they went into the country it was not in an air-conditioned machine which separated most of their senses from mother nature. They walked and felt the living earth under their feet and the air passing over their faces and they listened to every sound. We can watch each of their senses responding to its appropriate stimulation and in doing so draw courage to expose our own senses to a similar experience.

Fynn and Anna used all their six senses, not only touch, taste, hearing, smelling, seeing but common sense as well. With this last sense they harmonised the others and focused them into an act of intuition. They communicated with Mother Earth with every faculty and then understood her speech. It was never mere curiosity that drove them to ask questions and search for the answer with all their senses alerted and wherever possible magnified by primitive, home-made apparatus. Common sense guided them to the divine presence behind the symbols of nature and they looked inwards and found Him. This is the true climax in every sense experience: the doors are opened and then we see, as Blake taught us, the infinite world and the divine glory. But these doors open gradually, and much of our time and patience are used up in making a full, sensual relationship with God and His world.

Touch

Take the sense of touch as one of these doors, in many ways the first door of the senses to be opened and the one which gives us our clearest vision and intimacy with the earth. As always, nature takes the initiative and touches us first with the winds and changes of temperature to activate the skin, and the marvellous variety of textures of our being. Intimacy comes by exposing the faculties of the sense of touch to all these influences. It is not only a question of learning to accept them all gladly, ice and snow, cold and heat, winter and summer, but being sensitive to the different experiences these touch sensations bring. Touch is the first rung on the ladder of intimacy, but only truly felt when we go out naked to handle the earth and expose ourselves to her touch. There are so many ways of doing this. Life is an unending exploration of the physical body of the world.

Often the simpler ways are better than the more sophisticated opportunities opened up by machines. Gardening can be an intimate exploration of the earth. Housework where the hands replace the machine is another. There are touch explorations of the body through the disciplines of yoga, the T'ai Chi Ch'uan: and a simplified form of this in 'pushing hands'.

Pushing hands is a remarkable exercise in the art of exploration of the body of another through the sense of touch. It is done with a partner and comprises four simple movements: ward off, rollback press and push. In this movement each probes the tensions and vulnerability of the other and tries to discover hidden weakness and strength. This experience of shared vibrations leads to a state of deep understanding in which the partners eventually become doors in each other opening on to God.

Sexual intimacy is another touch experience which comes to many forms of fruition in terms of sense awareness. The Bible describes it in its most complete form as a way of knowing another. This is where it led the two lovers in the 'Song of Songs'. With Anna and Fynn there was an equally deep relationship of touch and knowledge but this without the use of the genital area. Fynn's admirer, Vernon Sproxton, who writes the sympathetic introduction to the book emphasises this part of the relationship and adds this wise comment:

'He is not among the ever-sanctified. But there is about him a touch of that engaging, wide-eyed, winsome innocence which mankind must have had before the Fall, and which would permit a youth and a young girl to snuggle up in bed together in a way which was completely innocent (there the word is again) of any sexuality. In fact the simple honesty of their relationship reminded me of the subintroductae — those virgins who slept with the early Christian fathers without intercourse taking place — which had to be abandoned in the fourth century because Cyprian and others were worried about scandals. . . .' (*Mister God this is Anna*, pp. 9–10)

The discovery that Fynn and Anna made in their own pilgrimage of intimacy through touch is one which is being made on a much larger scale today, where people are being encouraged to find a way to 'spread their sexuality throughout their entire bodies' and if they succeed then 'such bodies could not then be exploitable as machines' (Martin Seymour-Smith *Sex and Society*, p. 432). This is an exploration for which religious communities seem specially geared and it may well be good for them to engage in this kind of study rather than trying to duplicate work much better done by parish clergy and welfare workers. It is not enough to try and impose a past interpretation of chastity on the twentieth century, with its very different obstacles and opportunities. Certainly the end of sexual intimacy is not the satisfaction of one limited area of consciousness in terms of orgasm, which in spite of present-day emphasis is not essential, to either partner, but the indwelling of two egos in the physical creation reaching a climax of intimacy with God Himself.

Touching the earth with full understanding is always a healing experience as Kipling shows in this description of Kim's first contact after his nervous breakdown. The Sahiba is there to underline that it is Mother Earth who heals.

'Said the Sahiba, to whom watchful eyes reported this move: Let him go. I have done my share. Mother Earth must do the rest. . . . There stood an empty bullock cart on the little knoll half a mile away, with a young banyan tree behind — a look-out, as it were above some unploughed levels; and his eyelids, bathed in soft air,

grew heavy as he neared it. The ground was a good clean dust – no
new herbage that, living is half-way to death already, but the
hopeful dust that holds the seeds of all life. He felt it between his
toes, patted it with his palms, and joint by joint, sighing luxuriously,
laid him down full length along in the shadow of the wooden-pinned
cart. And Mother Earth was as faithful as the Sahiba. She breathed
through him to restore the poise he had lost lying so long on a cot
cut off from her good currents. His head lay powerless upon her
breast, and his opened hands surrendered to her strength.'
(Rudyard Kipling, *Kim*, p. 306)

From this touch-contact with Mother Earth all Kim's other senses
revived and he was prepared for the enlightenment to which the Lama
was soon to lead him. This is the path of intimacy with the earth and
its Lord which all must take. First, what Rimbaud called, 'the dis-
ordering of the senses' and then their renewal sense by sense, beginning with touch, as they come into a restored relationship with nature.
Much of Wordsworth's life and poetry witness to this truth. This was
the journey taken by Fynn and Anna through the living earth of the
East End as they exposed themselves receptively to its teaching.

Sight
Kim looked as well as touched. The earth is a wonder to be gazed
at. So God does. Having created it He looked on it and saw that it was
good. His looking was not the casual glance of a distracted spectator
but the loving regard of the Father at what He had made. This is the
sense of sight exercised at its deepest level, but there are other
superficial levels through which God's children must pass on their
way.
The stages of this looking are expressed in four Greek words for the
use of the sense of sight which describe also four degrees of intimacy
with the object. There is the word *blepō* which is a physical regard of a
physical object. In Indian thought this is spoken of as *trātaka*, an
exercise to focus the eyes on one object. This is a part of Dante's
teaching to 'look well'. It is the essential preliminary of the other forms
of looking: *horáō, theáomai, theōreō*.
These three words describe that deeper, inward looking which leads
to understanding. It happens after the physical eyes have come under
the control of the outside object which stimulates the eyes of the
heart, that 'inner eye', the 'third eye' which sees below the surface of
the outside object and makes of it an inner image. This is not a
photographic process but a work of the imagination which is seen
most vividly in the images of the artist, the poet, the musician.

Wordsworth found that the inner image often took geometric forms, what in India are called *yantras,* and through these he penetrated to the inner reality of sight. He regrets that for himself he failed to master this mode of communication, but he gathered pleasure from even his rudimentary knowledge and found in it 'both elevation and composed delight'. The Greek stylised figures, *kouroi,* are another form of this inner image generated by gazing on what Blake called 'the human form divine'. This image goes to the essence of sight, the inner presence and meaning, to the presence chamber of God Himself.

When nature is looked at in all these ways she too reveals the inner structure of her being. This leads into a world of mystery rather than of immediate understanding, to a situation of *koān* rather than of clarity. Into this world Fynn and Anna went unafraid. They even invented a vocabulary of their own and a new apparatus, the mirror book, to handle the wonders they found. For them it was an opening of doors in heaven, a discovery of Mister God.

Modern scientific instruments when used with the full range of sight wonderfully increase the possibilities of visual intimacy with nature. Scientific discipline, too, trains the powers of perception and arranges concepts into symbolic order of thought. It also provides a language of communication which is a kind of shorthand to lighten the burden of perception in the mind. The contemplative has much to gain in mastering the methods of at least one of the sciences. Edward Wilson and his artistic achievement at the South Pole journeys shows how much could be gained from combining a scientific mastery with the artist's skill. His drawings are masterpieces of scientific precision and imaginative insight. They helped to bring him into an intimacy with the Lord of creation, so movingly revealed in his last letter home.

The artist, the poet and the musician develop the sense of sight, creating from its materials those imaginative images which illuminate the object and reveal its inner meanings. Wordsworth describes this process with experienced insight in 'Tintern Abbey'. It comes when the gleams of thought have been half-extinguished, when memory has grown dim and faint and the mind balances in a state of perplexity. At that stage 'the picture of the mind revives again' and this supplements the visual experience with pleasing thoughts, leading to intimacy with the still, sad music of humanity', to a presence and joy, the sublime sense of the divine. In the hands of the contemplative all this becomes material for his attainment of the glory beyond the open door of heaven.

Taste

Fynn's mother, like Mother Earth, came to him most effectively through the sense of taste. She was given to making stews and through these stews she achieved the miracle that in her house nobody was ever ill. This made possible all his other discoveries into the mysteries of Mother Earth. His mother did not take him the whole way described by the psalmist of 'Taste, then, and see that the Lord is good.' (Ps 34:8) but she set him on the way. She presented nature to him as something to be eaten and enjoyed.

This is one of the most effective ways to intimacy with creation and its Lord. It is the way shown by the Lord in the eucharist and a way that has proved much more effective than the verbal niceties of doctrinal definition or the warmth of controversy. 'Take and eat this.' What follows is a feeding on the Lord in various degrees of intimacy.

It is a misunderstanding of this mystery of the sense of taste when the eucharist is separated from other forms of eating. All are modes of intimacy with the Lord. The family meal is such an occasion and St John in recording the feeding of the five thousand makes this clear. It was a physical renewal in which the hunger of the crowd was completely satisfied. But it was also an act of contemplative intimacy with the Lord for the crowd had a deep insight into the mystery of Jesus when they said: 'Surely this must be the prophet that was to come into the world.' (Jn 6:14) Our Lord Himself developed this insight with the discourse which followed the miracle in which He revealed Himself as the loaf of life, the indwelling presence in all food.

All intelligent use of the sense of taste leads to this intimacy. It brings contact with the life of the earth and this leads on to union with the life of God. M. C. Fullerson in her impressive meditations on food and eating expresses the need for this contemplative treatment of all meals:

'Somehow I must come to see His life in everything, for indeed it is His life in air and earth, in vegetable and grain and fruit. I live surrounded by His Being. I live because of it. In order to bring a whole dedication at the moment of partaking of the symbols of Bread and Wine, I must acknowledge His Real Presence within and without — at all times and in all things. When this was finally a realized and accepted truth, my body was healed.' (*By a New and Living Way*, p. 39)

This was experienced in more down-to-earth terms by Fynn and Anna. They first met over a meal of hot-dogs, eaten from a paper bag. Under these conditions they broke down the barriers and found they loved each other. This meal was the beginning of their three years' exploration into God. Over that hot grating and with that simple food they found each other and the Lord.

So it was, with greater elegance though not greater reality, with the Lover and the Beloved in the 'Song of Songs':

'He took me into the wine-garden
And gave me loving glances.
He refreshed me with raisins, he revived me with apricots;
for I was faint with love.' (*Song*, 2.4–5)

The hurry that sometimes accompanies the eating of school meals and community meals, the use of unnatural foods, forgetfulness of the ceremonies which should accompany the eating of all food, have all obscured the relationship between food and contemplative intimacy. Something like the Japanese tea ceremony, perhaps, is needed to restore this great mystery to its challenging place in daily life. Not all at once can we expect to achieve this restoration of the place of taste and food, but there are ways of moving in that direction. Hot-dogs in paper bags can be eaten with the style of Fynn and Anna. All food can be an opportunity for intimacy with life and its source. And the silence that concludes every meal is the chance to meet the Lord in the heart by faith and thanksgiving.

Hearing

There is a strong tradition both within and outside of Christianity that creation is the expression of sound. 'The Lord gave the Word' and from Him everything else follows. Even more explicitly the psalmist says:

'The Lord's word made the heavens,
All the host of heaven was made at His command.' (Ps 33:6)

The whole universe is not only a structure which corresponds to the sense of sight: it is also a structure which satisfies the sense of hearing.

The sound emitted by the universe is both audible and silent. Both forms of sound are present in each utterance, the verbal expression and the silence which follows it. The Lord speaks in both ways. Scott and his expedition had vivid experience of both communications. He writes of it with unexpected intimacy when describing the midwinter celebrations on June 22, 1911. There were the talkative, singing activities in the hut in which Scott took a full share even to the extent of making a speech. And then he slipped away outside and was overwhelmed by the silent beauty of the night. He writes of it with stimulated imagination and reveals the deeper part of his poetic nature.

'It is impossible to witness such a beautiful phenomenon without a sense of awe, and yet this sentiment is not inspired by its brilliancy but rather by its delicacy of light and colour, its transparency, and above all by its tremendous evanescence of form. There is no glittering splendour to dazzle the eye, as has been too often described; rather the appeal is to the imagination by the suggestion of something wholly spiritual, something instinct with a fluttering ethereal life, serenely confident yet restlessly mobile.' (June 22. Midwinter – *Scott's Last Expedition*)

There is an art in listening to the sounds and silence of the universe. It requires selection and a developed sense of hearing. Anna showed this in many ways. She liked the night because then 'the sights and sounds of the daytime got into manageable size'. They didn't get muddled up and you could hear them. She could interpret what each sound was saying. As Fynn put it: she captured sound. She heard God's voice speaking in the silences. As did the Beloved in the 'Song of Songs':

'I sleep but my heart is awake.
Listen. My Beloved is knocking.' (*Song*, 5.2)

Listening is the response of the sense of hearing to the sounds of creation. In many ways it resembles Dante's admonition to look well. It requires that sensitivity which Patanjali equates with a high state of contemplative skill – discrimination, selecting what is significant from mere noise – then following the selected sound into silence, a silence which is vibrant with meaning and quite different from the Zen search for nothingness. In that silence the Lord knocks.

Smell
In the lower orders of creation the sense of smell is the way to most intimate knowledge. Animals use this sense to communicate with each other and each part of the vegetable creation has an identifying smell. Human beings can similarly communicate with creation and each other and God. Incense has always played an important part in worship. It is prayer made odorous. St John uses it as a special stimulant of the memory when he recalls the anointing of Jesus in the house of Mary and Martha, six days before the passover. He recalls that 'the whole house was filled with the fragrance.' (Jn 12:3)

Wordsworth confirms that it is through the memory and memory-images that we reach deep intimacy with creation. Such images are powerfully made through the action of the sense of smell. They both recall and re-animate the past and bring to the present an intensified lustre and meaning.

The full impact of nature's communication through smell is reached in breathing, what the Eastern teachers call *prāṇāyāma*. This is more than physical breathing. It is a deliberate communication with the essence of life which comes through smell, holding it by a system of stops and rhythmical breathing, aiming at the most sensitive relationship with the Spirit of God who both breathes in creation and in the human body trained to respond to Him. The mastery of *prāṇāyāma* requires a long training and an understanding translation of the Eastern symbolism of the body centres of consciousness. These centres are at the base of the spine, in the genital area and the solar plexus. These are sometimes called the vital centres, since they are related to the mystery of our physical life. Then there are the imaginative and rational centres in the heart and at the throat. And finally the spiritual centres in the forehead and the crown. Some may dismiss this analysis as pure fiction but it is firmly embedded in our own tradition. The Sarum prayer: 'God be in my head and in my understanding: God be in my eyes and in my looking: God be in my mouth and in my speaking: God be in my heart and in my thinking: God be at my end and at my departing' – is one place where it shines through. The names of the physical centres of the body: sacrum, solar plexus, heart, forehead or temple and crown – also hint at deeper meanings. And churches, which are symbols of the human body, have similar overtones in such words as: nave, choir, corona. All these centres are energised by breathing. They are areas where intimacy with the outside creation achieves the intensity of orgasm. And the instrument which leads to this is the full, pelvic breathing of the Spirit implied in the discipline of *prāṇāyāma*.

Common sense

The senses never communicate with creation singly. There is a system of what is sometimes described as a central mechanism which links up the sensations communicated separately and harmonises them into a single awareness. We find this working in practice in the form of common sense. It is a faculty not confined to sophisticated communities or highly educated people. In fact in such conditions it is often notably absent and instead a schizoid situation, where the information communicated by the senses is confused, is found. Blake would no doubt have included this under his description of the doors of perception as being in a state of obscurity. Common sense was brilliantly present in Fynn and Anna. In their sense perception there was an outstanding capacity for sense coordination.

The mirror-book is a good example of this. It was designed to improve the range of the visual sense. It provided experimental situations which could have led to pure phantasy but Fynn and Anna always kept their feet on the ground and their hearts in touch with God. They reasoned out the various figures the book gave them. They managed with a torch to get the light inside. They drew logical conclusions and joined them with other facts and experiences. They never tolerated an unresolved contradiction. What was intended to be an extension of the sense of sight became, through the co-ordination of other sense experiences, an instrument of common sense and that common sense a way to God.

This sixth sense is often at a discount with the over-intellectualised. It is replaced by complicated mental patterns which often lead to wrong conclusions and rarely to deeper intimacy with God and His creation. Common sense controls the New Testament and dominates the life of our Lord. Time and time again he reduced mental problems to sense experience and then drew His conclusions by the application of common sense. Bring me a penny, He demanded of those who wanted to involve Him in a political argument and from the evidence of the coin He reached the right conclusion. Look at the lilies, look at them well. And from what He sees He concludes the presence and nature of God.

Of all the disordered senses common sense is the most disordered and needs the most repair. Often it is so concealed that it hardly seems to exist. Often it is used last when it could have solved the problem with a single glance. Fynn and Anna were frequently tilting at the absence or distortion of common sense in those appointed to teach them. The clergy came in for some hard knocks, and so did Anna's teachers. It is in the little ones of God that common sense most flourishes.

In all traditions there is a belief that above common sense is a divine understanding which provides a standard of truth by which all the senses and understanding may be measured. In the Indian tradition this cosmic intelligence is called *mahat*. It is more than a supreme reason. It is a co-ordinator and interpreter of the senses as well. In the Christian tradition there is the teaching about the logos who is the supreme reason, the truth which is in all things. By this power both human reason and feelings are judged. It assures us of the rational nature of all things and their mutual relationship. The writings of the great Indian teacher, Sri Aurobindo, describe this truth in a form which combines both eastern and western traditions. He used the phrase 'Universal Mind' to present his meaning, and he gave to this power an active intervention in creative activity. He thought that perception could only reach its open awareness by communicating through this intelligence. In other words, that it was not so much a question of opening the doors of perception as of using the universal mind to penetrate the mystery of creation. At a certain development in conscious perception, he wrote, there was a change of consciousness in which the senses became united with the universal mind and perceived through him:

'From the moment, in principle, the mental being in me became a free Intelligence, a universal Mind, not limited to the narrow circle of personal thoughts as a labourer in a thought factory, but a receiver of knowledge from, all the hundred realms of being and free to choose what it willed in this vast sight-empire and thought-empire.' (*Sri Aurobindo or The Adventure of Consciousness*, p. 49–50)

It was this experience which he saw as the full cleansing of the doors of perception, the restoration of common sense and his teaching in many ways reflects the teaching of the Christian tradition and its distinction between acquired and infused contemplation. Briefly this means that man can in co-operation with the Spirit develop his sense and mental faculties: then comes a traumatic experience or dark night in which these are suspended but, if the exploration is continued, these faculties are taken over by the logos who Himself renews them. Wordsworth puts this same truth into poetic form:

'... that serene and blessed mood,
In which the affections gently lead us on,
Until, the breath of this corporeal frame
And even the motion of our human blood
Almost suspended, we are laid asleep
In body, and become a living soul:
While with an eye made quiet by the power
Of harmony, and the deep power of joy,
We see into the life of things.' ('Tintern Abbey')

Our supreme response is not to do the work ourselves but to open to the Logos who knocks.

THE IMAGINATION

The greatest and most mysterious power of God is His imagination. He understands Himself by generating an image and that image is called in Christian tradition His Son, 'the image of the invisible God.' (Col 1:15) St Paul describes him as 'the full and perfect image of the Father.' (Col 1:15) He is also 'the primacy over all created things.' (Col 1:15) He is a perfect likeness of the original: God from God, Light from Light, true God from true God ... one in Being with the Father. Through this same power of imagination God images forth the whole of creation, including man, made in His image though not given by created right a participation in the divine nature.

As a gift from God man receives the power of imagination by which he can make and receive images. Blake saw this creation of images as his greatest function.

'I rest not from my great task.
To open the eternal worlds, to open the immortal Eyes
Of Man inwards into the Worlds of Thought, into Eternity,
Ever expanding in the bosom of God, the human imagination.'

('Jerusalem')

And again:

'And I know that This World is a World of imagination and vision. I see Everything I paint In This World, but Every body does not see alike. To the Eyes of the Man of Imagination, Nature is Imagination itself. As a man is, so he sees.' (To Dr Truster, 23 August 1799 — *Complete Writings: William Blake*)

But Blake also realised that the power of imagination was impaired in every man. The miser saw more beauty in a guinea than in the sun; and a bag worn by money more perfectly proportioned than a vine filled with grapes.

Anna saw this imaginative blindness as almost universal when she looked at the broken-off stump of an iron railing and asked the passers by to stop and write down big what they saw — each of them refused. And she summed up their imaginative sickness and her own imaginative health by saying:

'I know what I see and I know what you see, but some people don't see nuffink.' (*Mister God this is Anna*, p. 52)

The imagination and the images it makes are the means by which we see the meaning of the sense-dialogue between ourselves and the universe. When we are using our imagination with contemplative awareness, we are nearest to the activity of God and enter into the closest intimacy with Him. This great privilege is one that is not developed by all and in some it is gravely damaged. Fynn and Anna show us how it is used and how it can be so developed that very ordinary people become poets and achieve the vision of God.

The first condition for this imaginative activity is the faith to see all created things as symbols. Only when created things are seen in this way can they become the raw material of the contemplative image. That is how the Church sees both the creation and the articles of her faith. They are symbols, outside forms with inner meanings. They are what the New Testament means when it calls events signs and mysteries. Anna saw the broken-off stump in this way and it led her to the second stage of contemplative intimacy.

That second stage is the making of two kinds of images: the percept and the concept. The percept is the interiorisation of the object by the senses. It is the nearest the senses come to a photographic reproduction, with the exception that it also reproduces emotional tone. Thus is the object made available for the making of the second image, the concept.

In forming the concept image more imaginative exercises are involved. The image is related to others in the memory. This is the process of association. The Holy Spirit also co-operates in making an image which will interpret the secret of the symbol and energise it as an instrument for communicating the divine presence. This was the image Anna had of the iron stump. It was a percept animated with the glory of God. As Fynn was able to see: 'It wasn't dark behind those tear-filled eyes, but a blaze of light.' And from it he could draw the conclusion that 'God made man in his own image, not in shape, not in intelligence, not in eyes or ears, not in hands or feet, but in this total inwardness. In her was the image of God'. (*Mister God this is Anna*, p. 53) He might even have gone further and seen man's glory as a fellow-worker with God in the making of the images through which He is known and revealed.

There is one other important fact about the imaginative faculty. It does not always operate in the same place. Sometimes it makes images of movement; sometimes images of emotion; sometimes images of sound; and of course, visual images as well. It would seem that these different images are made at the different centres of consciousness. The vital centres in the lower part of the body make images of movement and emotion. The heart centre is the origin of the visual images. In the top centres of the body the images resemble what St Theresa called the intellectual images, images without identifiable shapes, appealing to the faculties of the supraconscious, and of immense power and intimacy. Fynn and Anna with their fearless physical and mental intimacy were able to use all these centres in their imaginative life. They even penetrated to the higher centres where images become light and reason becomes intuition. Images made with the energies of all the centres can take us into all degrees of intimacy: with the earth, with heaven, with God Himself. The divine humanity of our Lord is there to prove this and also to stimulate us to develop to the full the infused power of imagination.

Sleep

There are two ways of using the imaginative faculty to achieve intimacy with God: contemplative prayer and sleep. Both are really the same activity under different conditions of consciousness. We shall often be considering the first of these ways so that this is not the place to go into it in detail. Sleep is a form of contemplation imagination that needs more enquiry.

It is a pity that psychologists have most often studied sleep using disturbed models for their purpose. In Jung's *Memories, Dreams, Reflections* (Collins and Routledge & Kegan Paul, 1963) dreams are used as a means of confrontation with the unconscious, and since that unconscious is disturbed what is recorded very often takes the form of nightmares. It is far removed from our quest for contemplative intimacy with God and His creation: and where Jung has explored with great insight and restraint others have followed far less skilfully and with dangerous disclosure. The sleep which reproduces such dreams is not the sleep we are thinking of as a generator of contemplative images.

Fortunately there are other sources of material. The Bible is one such source. Here the dreams of normal people are recorded, with implications of their power to lead to divine intimacy. The Old Testament shows much of this evidence. In the New Testament we have the dreams of Joseph, of the wise men, of St Peter: all of them reveal contemplative forms in sleep. There is a remarkable analysis of this kind of sleep by the great Indian teacher, Sri Aurobindo. He gives some of this teaching in *The Adventure of Consciousness*.

Aurobindo expounds his experience of sleep in a chapter entitled 'Sleep and Death'. The association between these two states is important and is one of the leading ideas in his teaching. Death for him is sleep prolonged. The experiences of each state are very similar. We need to bear this in mind. This was also the attitude of our Lord; it is implied in the service of compline which is both a preparation for sleep and for death.

The first principle of Aurobindo's teaching is that sleep is a mode of consciousness. Waking life is one such mode, limited and incomplete. Sleep widens the horizon and opens the ego to new experiences. It supplies a range of new symbols which require the same kind of interpretation, using images, as that which is required in waking life. To begin with the dimension of sleep communicates very little, beyond a more vivid contact with the unconscious activities of the body. As the inner life develops under spiritual discipline so 'we pass from animal sleep to a conscious sleep or sleep of experience.' (Ibid, p. 126)

Aurobindo writes of the sleep of experience in the second part of his teaching. He lays down the principle that the extent of this experience depends upon the degree of waking consciousness achieved. We can only respond to the experiences of sleep in proportion to our response to the experiences of waking life. Sleep then opens a vastly wider range of experience which can be explored 'by a clear austerity, and the absence of desire, the silence of the mind'. (Ibid, p. 127) Without these qualities the sleeper becomes the 'toy of all sorts of delusions'. The experiences offered by sleep require much more than the language of waking life for both understanding and communication. Sleep stimulates all the centres of consciousness and leads right up to the supreme light of the Spirit, to the divine presence where God Himself is given and the whole being re-charged with His life. Aurobindo insists on the need to emerge from the experiences of this kind of sleep gradually, to avoid trying to recall them with too limited a verbal precision, and to be sensitive to the variety of light in which dreams are presented. Indeed, he interprets dreams as the counterpart of the image activity of the imagination in waking life.

Sleep is more than an experience in which the dreamer is a spectator. It is an action, and, as the consciousness grows, so the power to take a vital part in the action of dreams grows. This action is both in the emotions and in the will. In the emotions it develops into an emotional harmony with God who is Ananda in terms of joy. In the will it becomes a co-operation with the spirit of God manifested in the dream images. Sleep then becomes an active participation in the total life of the universe and our decisions and actions during sleep have their effect upon the waking life of earth.

The teaching of Aurobindo about sleep can be paralleled in other traditions, especially in the Christian tradition. The dream of Joseph is an example. In his sleep he entered into the highest level of consciousness, the dimension of angels who have a direct vision of God. There he was able to make a projection of his problem in terms of anamnesis. This made his whole situation present before God: he saw it in the light of God. He mastered his fear and achieved the courage

needed to carry out his decision. He rose from his sleep with his whole
being renewed, ready to fulfil the demands imposed on him by this understanding of the will of God. Such dream situations are offered to us
each time we sleep. In proportion as we are trained to respond to the
enlarged experiences of sleep consciousness, so we enter a relationship
of intense contemplative intimacy both with God and the enlarged universe which sleep brings.

Shakespeare's description of sleep contains all of this teaching in
miniature:

'Sleep that knits up the ravell'd sleave of care,
The death of each day's life, sore labour's bath,
Balm of hurt minds, great nature's second course,
Chief nourisher in life's feast.' (*Macbeth,* act II, sc. 2).

Fynn describes imagination as an inwardness and this goes for
sleep as well. It is a turning of the senses inwards and in proportion as
they are trained to act inwardly they find themselves surrounded by a
wealth of symbols. Out of these are formed the sleep images we call
dreams. If the senses are disorientated in waking life these dream images will be nightmares. But if the senses are trained in the arts of
selection and concentration these dream images will be bridges leading
to intimacy with a greatly enlarged area of consciousness and to a
deeper relationship with God. Sleep and dreams offer this enlarged
contemplative intimacy to those who are trained in waking life to use
their conscious environment in this way.

But it is in sleep that the whole being learns to act in God. It absorbs the joy of the Lord and identifies with His will. This is then
translated into waking action. At present the experiences of what is
called extrasensory perception (ESP) are still being explored and
dogmatic conclusions cannot be reached about them. But the fact of
ESP is established beyond all reasonable doubt and it is in the witness
of dream experiences in many lives that we find the most conclusive
evidence for this kind of communication and influence. The Wise Men
dreamed of the decision of Herod before it was carried out and took
action before the situation had arisen. Pilate was warned through his
wife's dreams and in his unbelieving foolishness ignored their message.
We may not have this kind of intimation, nor the chance to act in such
vital ways, but we all know the restoring power and the divine peace
of sleep which is so near to God that images are replaced by light:
these are reassurances that in sleep we move away from the fantasy
world of consciousness into the outskirts of the real world of the
superconscious and into the very ante-chambers of heaven itself.
Death for those trained to use sleep in these ways is but the stabilising

of life in a world that has already been often experienced.

Thus the doors of perception are opened by sleep to those whose senses and imaginative faculties have been cleansed.

The emotions

We have already seen how creation is personified in many traditions under the image of Mother Earth and how that image reaches a special clarity in the figure of Our Lady. This image visualises creation under a shape which offers the closest intimacy which we have seen developed in many ways. But the Mother Earth image is more than visual. It is emotional. Sense contact with this symbol must always be emotional as well as mental. The intimacy is certainly contemplative, but it is lovingly contemplative in the sense that it uses all the emotional capacities of our nature.

Mother Earth presents herself visually in muted forms to match our obscured perception. She similarly reduces her emotional impact to the measure of our emotional response. This is not a deprivation: it is a merciful dilution. We have to use our emotions with a growing response and in this way we develop that loving contemplative intimacy which is the goal of our prayer.

Fynn and Anna made this pilgrimage in their imaginative life with images which were glowing and vibrant with life, emotionally energised with a variety of joy, grief and fear, with love always at hand to bring them into harmony. Anna had her special movements of joy: she had no scruples about expressing her love: and tears were unashamedly used when they were needed. So the concept images they made brought them into contact with Mister God through His works in living and loving intimacy.

This employment of emotional images follows from observing the instructions St Ignatius gives for the practice of contemplative prayer. Often the Ignatian exercises have been understood in terms of a mental exercise of discursive meditation. The following instruction makes it quite clear that they were intended to be much more.

'We contemplate rather than meditate when, after the memory has recalled the whole, or some detail, of the life of our Lord Jesus Christ, the soul, in a state of profound recollection, employs itself in seeing, hearing, considering the different circumstances of the mystery, for the purpose of being instructed, edified and moved by it. This contemplation takes the name of 'Application of the Senses,' when the soul nourishes itself at leisure, and without the employment of the understanding, on all that the mystery offers it to see, to hear, to taste, to feel, almost as if the fact present to the

imagination passed before the eyes, and affected all the bodily senses.'
(*Spiritual Exercises of St Ignatius*, p. xii)

The human emotions are infinite and vary with each person and situation. Yet there are some basic emotions which are the foundation of all the others. This is taught by many traditions. St John of the Cross, following the western tradition reduces them to four: grief, joy, hope and fear. In the eastern tradition there are three principal emotional states, or *gunas*: the lethargic (*tamasic*), the sanguine (*rajasic*) and the balanced (*sattvic*). The most stable of the emotions is joy which energises the higher forms of contemplation known as *sānanda samādhi*. Wordsworth has his own way of saying much the same thing, but in doing so he brings together both traditions.

'From Nature doth emotion come, and moods
Of calmness equally are Nature's gift:
This is her glory; these two attributes
Are sister horns that constitute her strength.
Hence Genius, born to thrive by interchange
Of peace and excitation, finds in her
His best and purest friend; from her receives
That energy by which he seeks the truth,
From her that happy stillness in the mind
Which fits him to receive it when unsought.'
('The Prelude', book XIII, 1–12)

This interchange between Mother Earth and ourselves in full emotional life is an art which demands life-long growth. The more effervescent emotions are the concern of youth: then follow the deeper emotions of manhood and finally the 'calm of mind, all passion spent' which marks old age. Anna in her brief life seems to have covered the whole range in less than eight years, but she was exceptional. Fynn stumbled on more slowly. Most of us we need the full span of contemplative life to achieve full emotional development. It is a response in both waking and dream consciousness to the emotions nature so certainly evokes from those who share her life.

Expressing these emotions is something much bigger than words. Our images require the same emotional stimulus that Mother Earth gave us when they were being received from her. Just as all the senses were stimulated by nature, so we have to stimulate the image with all our senses to make it come fully alive. Anna's attitude to seeds exactly illustrates what this means. She looked at the flower-filled park and realised that it could be reproduced from the dark grains of seeds in her hand. Then she planted them, pouring into the operation all her love and admiration for Mister God who had thought of the miracle first. We share in something of this process when we make images of God's world and bring them to life.

The life we breathe into our images is the *prāṇā*, the *chi*, the Holy Spirit. He fills our being: we direct His energy to the lifeless work of our imagination and the structure stirs into life, the dead bones begin to live. The image must then be, as St John says, seen with our own eyes functioning at their fullest concentration, gazed upon with those inner eyes of intuition and felt with our own hands. Even that is not enough. It must be loved, whether it is an image of beauty or an image of darkness. And the emotions corresponding to the senses must be focused upon the image so that it lives in its own right and becomes a temple of the living God and an instrument of His power.

It is this living image which becomes the way to our deepest loving, contemplative intimacy with Mother Nature and the God and Father of us all. Once matured it acts with sacramental power, communicating the presence it images, enabling us to touch and taste and see and love the living Lord.

In making these mature, living images poetry and music play a special part. Anna and Fynn had little use for poetry. But music as an enrichment of images they fully understood. Fynn's piano and performance were mediocre, but they were enough to inspire Anna's imagination to its fullest pitch. The music was more than an emotional experience: it led to exciting discoveries in the visible and sound worlds. She was not content to listen: she started to compose, making games and music at the same time, opening up new worlds for her imagination to conquer.

Music does this for our contemplative intimacy with the earth. We can go back to plainsong and listen to the way our predecessors used it, and from them learn the value of simplicity. One of the disasters to the growth of contemplative prayer in Christian worship came with the modern organ and the use of heavy orchestration. The simpler folk tunes, which were so powerful an instrument for expressing emotion, were ousted by melodies with harmonies which obscured the direct communication with the devotional images. We have had our liturgical revolution: we now wait for an even more significant one, the replacement of our present religious music by more contemplative forms.

THE WORLD AS IT IS

Images interiorise the outer symbols and emotional energy brings them to life, but this is not the climax of our contemplative intimacy with the earth. There is a further process, identification with the image. This takes place in various degrees of intensity which are all modes of love. The image must be loved and the love goes beyond the image to the Lord who is its indwelling presence.

In the West there has been a suspicion of an over-identification of God with His creation. Poets and mystics, like Traherne in his 'Centuries of Meditations' have always been prone to emphasise this relationship. The fear is of pantheism. What is noticeable in Traherne is even more apparent in Wordsworth and Shelley. Wordsworth could write of:

> 'Something far more deeply interfused,
> Whose dwelling is the light of setting suns,
> And the round ocean and the living air,
> And the blue sky, and in the mind of man:
> A motion and a spirit, that impels
> All thinking things, all objects of all thought,
> And rolls through all things.'
>
> ('Tintern Abbey')

He did not confuse and limit God to nature. There is a world of difference between recognising the divine present in nature, and worshipping a God limited to nature. The Christian doctrine of the Trinity is the safeguard against this error and preserves both Traherne and Wordsworth from pantheism.

In the East much greater freedom has been observed in describing the relationship between God and His creation. It is frequently mentioned in the Bhagavad-Gita. Here is a typical example:

> 'Who sees his Lord
> Within every creature,
> Deathlessly dwelling
> Amidst the mortal:
> That man sees truly.' (*Bhagavad-Gita* XIII)

It occurs in a spectacular experience of Aurobindo which he describes in his *Adventure of Consciousness*. He had been arrested for being implicated in a revolutionary plot, and imprisoned in solitary confinement for one month in Alipore jail. There he waited in vain for some manifestation of God. He was brought to trial and as he stood in court he was directed where to look. As he looked he had this insight into the divine presence:

'I looked and it was not the magistrate whom I saw, it was Vasudeva, it was Narayana who was sitting there on the bench. I looked at the Prosecuting Counsel and it was not the Counsel for the Prosecution that I saw; it was Sri Krishna who sat there and smiled. "Now do you fear?" he said, "I am in all men and overrule their actions and their words.' "

(The Adventure of Consciousness, p. 162)

This might very well be dismissed as pantheism, for God is recognised as present in His creation, but even these examples do not limit God to His creation. There is no deification of the creation because it is the dwelling place of God. He is like the poet, greater than anything He has made and ultimately apart from it. Yet this insight greatly enhances the wonder of the earth and makes it capable of being used as a gateway into God.

This seems to be what our Lord meant when He took a loaf and said 'This is my body'. He revealed creation as His body, the instrument of His presence and manifestation. The Church has understood this and, in the Eucharist, offers the creation not merely to be contemplated but to be eaten and assimilated, to be used as the bridge which connects man and God.

When we attempt to identify with the images we make of creation we do this because the Lord says this is the ultimate meaning and purpose of the earth He has made. This process of anamnesis by means of an animated image offers us the most complete intimacy we can achieve with God and His creation. We can feed on Him in the heart centre of consciousness by faith with thanksgiving. This is the highest expression of love, the most complete identification.

The Eucharist is the supreme model of this identification and it guards us adequately from the danger of pantheism. It is the model of an intimacy with nature which is universal. All creation is God's body. He indwells all of His creatures. His Spirit is present in all that He has made. Therefore our intimacy with creation must never stop short at contemplative admiration. It must never degenerate into the sentimental relationship which the phrase 'pathetic fallacy' suggests. It must lead to a living and loving intimacy in which the limited ego is fulfilled and united in the personality of God. Every part of creation possesses the power to lead us in this way. We respond adequately when we have reached this degree of intimate union.

Anna and Fynn were certainly not emotional mystics, nor were they poets in the sense of having the fantasy part of their being highly developed. They had their feet firmly on the ground in the East End. Yet here, out of the materials provided by Mother Earth they made their images and quickened them with inspired enthusiasm and used them for penetrating to God and His kingdom and becoming part of it all when they arrived. 'God', said the realistic Anna, 'is in my middle'.

4
Love Me: Love them

Anna by-passed all the theological non-essentials when she summed up her knowledge of God's requirements to the questioning local parson in these words:

'God said love me, love them, and love it, and don't forget to love yourself.' (*Mister God this is Anna*, p. 33)

And to avoid any uncertainty about the meaning of 'them' she went on to particularise: 'I know to love Mister God and to love people and cats and dogs and spiders and flowers and trees with all of me.'

What she said she carried out for she was surrounded by a varied collection of animals and she understood and loved and found God in them. Not only was there Mother Earth to make possible intimacy with God but also all of her creatures. She looked and saw Mister God in His creation and in His creatures too.

HIS CREATURES

Anna was not discovering something new. In the East animals have always played an important part. The little Indian girl who touches the sacred cow and reverently collects its urine and excrement is expressing an approach to creatures which is almost divine. The Lord manifests Himself in them. This is even more clearly expressed in the animal figures outside of the temples – the animal symbols of bull and monkey and tiger which are treated with the worship of divine manifestations. The almost universal practice of animal sacrifice is another expression of this theme. Animals were given to God because it was felt that they had a special capacity for union with Him. As they were transformed in the sacrificial fire so they were supposed to make atonement between God and man. This is one of the messages of the Old Testament sacrificial system and it abounds in the psalms which were its verbal accompaniment. Yet another relationship between man and animals appears in the 'Song of Songs'. They share in human intimacy: they provide simile after simile of human experience:

> 'Your eyes behind your veil are like doves, your hair like a flock of goats streaming down Mount Gilead; your teeth are like a flock of ewes just shorn which have come up fresh from the dipping; each ewe has twins and none has cast a lamb.' (*Song,* 4:1)

But it is in the New Testament and especially in our Lord's teaching and example that the place of animals in contemplative intimacy is most clear.

They were present at all the important moments of His life. At His birth shepherds were watching over their flocks and were the first to worship Him. In St Mark's account of the wilderness temptations he makes the important comment that in the loneliness and struggle of the wilderness the Lord was among the wild beasts. This need not be interpreted in any hostile sense: the wild beasts were His companions. They were present and sustained Him. Fishermen and fish played an important part in His ministry. Towards the end of His ministry He rode into Jerusalem on an unbroken colt. And then like the Buddha, He released the sacrificial animals and birds and for ever saved them from the function of mediating between God and man with the proclamation: 'My house shall be called a house of prayer for all the nations.' (Mk 11:17) After His resurrection the relationship between the Lord and His creatures continues. In the vision of the heavenly worship of the Apocalypse St John writes:

> 'In the centre, round the throne itself, were four living creatures, covered with eyes, in front and behind. The first creature was like a lion, the second like an ox, the third had a human face, the fourth was like an eagle in flight.' (Rev. 4. 7–8)

The creatures are there no longer as silent companions but as participants in the very worship of heaven.

Our Lord's teaching is impregnated with metaphors and similes from the lives and actions of the creatures. He uses the symbol of the shepherd and applies it to Himself: He uses the ways of sheep to describe the ways of His people. They do not listen to the words of complicated arguments: they hear the sound of His voice. He makes magnificent use of the relationship between the shepherd and the flock to expound His own relationship to His people. He is the door of the sheepfold: He stands by them in danger: He lays down His life for them. If God is integrated in the earth how much more completely is He integrated in the lives of His creatures. In their presence we are in the presence of the Lord: in their life and ways we are looking upon His life and ways.

This was deeply understood by the early Christians. In choosing a symbol for the Lord they modified the Greek *kouroi* figures and called Him their *Kurios*. But they went even further. Their chief symbol for the Lord who chose fishermen for His first disciples and knew the ways of fish so well that He could catch them when the professionals failed was the fish (*ixthus*) which was a secret anagram for the deepest mysteries of His being: i = Jesus. x = Christos. th = *theos* (god) u = *huios* (son) s = *soter* (saviour). The later Christians chose animal symbols for other mysteries of their faith: the eagle, the lion, the pelican, the goat and of course the lamb. The following is an extract from a description of the female goat which appears in the 'Bestiaire du Christ' and has been reproduced and hung over the stable of the two Anchorhold goats, Daisy and Anna:

> 'When the female goat climbs the highest peaks, not only does its field of vision enlarge but it is said that its visual acuity to distinguish details grows extraordinarily as well. Therefore it surpasses all creatures in its ability to take in with one look the most immense vistas and their most minute features. It symbolizes the highest perfection of the searching and penetrating gaze of Christ, who as God, sees all in the past, present and future.' (*The Symbolic Animals of Christianity*)

CONSIDER THE CROCODILE

Animals both in the Eastern and Western traditions were not merely looked upon as sources of food, though that was one of their important functions: they were also symbols revealing secrets about God and man, instruments for establishing intimacy between them. In these roles they had a vital part to play in the life of man, so vital that often they were used as symbols of the gods.

Yeats in his poem 'The Indian Upon God', touches lightly on one of their most important functions in human thought. He writes:

'I passed along the water's edge below the humid trees,
My spirit rocked in sleep and sighs and saw the moorfowl pace
All dripping on a grassy slope, and saw them cease to chase
Each other round in circles and heard the eldest speak:
Who holds the world between His bill and made us strong or weak
Is an undying moorfowl, and He lives beyond the sky.
The rains are from His dripping wings, the moonbeams from His
eye.
. . . A little way within the gloom a roebuck raised his eyes
Brimful of starlight and he said: The Stamper of the stars,
He is a gentle roebuck, for how else, I pray, could He,
Conceive a thing so sad and soft, a gentle thing like me?

We can smile at this poem but it hides great truth. It is part of St
Paul's theme that the visible things of creation manifest the invisible
attributes of God and how better can this be done than through the
varied characteristics of His creatures? This is part of the argument in
Job. He is told to consider the chief of the beasts, the crocodile, and as
he does so he reaches one of the greatest moments of insight into the
being and work of God.

'I know that thou canst do all things
and that no purpose is beyond thee.
But I have spoken of great things which I have not understood;
things too wonderful for me to know.
I knew of thee only by report,
but now I see thee with my own eyes.
Therefore I melt away;
I repent in dust and ashes.' (Job 42:2–6)

Through animals and their lives God reveals Himself. The psalmist
sees God's loving providence as he considers the lions roaring after
their prey. Our Lord sees it in the smaller things, the care for the
sparrows. Anna saw Him in the cats and dogs and spiders she was
commanded to love. Blake went even deeper and found animals
posing the profound questions of life and God's relationships. He
shows this happening as he contemplates the lamb and the tiger. They
evoke the same question and reduce him to the silent wonder of faith.

To the lamb: 'Little Lamb, who made thee?'
To the tiger: 'Did He who made the lamb make thee?'

There is a disarming simplicity about these questions, but they carry the questing mind of the poet to the ultimate issues of human perplexity. Animals have the strange power to do this, and, when we surrender to them, we find ourselves not left in an exasperating state of doubt but in the divine presence, willing to rest in a God who can do all things.

It is this function of animals to reveal God which should be the main reason for our protest against their misuse and exploitation. Hens under battery conditions cannot illustrate the Lord's parable of Himself like the mother hen longing to gather her young under her wings. Wild animals in unnatural zoo conditions are denied the freedom to live as God wished them to. The over-domestic pet, hindered from contact with nature, obliged to make unnatural relationship with human mental disorders, is a parody of the free creature manifesting the work of God. Blake's 'Auguries of Innocence' speak for all of us who see God's creatures as the Lord made present in them.

> 'A Robin redbreast in a cage
> Puts all heaven in a rage. . . .
> A horse misus'd upon the road
> Calls to Heaven for human blood.
> Each outcry of the hunted hare
> A fibre from the brain does tear.'

Every exploitation and misuse of animals dim the glory of God in them and injure a part of man's nature. They prevent him from seeing God in the creature and hinders the intimacy between man and God which the free creature can give. This seems the true basis of our protest against man's outrages against animals: it exceeds the ecological reasons for our protest.

Instincts

Through contemplating the crocodile Job came not only to know God: he came to know himself. Animals have much to teach man about himself and his place in creation.

Martin Seymour-Smith in his recent book makes an observation about Freud and his methods whose important element of truth needs to be applied when we are considering his analysis of man and his predicament. He writes:

'Freud's theory, in its earliest as in its final form, is a metaphorical construct – a massive and regular fiction derived from his clinical experience of himself and of a number of Viennese middle-class

neurotics living in the final, rotten-ripe period of a great empire.'
(*Sex and Society*, p. 49)

We might regret the limitation of Freud's theories, especially his
concentration on the libido with its almost exclusively sexual instinct
and wish that he had taken more notice of the evidence animals could
supply of this part of our nature. For one of the great contributions of
animals to man's knowledge of himself is that they tell us a great deal
about the structure and function of the instincts which we share with
them. And they present us with them in a much clearer and more
unspoilt form than Freud or his fellow psychiatrists could ever observe
in the middle-class neurotics they studied.

Animals confirm that there is a sexual instinct. In this they agree
with Freud who, in the early form of his teaching, seemed to suggest
that this was the only driving force in the libido. He did moderate this
theory a little later and even went as far as to say 'in the last resort we
must begin to love in order that we may not fall ill'. But animals tell us
something very different about the sexual instinct and its activities. It
is certainly not the only instinct, nor is it the instinct most often in action. The sexual instinct is under strict biological control. In many
creatures it only dominates at certain periods; for long spaces it is
quiescent. It is an instinct which starts off a cycle of processes which
are essentially non-sexual in content. The sexual instinct seems to
appear when it is needed, for specific purposes, and for a time only: it
is certainly not the dominant instinct of life.

Although it would not be right to restrict the activity of the human
sex instinct to the animal dimension it is equally wrong to draw one's
conclusions about it from experience with the neurotic. Animal sexuality gives us a picture of undisturbed physical sexuality, and this is a
good basic model to work from. It shows us the sexual instinct as one
among many. It shows us sex as a drive which leads from physical intercourse, from *eros* into other activities and relationships. It shows us
the sex instinct as more than the drive of the individual libido: as a
force acting on a collective and universal rhythm, drawing its inspiration from more than personal needs, linking fragments of creative life
into a universal and cosmic whole. Sexuality for animals is an instrument for common intimacy. This may very well be its normal and
healthy expression in man. In forming our ideas of the sexual instinct
and its expression we should take animals as our models for sex in its
more primitive and normal forms.

But animals reveal other and more powerful instincts. Hunger,
anger, fear, curiosity and happiness are some of them. These they
show without camouflage and show us how these instincts should be

expressed. Each of them is a force driving the creature out of isolation into some state of intimacy, either with another or with the herd.

Hunger is an example. The psalmist places a great emphasis on the power of hunger to lead to God. 'The lions roaring after their prey do seek their meat from God.' (Ps 104:21) It also leads animals into relationships with each other. Most animals come together into herds driven by the instinct of hunger. This is an instinct that is much more continuously demanding than sex. For the animal, sex is occasional and cyclic: hunger is continuous and urgent, a matter of life or death. The well-disciplined human being finds this is true of his own instinctive life. Under the guidance of his instincts and protected from the media he finds that sex takes a minor place in the instinctive life and that there is nothing erratic or capricious about their healthful use. The lion has his own diet and it is different from that of the other creatures. Animals eat at prescribed times. There are periods for rest and rumination. A herd of cows grazes the field in a planned way, coming into a patterned relationship with each other and the field. These experiences are translated into human terms when the hunger instinct is allowed to control behaviour and is freed from the hidden persuaders of the advertising media. Above all the hunger instinct, responded to in this way, leads to human and divine intimacy. The eucharist is the most articulated form of this truth, but every meal governed by the instinct of hunger can be so, too.

So it is with the other instincts: anger, fear, curiosity and happiness. Animals reveal these instincts in their most vital form and also show the best ways of using them to further the development of life. Konrad Lorenz has shown the value of carefully studying this sequence of instincts under the general heading of aggression (*On Aggression,* Methuen, 1966). He shows animals not only responding to the stimulation of anger and fear, but using them to strengthen their intimacy with each other. The instincts uncover not only libidinal energy but also an infused response pattern which is integrating rather than destructive. In human life it is possible to direct these instincts in a similar way. Dance movement resolves a great many anger and fear situations and blends them into a harmony of joyful relationships. The instincts used in this way are not volcanoes of fearful and destructive energy: they are power sources for the building up of the community. The Bible writers had no difficulty in ascribing all these instincts to God Himself, but because they understood the action of these instincts in animals the image of God they produced was not one of destructive tyranny but the psalmist's image of a loving and powerful Father who could be angry and forgiving and whose life was the essence of joy. To such a harmony these instincts lead man when they are expressed in the life of the balanced human being, and their inbuilt patterns and responses are allowed to operate without hindrance. All this does not ignore the fact that man's instinctive life has been seriously damaged and needs cure, but it does recognise that the instincts have not been irreparably destroyed and that to get a true idea of what they are in their undamaged state, how they should be used and where they lead we can learn from the less damaged instincts in animals. Animals reveal much we need to know about the unconscious, about the vital centres of consciousness at the base of the spine, in the genital regions and in the solar plexus.

Language of instinct

Animals express the basic instincts without words. They use a language of signs, sounds and movements. It is a language which has to be learnt before we can penetrate to the secrets it reveals.

Gerald Durrell is one of our contemporaries who has lovingly mastered this language and shares his understanding with the readers of his animal books.

In *Menagerie Manor* (p. 117) he describes a watch of several hours at the hatching out of a small tortoise. He thinks the time well spent for, as he watched the process, he found himself mastering the language of movement and sign. Using his hind feet to make a hole in the egg the small tortoise would every so often swivel himself round to look out rather anxiously with his little wrinkled face on the great world he was preparing to enter. Durrell found humour in the face and the situation and responded to the reassurance of the world as it prepared to welcome this new tortoise.

Durrell shows us that animals speak through their bodies. Changes in the outward appearances of animals can be read as messages of their needs and emotions. Many animals will show aggression by swelling visibly before their enemy. Others will shrink away when showing fear. Animals constantly speak to man and each other in these ways. It is a language of signs which, once understood, makes possible a conversation with creatures normally classified as dumb.

But animals speak most clearly in movement, posture and stillness. Anna understood this as she communicated with her East End menagerie. There was Bossy, the cat: about twelve pounds of fighting fury until she came along and then they spoke to each other in the process of eating and she taught him to make his meal last about five minutes instead of the usual five seconds. The result was intimacy between them.

Animals speak through movement and provide us with models for many of our own movements. It is in imitating some of their movements that we correct our own and also find harmony with creatures. This has been discovered by people dancing the 'T'ai Chi Ch'uan', a dance largely built up from observing animal movement. Birds and squirrels will approach with complete confidence when these movements are being performed and the dancer finds that their consciousness opens out to him as he moves. Many Yoga postures are based on animal postures and movements and again these help the performer to enter into a deep relationship with creatures and at the same time to share in the unrestricted intimacy which such postures give with the rest of creation. The 'Alexander Technique', largely a series of remedial postures based on the sound physical principles so clearly exemplified in animals was designed to correct obstacles in the throat centre. In unspoilt and primitive communities, such as still exist in Indian villages, it is a common sight to find dancers dressed like animals and imitating their movements. Animal postures were used in medieval times to communicate truths. The Lindisfarne Gospels illustrate this: where the first page of St Mark's Gospel is illuminated with a winged lion in stylised posture, speaking truths beyond the range of words.

Animal movements not only communicate intimacy between them and mankind: they are also an instrument of intimacy between ourselves and God. In Job there is the command to look well at the crocodile and Job does so. He examines the strength in his loins, the muscles of his belly, the tail as rigid as a cedar, the bones like tubes of bronze and the limbs like bars of iron. He watches him in stillness and movement: concealed under the lotus, his prowess and grace of movement, the lashings of his tail. And he is led beyond admiration for a marvellous creation into the very presence of God. That is the ultimate communication of animal language in posture and movement: it is an intimacy with God. Some contemplatives reach this conclusion and admit it simply like the psalmist who wrote: 'O Lord, how manifold are Thy works: in wisdom hast Thou made them all.' (Ps 104:24) Others, like Gerald Durrell watching the hatching of a tortoise, are more scientific and reserved, but there is still that wonder which Wordsworth describes as the outer door of the divine presence chamber.

> 'There was a time when meadow, grove and stream,
> The earth and every common sight,
> To me did seem
> Apparelled in celestial light,
> The glory and the freshness of a dream.'
> ('Ode on Intimations of Immortality')

Some never lose this awareness and when they do the glory of a bird's flight or the patient strength of an animal under perfect control recalls them to the recognition of God's presence, His glory and His Love.

HAVE DOMINION

Animals offer a way to contemplative intimacy which is wider than themselves. In instinct, movement and posture they reveal wide vistas leading to God and man and the whole creation. But they share in the imperfection of nature, their faculties are imperfect, their communication obscured. They need man's help; they wait the general renewal of all creation.

The Bible traces the need of animals for man's help to a creative condition implanted by God Himself.

> Then God said, 'Let us make man in our image and likeness to rule the fish in the sea, the birds of heaven, the cattle, all wild animals on earth, and all reptiles that crawl upon the earth.' (Gen 1:26)

Animals need man for their perfection; he must play his part in ruling them and sharing with them his higher faculties. Only when these are added to the instinctive faculties of animals do they achieve their full stature.

This Exupéry understands and beautifully describes in his account of the taming of the fox by the Little Prince. It is the fox who recognises his need to be tamed and helps the Little Prince to meet it. He knew the meaning of being tamed, 'establishing ties', and he knowingly accepted the relationship it would forge between himself and his tamer.

> 'To me, you are still nothing more than a little boy who is just like a hundred thousand other little boys. And I have no need of you. And you have no need of me. To you, I am nothing more than a fox, like a hundred thousand other foxes. But if you tame me, then we shall need each other. To me, you will be unique in all the world. To you, I shall be unique in all the world.' (Antoine de Saint-Exupéry, *The Little Prince,* p. 64, Piccolo, 1945)

The fox then describes what must be done to tame him. The Prince must approach slowly and win his confidence. He must avoid words, remembering that 'words are a source of misunderstandings.' He must also keep in mind that 'it is only with the heart that one can see rightly; what is essential is invisible to the eye.' And he must communicate regularly, with a closer intimacy every day.

In these brief instructions the fox summarises many of the actions that go to the taming of an animal and the establishment of intimacy. It is a work of contemplative understanding and complete sympathy. It is possible because in both the animal and his tamer there are shared needs and mutual responsibilities. The tamer becomes responsible for the creature he has tamed and the creature finds his range of intimacy enlarged to include all the world. This is the fox's greatest discovery:

'If you tame me, it will be as if the sun came to shine on my life. I shall know the sound of a step that will be different from all the others. Other steps send me hurrying back beneath the ground. Yours will call me, like music, out of my burrow.' (ibid, p. 67)

Taming brought the fox not only into intimacy with his trainer but with the whole creation. His experience is a commentary on the mysterious statement of St Paul: 'For the created universe waits with eager expectation for God's sons to be revealed ... the universe itself is to be freed from the shackles of mortality and enter upon the liberty and splendour of the children of God.' (Rom 8:19)

It is a two-way service: the tamer and the tamed serve each other and in the work grow in mutual intimacy.

Understanding is the first step in the process. It is an act of contemplation in which all the senses are concentrated on a limited number of creatures. This limitation is essential. The world is full of a multitude of creatures and if one tried to achieve intimacy with them all the most that could be hoped for would be a shallow and distracted knowledge. Animals, like other objects of concentration, need to be selected and then separately contemplated. One has to place a frame or *mandala* around a few and, within that area, look well. In deciding which animals to contemplate in this way it is usually best to specialise on those nearest at hand. This is what our Lord did, and, in doing so, achieved an intense intimacy. He does not talk about elephants and tigers: He speaks of sheep and goats and hens. Anna limited herself even more strictly. For her it was the doings of Bossy and Patch she watched and mastered. This contemplation of creatures near at hand ensures that they are known at the sub-conscious level, through the memory of childhood as well as the experience of adult life. They become integrated into our thought patterns and we grow together in intimacy and understanding.

Contemplate a few chosen creatures: it is the best way to achieve understanding, and contemplate them with all the senses. Look at them well. Look at them outside as separate from ourselves with a life and character of their own and with much to communicate. And then make the internal image of them in their total surroundings as creatures of God sharing the life of the same garden as ourselves. This demands a great activity of the imagination. The scenery has to be filled in around the animal we contemplate. This involves surrounding it with its background, and finding the point where God impinges on its life. The psalmist did this with his lion. It was in his hunger that the lion met God. This contemplation of the animal with the eyes of the body and the eyes of the heart is a long, slow process which must never be rushed. This the fox taught the Little Prince. He had to be very patient, to sit a little closer every day.

Touch is one of the most intimate senses for reaching contemplative intimacy with animals. They must always touch first. It is humiliating, but unless one is prepared to wait for this to happen hours of patient watching may be lost. The hand may be stretched out but not with any sign of threat or compulsion. A little closer every day and then the moment of contact.

Touch sets up a current of intimacy between the creature and the tamer which grows stronger every day and communicates more deeply than words. In India it is a frequent sight to see the cow walking with complete assurance whilst the children and Parsee business men stepped forward to touch it. Thousands of years went to the making of that intimacy. We must be patient.

The senses of smell and taste and hearing come to sharpen our contemplative relationship until gradually the animal comes alive within the heart, and the inner image begins to communicate secrets about the animal and its maker to us. The New Testament writers understood this: so did the Christian contemplatives of all ages. It comes out especially clearly in St Peter's vision on the house top at Joppa. There the sail cloth full of creatures of every kind came down and as Peter contemplated them, he reached his moment of insight when he saw the whole of creation cleansed by the work of Christ. (*see* Acts 10:9–16) St John used animals similarly in his great contemplative masterpiece of the Apocalypse. They played an important part in the life of St Columba: St Francis's ministry was almost as much for animals as for human beings. In his lovely Canticle of the Sun he reveals how deep was his intimacy with creatures and how much they gave to him.

St Francis illustrates the emotional level that the contemplative intimacy with animals opens. Their language is never verbal, and therefore the images with which they communicate appeal immediately to the emotions. The singing of birds is the stimulus of joy: the roaring of the lions evokes fear: the curiosity of the goat, as the medieval writer knew, extends the human vision. The restricted emotions of human beings are enormously widened by contact with the emotions of animals, and this leads to the emotional contact with God which Job attained and which enabled him to break through the limitations of his rational faculties.

The fox ended his relationship with the Little Prince in tears. The images they had made of each other had to be withdrawn. But the fox saw that the contact had been worth while, for it led them both nearer the heart of each other and the mystery of life. It opened the fox's eyes to 'the colour of the wheat fields', to beauty, to truth itself. He told the Little Prince that the contact with himself would help him to understand his roses, that his own were unique in all the world because they alone could reveal the mystery of his life to him.

This is what contemplative images of animals can do for us. The making of them is a focusing of our powers of concentration. They energise our emotions. They provide us with a luminous centre which reveals not only the creature with outstanding clarity but, when the image is withdrawn, leads on as it led Job into the presence of God Himself. Such contemplative understanding of the creature is a door opening into heaven and God. We are tamed and raised as we learn to understand and tame the creature. Whether man likes it or not he is destined to have dominion over the creatures. Exupéry's fox accepted this. Anna exercised it with gentleness, but she taught the cat Bossy not to bolt his food. All the same, there is a great difference between ruling and leading animals and crushing and exploiting them. The first approach, like dictatorship, leads eventually to rebellion, and is the death of intimacy. The second develops the capacity for intimacy in the leader and gives him the trust and cooperation of the creature he leads.

There is a large natural reserve park in Madhya Pradesh where animals are allowed total freedom and protection. They use their freedom well and achieve a balanced life. It was an unforgettable experience to spend an afternoon and evening in a *machan* watching nature about her business. Law and harmony reigned. Yet something was missing. There was a sense of isolation, of being an intruder in a life one longed to share. Human participation in that life, with man taking a restrained and legitimate part would have added to the happiness of both man and beast. But how can this be achieved?

Partly by man providing animals with the right conditions for their life. This was being done by the park keepers. They were responsible for applying the rules which gave the animals their freedom. What was lacking was the deeper intimacy.

This is only achieved partially at present. It is achieved by the rider who controls his highly trained horse with mental images and the slightest pressure of his knees. It is achieved by the shepherd who directs his dog in a work of mutual control, without seeming to give any orders at all. But it is not achieved by the animal trainer who bribes and frightens the animal into submission and replaces the animals' understanding and instincts with his own.

In the popular book *Born Free* there is an account of a long and understanding relationship between a woman and a lioness. It is a classic example of an intimacy achieved through wise and restrained leadership. The lioness was not deprived of her freedom: the trainer always led from a position of weakness and the result was an intimacy which began to show the first glimmerings of what we mean by love. Mrs Adamson was as much developed in her capacity for intimacy as the lioness she led. Perhaps as man develops in true leadership, so animals will develop in their response and grow more nearly able to share in the life of those who lead them. The mature relationship between animals and mankind is not isolation but integration into the one family. Such an achievement will raise both parts of creation into the presence of God.

The deeper the human-animal relationship, the deeper grows man's power to relate to them and to his fellow-men. Kipling found this and so did George Orwell.

In his *Jungle Tales* Kipling combined a very profound understanding of animals with a superb imagination: the result was that he got to the heart of animals and used them to reveal the heart of man. He was spectacularly successful in his portrayal of one of the most critical stages of mankind, the pre-adolescent boy, and he shows the introduction of Mowgli to animals as his preparation for the ways of men. Mowgli became a man because he shared the full physical and emotional life of animals. Like the fox and the Little Prince he reaches a stage where this intimacy has to change and he goes away to the rational world of men, but how sanely he was developed and what a splendid manhood he carried out of the jungle into the world. Something of that kind happens to each of us as a result of our full intimacy with animals. They carry us through the processes of our physical and emotional growth and take us to the point where we can begin our mental and spiritual pilgrimage. Such is Kipling's insight and it is confirmed in the experience of the most contemplatively developed human beings.

George Orwell, in *Animal Farm,* approached the relationship between man and animals from a different angle. He projected on to animals the inadequate mental development of man. In the animals this inadequacy assumed monstrous proportions against the background of their balanced physical and emotional life. All those animals who tried to absorb the rational life of man became deformed caricatures of men. The pigs were no longer pigs, they were sensual dictators: the dogs were exploited to supply the force needed to apply injustice. Human and distorted mental states not only showed up in their naked ugliness: they also destroyed the animal bodies on to which they had been grafted.

What is the lesson of this magnificent satire? It is the truth that animals in their true natures communicate with the source of life in a beautiful harmony. Men in their true natures communicate with the source of life in a beautiful harmony. But when these natures are distorted they can no longer consort together in a complementary intimacy which raises them both. When their distorted natures are brought together they contribute to a mutual destruction and the break up of all intimacy with each other and of their common life in God. This truth, enunciated with such power in *Animal Farm,* is a warning that contemplative intimacy between men and animals is not an optional or unimportant achievement: it either raises them both to a higher relationship with life, as Kipling teaches, or it leads both over a precipice of destruction. The miracle of the Gerasene swine is the Lord's dramatic statement of this truth: 'And the herd, of about two thousand, rushed over the edge into the lake and were drowned.' (Mk 5:1–13) Men and animals need each other in their ascent to God: when they fail to develop their full capacities, intimacy is impossible and destruction follows. This is the grave basis of the Christian protest against the exploitation of animals and the misuse of the rational faculties of men. We rise and fall together.

We share our instincts with animals, always remembering that our instincts compared with theirs are nearly always distorted by the influence of the environment in which we live. Our instincts of movement have been damaged by bad habits. The other instincts of sex, hunger, fear, anger and curiosity have also been damaged. We have only to compare the action of these instincts in animals to see how seriously distorted they are in most human beings. One of the most effective ways of restoring these instincts to their intended health is to co-operate with the instincts of animals in movement.

This process of restoration is impossible without the grace of the Holy Spirit. The animals are themselves the work of the Spirit and in them He lives and moves. When with this understanding we turn to them we are turning directly to the Spirit and using His grace.

Animals are not creatures of one instinct, nor do they limit their instincts to one centre of consciousness. Each instinct is capable of
movement and transformation to strengthen the others. Sex is one of
many instincts. The hunger instinct is much more continuous and
frequent. And fear and anger and curiosity play a regular part in the
instinctual life of animals.

It is by contemplating and identifying with the balanced instinctual
life of animals that so many of our own unbalanced and over-
stimulated instincts are brought under control. Fynn noticed this with
Anna who was brought up in the open life of the East End 'when sex
with a little 's' was as natural in its right place as the air we breathe. It
hadn't got the self-importance of a capital 'S' nor for that matter its
problems.' (*Mister God this is Anna,* p. 85). She had no isolated sex
problem nor did the other instincts cause her undue difficulty. She
could handle hunger without diet fads and the same was true with fear
and anger. Her unrestricted life with creatures put her in touch with
these instincts and also showed her how they were being successfully
handled and balanced every day. Intimate contact with animals gives
us this healing and takes us further, for in sharing the movements of
animals we come to participate in their blending of the instincts into a
harmonious whole.

When primitive peoples wish to do this, they sometimes put on a
mask of the animal or the plumage of a bird. In this way they lose
their own identity and blend with the creature. They imitate its
movements in a ritual dance which leads to complete union in physical
movement and emotional and instinctive life. The result is not
degradation but a kind of emotional and instinctive catharsis. The
dancer comes out of his induced trance restored.

It is not suggested that this method of sharing the life of an animal
should be imitated without modification. In the West we cannot be so
spontaneous. We need the concealments of art, but even then the
experience can be much the same. Yoga postures are based often on
animal movements. When they are performed with mental concentration on the particular animal much of the animal's strength and health
are transferred. This is even more true of the T'ai Chi Ch'uan which is
rich in animal imagery. Its main image concerns the mastery of the
tiger nature, not in terms of repression but of transformation. Many of
his virtues can be absorbed on the way: his instincts, his strength, his
courage. What has to be added is that contemplative clarity which is
man's special gift to the animal nature. Other creatures have subsidiary parts in the dance: the sparrow, the stork, the monkey, the
golden cock. The various movements bring intimacy with each
creature, an intimacy which begins by healing and then leads on to the

development of an emotional relationship of love. As the dance weaves out all these complicated relationships, so the dancer moves into a transfiguring ecstasy which does not end with the creatures but leads on to a full share in their work of bringing mankind to loving intimacy with God.

A way into God

Creatures lead man into God. This is the climax of our relationship with them, and it is shown in the Bible in the remarkable place and work given to the dove. In the Old Testament it is the creature which reassures man of the merciful character of God. The creation saga speaks of God in terms of its movement: He broods over the face of the waters of chaos. (Gen 1:2) This is the creature that brought back the olive leaf to the ark and announced that the flood was over. (Gen 8:11) In the New Testament it plays a more prominent part.

John the Baptist used the dove as an object of loving contemplation, and it became an instrument of healing and insight. The contemplation of the dove was needed to soften and balance the harsher instincts of his character. From a fierce and condemning prophet he grew into the gentle and retiring friend of the bridegroom, Christ, content in the lowest place: 'As he grows greater, I must grow less.' (Jn 3:29) Through this contemplation he saw heaven opened and came to understand the presence and work of the Spirit. He saw the mystery of the Spirit as the divine life coming from heaven to earth and flowing from Christ into the world. Through this he was led to see the full stature of Christ, again in terms of animal symbols: the Lamb of God who is taking away the sin of the world and is God's chosen one. (Jn 1:34). To these great heights did John's intimacy with the dove in contemplation lead him.

There is a world the creatures can help us to develop and use in this way.

There must be a deliberate choice of certain creatures for this contemplative intimacy.

Creatures of a particular symbolism occupy an important place in the Church. For instance, the eagle is associated with St John. In him many of the qualities of the eagle are signified. Contemplation of the eagle is one of the ways of contemplating St John and His master. This use of symbols can be newly applied today. A creature can open for us the secrets of ourselves and of God. In recent times this has been done by Richard Bach in his story *Jonathan Livingston Seagull* (Turnstone Press, 1972).

Under the symbol of a seagull Richard Bach describes man's predicament and the way of his growth. He identifies man with the seagull, and breaks through to an astonishing insight into the meaning and purpose of life. But the seagull has a shadow self, too, which is in each of us. It is represented by that majority that dodges and fights for food, the crowd who don't bother to learn more than the simplest facts of flight – how to get from shore to food and back again, that majority for whom flying does not matter so much as eating. The symbolic Jonathan opts out from them and, concentrating on flying rather than eating, makes discoveries which put him ahead of his time and lead him into the secrets of a full instinctive, physical and emotional life. It is a work which resembles the courageous explorations of Aurobindo in the East, an exploration to which all of us are challenged.

Masefield, in these lines from 'The Everlasting Mercy', shows the glory of complete intimacy achieved through the ministry of creatures with Christ Himself.

> 'O glory of the lighted mind,
> How dead I'd been, how dumb, how blind.
> The station brook, to my new eyes,
> Was babbling out of paradise;
> The waters rushing from the rain
> Were singing Christ has risen again.
> I thought all earthly creatures knelt
> From raptures of the joy I felt.'

Here are all the elements of creaturely and human intimacy: the contemplative awareness, the emotional harmony, the divine insight of joy making that degree of contemplative joy, *sānanda samādhi,* which is the highest union with God on this side of death.

We have confirmed this at the Anchorhold by gradually bringing creatures to share our life. Bees came first, 'the singing masons building roofs of gold', and they brought joy. Then the hens, models of the relationship between the Lord and His people. And finally the goats with their special power, like the Old Testament goat of Azazel, to take away from the family frictions and separation and inject into us their robust independence and strong sense of humour. We have found these goats do for us what they used to be allowed to do in a herd of cows: they bring emotional harmony and strengthen community life. They have always served Indian families in this way: now two of them serve us.

There is in the Basilique Saint-Sernin in Toulouse a marvellous 12th century sculpture of Christ en Majesté. The figure is enclosed in the traditional framework of the mandala: at the four corners there are

Christ in Majesty
Basilique Saint-Sernin
Toulouse

carvings of four tamed creatures, forming as it were gateways into the image and protecting it from danger. These are symbols of the full contribution of animals to human happiness. They not only offer intimacy with themselves and open up ways of intimacy between human beings: they are doorways into God Himself. This idea is admitted in all the great contemplative traditions. This carving is an example of its place in Christianity, but it is also expressed in the carved elephants outside the Buddhist caves at Karla, the Hindu animal figures of Marūthi, the sacred bull and the snake in the Oriental traditions and the dragon in China.

Lewis Carroll in his allegory *Alice in Wonderland* emphasises this truth and, in the adventures of Alice, shows how man must respond to animals in order to receive the full range of intimacy they offer. Alice comes to intimacy with truth through a variety of creatures and a variety of responses. She may not be a formal contemplative, but she demonstrates ways of reaching intimacy with creatures that the contemplative might well learn.

First, she always adapts herself physically to the animal she is meeting. This is a principle understood by Exupéry's fox. 'First you will sit down a little distance from me,' he advises. You will, in other words, come down to my level. So with Alice, who had her own ways of changing her size. Only when she was physically in harmony with her animals was the beginning of intimacy possible. A great many things have to be thrown away before the contemplative can begin to make contact with the animal of his choice. Like His Lord, he has to learn to empty himself.

Then Alice balanced reason and imagination in her relationships. She tried to take on the mind of those she talked to. She talked from their point of view. Then she identified with their emotions and used her imagination to become like them. So she was able to talk to such an elusive creature as the Cheshire Cat because she was roughly his size and had absorbed his thoughts.

It is this interchange between reason and imagination that maintains the health of the contemplative and prepares him for union with God. The laws of life in the animal world must be mastered before any imaginative structure can be raised. It is no accident that some of the greatest naturalists have been also men of deep prayer. This was true of Edward Wilson and was manifest in his art. His masterly drawings of penguins and the birds, made during the Antarctic expeditions, are based on patient study and exact knowledge. They reveal to the scientist all he wants to know about the structure of the creatures. But these drawings are also alive with the love and imagination of a man who saw the animals as creatures made by God and used them to enter His presence. This entry in his diary for 27 October, 1911 shows Wilson at his most sympathetic and intimate:

'At the Great Razorback we were in the midst of a nursery of young Weddell Seals, all born within the last 4 or 5 days and some only a day or so. They are jolly little woolly haired yellowish animals with great big black eyes. The old mothers took no notice of us, except one which lolloped in a great hurry after our sledge and viciously bit the end of it. I found one baby seal had got frozen into the ice — it was quite alive but lying in a pool of thaw water, so I freed it and put it back with its mother who continued to snooze a yard off and showed not the slightest interest. When I got back to the hut I found that I had got a touch of snow glare, as I had marched without goggles, and I spent a lively night in consequence.'
(Edward Wilson, *Diary of the Terra Nova Expedition to the Antarctic 1910–1912,* p. 190)

Here is all the precision of the scientist coupled with the sympathy of the contemplative and his last letter to his parents, with his reassurance that his love for them has deepened and his confidence in the divine presence and mercy, shows how near he had grown to God. Wilson is a classic example of the way in which intimacy between man and animals develops humanity without in any way sacrificing its specifically human virtues. The instincts, the emotions, the physical powers are all brought into harmonious development and at the same time the rational faculties are not reduced. Emptying the self does not reduce the self but rather raises it to the measure of the stature of the fulness of Christ. There is no sign of the human being lost in the contact with the creature. He is raised to his full powers. He is made capable of his own intimacy with God.

5
Love yourself

When we speak of intimacy between human beings we leave behind many of the simplicities we have been considering in dealing with human beings and animals. We enter a confused area where strife and separation often seem to prevail, and where even the elect fail to achieve the intimacy of one communion and fellowship and fragment into warring sects and discord. Even the great achieved intimacies of an Antony and Cleopatra, of a Helöise and Abélard are more imperfect than perfect, and are destroyed by death.

But there is one exception. The perfect intimacy has been achieved. The Son of God took humanity into Himself and at that point raised human nature to a perfect intimacy in the person of Himself. What Aurobindo spent his life trying to achieve has already been achieved by the Son of God: we are now in the stage Aurobindo so clearly saw would follow that achievement: this intimacy is being communicated by the Spirit to the whole human race. The embryonic achievement is infecting the whole universe and already, in the short period of less than two thousand years, our humanity is firmly embarked on a course which will culminate in the taking of the whole of our manhood, renewed and glorified, into God.

We are not then in a stage of uncertainty about the possibility of reaching this intimacy: we are already involved in it. Our inescapable situation is to respond to the conditions of intimacy under which we now live and to grow as far as we can into the greatest measure of participation with its victorious centre.

CHRIST THE MODEL

Perfect intimacy has been achieved in Christ. He is the model on which the intimacy of His members must be built. In studying Him and co-operating with His Spirit we embark on a course which will lead to a full share in that intimacy. That requires a careful examination of the structure of intimacy in Him.

The intimacy of Christ is internal and personal: it is also external and corporate. That is the basic pattern which we have to examine and reproduce.

The inner self

Christ was perfectly integrated within Himself. Whilst the storm raged outside He was asleep, perfectly at one in Himself. He went through the experiences of His life unshaken either by the ecstasy of the transfiguration, or by the demands of His passion, death and resurrection, and He went on to the glory of the ascension with the inner harmony of his life unmoved. How this happened and what was the inner essence of His peace are revealed in the Gospel narrative, especially in the intimate Gospel of St John.

St Luke's Gospel shows us that an adolescent decision created the pattern. At the age of twelve, when His inner life was beginning to form Christ made this vital decision. He rejected the opportunity of making a self out of the raw materials of His home, His friends and relations. He withdrew from them, leaving His mother and father perplexed. He went back to the temple and there made another rejection. He rejected the Old Testament image of God and an Old Testament relationship with Him. Instead, he turned to God in the image of the Father and to the image of his own ego under the image of His son and from the basis of that material spent the whole of His life in a perfect filial relationship in which his inner self was none other than the Father. At His death He revealed the strength of this inner intimacy when He concluded His earthly life with the words; 'Father, into thy hands I commend my spirit.' (Lk 23:46)

The full mystery of this inner intimacy is revealed in St John's Gospel, where we are shown Christ in constant intercourse with the Father. He had no other Self. The Father was the given self of the Son and the Son's response was not to make an image of the Father but to receive Him into His own heart and live in obedient filial love with Him. This is the secret of the intimacy of the Son of God with the Father. This is the explanation of His perfect achievement of true self-love to which He called all His followers. It is the model on which we have to build.

Contemplative Intimacy

The outer self

This is the secret of Christ's outer life as well. At the same time that
He decided to make the Father His real self He decided to accept as
that self all that belonged to the Father. In these cryptic words He
made this known to His mother: 'What made you search? Did you
not know that I was bound to be in my Father's house?'

The Greek is rather different. It means literally: 'concerned with the
things that belong to my Father.' This implies that what constellated
inseparably around the Father-Self are all the things that belong to
creation. In other words, the Self of Christ is the whole creation centred around the Creator-Father. This He lived out in a life which refused to withdraw from life, even when it crucified Him, which refused to
abandon that life even when His resurrected and ascended state made
that possible. In that life He still lives and works, transforming it to the
glory of God the Father.

EGO-SELVES

That is the total mystery of the self of Christ, and, as members of
Him, we share in that intimacy. But we bring to it our own self-struc-
tures. The stuff on which this Self has to be imprinted is already occupied by other figures. We do not, like Christ, come to our
adolescence with an empty, receptive matrix to receive the Father and
the kingdom. We have already started to make caricatures of our own
and, worse still, other influences from parents and relations, the
Church and the media have begun to stamp their impressions. Before
considering our reception of the true Self we must consider what are
the pseudo-self figures that have first to be recognised and transformed.

We could, in finding the outline of our pseudo-or ego-self, use a
method of personal self-examination. This is a method which has been
used in the Church with some success. It is found in the accounts of
the lives of the desert fathers – page after page of scrupulous self-ac-
cusation. In the sayings attributed to Arsenius there is a frequent and
embarrassing self-scrutiny. This method leads to an inadequate picture of the ego-self, and a risk of still further imprinting distortions on
the mind. This is the risk of using the analytical methods of the psy-
chiatrist. In digging into the unconscious, using the door of the ego
and its actions, there emerges a limited and unbalanced picture which
needs to be completed by the wider experience of other beings and the
more generalised knowledge which alone can link the picture to the
human whole. For however isolated we become, we are still members
of each other in a shared humanity.

A better way to study the ego-self is to use the lives and records of others. This is the method of the Bible. It transmits its message through a series of biographies and historical records. Through them it is possible to build a theology of God's ways and relationship with man, and to map the complicated nature of man in his attempts to relate to God and his fellows. This is the better way for our purpose.

The ego-self also appears in the lives of outstanding people who have shared their experiences in autobiographical form, Winston Churchill is an example. Others have left no memorial and yet have achieved an equally deep development. Besides those who have succeeded there are the many who have failed, often supplying psychiatrists with case histories for illustrating that dark analysis of human nature which disfigures much of Freud's psychology. Most important, there is the personal experience on which eventually we have to build our own conclusions of the way to intimacy for ourselves.

All these sources are open to us and are generally used but there is another, often omitted from the work of psychiatrists and theologians, which can give us better material than any provided by the limited experiences of life. This source is the imaginative characters of great literature, and, where the creative imagination is strong enough, the figures we ourselves make with this instrument. Shakespeare used such characters in his picture of life and wove them into dramatic patterns where they could be seen in the clearest perspective. He gave us the dramatic version of real life.

The characters of Shakespeare's plays could provide all the living material we need for studying the various degrees of human intimacy. Shakespeare has a depth and mastery for which one looks in vain in the unbalanced and inadequate characters of Hesse's work. But there is one great advantage in using Hesse as a source of illustration. He is contemporary and he has gained the attention of great numbers of our generation. Moreover, Hesse, is concerned with the contemporary problem of identity and relationship: he presents characters limited to this theme and specially suited to the purpose of our enquiry. In *Steppenwolf* he handles the theme of inner intimacy; in *Narziss and Goldmund* the same theme is treated, but with an emphasis on personal intercourse; in *The Glass Bead Game* the same theme is handled again, but in more corporate dimensions. Hesse may fail to find a solution to the questions he asks, but this again is where he is useful to us, for he encourages his readers to search for themselves, and not to look for ready-made answers. His characters and the movements of his plot provide what is needed in terms of objective examples for handling the highly charged subject of human intimacy whilst retaining the detached attitude needed for a balanced and unprejudiced approach. We shall draw on most of Hesse's work but especially on *Steppenwolf*, which requires a short introduction before returning to our theme.

Steppenwolf

In a note dated 1961 Hesse points out that 'of all my books *Steppenwolf* is the one that was more often and more violently misunderstood than any other'. He attributes this misunderstanding to the fact that the book fell into the hands of very young readers, although it was intended to describe his own experiences at the age of fifty. These young readers tended to identify themselves with the griefs and dreams of Steppenwolf whilst overlooking the other aspects of the story: the indestructible world, 'the positive, serene, super-personal and timeless world of faith'. They failed to recognise the other theme of the book, which is not only the story of a man despairing but of a man believing. Yet, while gently complaining of this general misunderstanding, Hesse concedes the liberty of his readers to understand the tale in their own way. This liberty we shall take, seeing in the story a remarkable analysis of a growth in human intercourse, leading through disease and crisis and ending not in death and destruction, but in healing.

Hesse sums up the predicament of the main character, Harry Haller, in this description which has a wide application:

'I have good reason to suppose that he (Harry Haller) was brought up by devoted but severe and very pious parents and teachers in accordance with that doctrine that makes the breaking of the will the corner-stone of education and up-bringing. But in this case the attempt to destroy the personality and to break the will did not succeed. He was much too strong and hardy, too proud and spirited. Instead of destroying his personality they succeeded only in teaching him to hate himself. It was against himself that, innocent and noble as he was, he directed during his entire life the whole wealth of his fancy, the whole of his thought; and in so far as he let loose upon himself every barbed criticism, every anger and hate he could command, he was, in spite of all, a real Christian and a real martyr.' (ibid. p. 15–16)

It is against this background that Harry Haller works out the problems of his inner life. Rightly he sub-titles the account 'For Madmen Only' and describes his record as 'Treatise on the Steppenwolf'.

The story is highly complex. Wisely the telling is not confined to words but to a series of images which greatly enlarge the scope of interpretation. Hesse in his preface realised that there would be many interpretations and pleaded that 'the higher indestructible world beyond the Steppenwolf and his problematic life' should not be forgotten. The story is much more than an analysis of a schizophrenic: it is about a man, believing rather than despairing, who finds a way to healing rather than to destruction.

The Steppenwolf achieves this intimacy through the reconciliation of the many warring elements in Haller's character. His achievement goes beyond the scope of one man: Haller is an aspect of everyman struggling to harmonise the fragments of his ego-self. In him we see our own biography spread out before us. To understand it we must first look at the fragments more closely.

The main dark fragment in Haller is the Steppenwolf, who symbolises his disordered animal nature. He is strange, wild, shy, sometimes violent, painfully alone. This animal nature was tamed not by a process of elimination, nor by a transformation of the warring elements. It was tamed by being incorporated into the other parts of Haller's personality. One of the main instruments for this rebuilding was the miracle of laughter. As he looks at the mournful image of himself in a glass his friend suddenly laughs and the glass itself goes grey and charred and opaque, the image disappears and he stands ready for the next stage of his integration. There is an immense fund of reassurance in this event. The animal nature need not be isolated and feared. Treated lightly and as part of a larger whole it contributes to that ultimate inner intimacy which is the foundation of the whole man.

Harry Haller's emotions had been starved from childhood onwards. So seriously were they impaired that he is incapable of warm, spontaneous relationships with others. His marriage had failed: he is introduced to the reader living the life of a recluse in isolated lodgings. In the healing of this part of his injured character the two women, Hermine and Maria, play a vital part. Hermine does not talk about the emotional life: she gives it, in the first stages by teaching Haller to dance. This prematurely old man of fifty, paralysed by the over-development of his rational faculties, is forced to learn to dance and as he does so his emotions began to thaw out into life. Maria leads him further in an exploration of the full life of the senses which had been so inadequately tasted in his youth. His frozen nature warms under this treatment and his aging body regains some of its youth.

Although much of Haller's life has been spent in developing his mind it is this faculty which is more fragmented and disordered than the others. The variety and imperfection of his intimacies show this. Hermine teaches him that, having in youth failed to master the full depths of mental intimacy, in maturity he has lost the power to relate fully to another person. Pablo shows him the unsatisfied sensual needs of his nature. Under the image of a magic theatre he watches phase after phase of his mental life played over: the man of revolutionary ideas, the cautious chess player, the aggressive wolf and the lover of beauty who achieves a deep intimacy with Mozart. One after another these images of his self are presented and destroyed. The last, which he sees in the form of Hermine united to his rival, Pablo, he destroys, only to find flowing out of the murdered body something that was deathly and yet 'it was beautiful, it rang, it vibrated. It was music'. (Ibid, p. 245) The climax of this journey into the fragmentations of his self ended with Pablo transforming Hermine into one of the pieces of the chess game and handing it to Haller. That gesture brings him as near understanding his predicament and cure as he reached in his life experience. He cries out:

> 'I understood it all. I understood Pablo. I understood Mozart, and somewhere behind me as I heard his ghastly laughter I knew that all the hundred thousand pieces of life's game were in my pocket. A glimpse of its meaning had stirred my reason and I was determined to begin the game afresh. I would sample its torture once more and shudder again at its senselessness. I would traverse not once more but often the hell of my inner being. One day I would be better at the game. One day I would learn how to laugh. Pablo was waiting for me, and Mozart, too.' (ibid, p. 252–253)

Hesse's portrait of the ego-self is a valuable contribution to the work of making our own assessment. Writing in a language which has been welcomed and partly understood by the present generation, he provides us with an instrument for understanding and communicating in contemporary language. His analysis is of great significance, – of greater significance than much which has come from the psychiatric case-books. Where he is not so strong is in his prescriptions for the renewal and transformation of the inadequate self-structure. We can sum up the main outline of his description of the self man has made and with which he unhappily has to live.

It is a self gravely disordered by infused and inherited influences. It is not here necessary to blame parents and relations and the world, which is a home we had little opportunity to plan. All that is necessary is to share Hesse's realism that much we have been given is bad and needs rejection. We may note in passing that even the Lord Himself early removed from His relations and friends in deciding the vital question of His true Self.

By adolescence the part of the ego-self which has been most dis-ordered by these influences is what pertains to its instinctual life. The decision of the adolescent's elders to repress the life of the instincts, and the failure to give them sound creative expression bring the adolescent to a state where the instincts have taken on a dangerous form which Hesse symbolises under the image of a wolf – not in its free and natural state, but a wolf frustrated and partly enraged to madness. Instead of the instincts of hunger and sex, of fear and anger, of curiosity, being in balanced and energetic tension they are in a state of dangerous frustration, bringing about that violent hatred of the ego-self which Hesse notes as the full development of this frustrated instinctive repression. Such a situation when fully developed makes impossible any creative intimacy with the self. As Hesse puts it, the will is broken. This is the first and most important point to grasp in making an image of the adolescent ego-self. Attempts have been made to construct an adolescent ego-self not damaged in this way, such as the Mowgli character of Kipling's *Jungle Tales,* and a very attractive image results. But it must be remembered that in order to do this Kipl-ing had to create the special conditions of an infancy and youth beyond the influences of human training, an upbringing solely under the control of the undamaged instincts of the jungle folk. The practical consequence of this is that when the ego tries to make its images of the self these images will always be instinctually lacking. The instincts will be those of the wounded and misused animal. They will be lacking in the joyful strength of the free.

Hesse shows a man in both periods of creative energy trying to make self images. These two periods are adolescence and the threshold of old age. Both periods of life are creative in this way: both need images in order to continue the next stage of the journey. The adolescent needs a self-image in order to face the years of manhood: the middle-aged man needs an image to help him face death. No wonder both adolescents and people of middle age have found a message for their state in *Steppenwolf.*

Because the instincts have been deranged, the images of both periods of life are distorted. In adolescence they are either reflections of a maimed ego or attempts to form the other part of the self in terms of the opposite sex image. In doing this Haller shares and exemplifies the common failure. His adolescent self-image is a deformity which evokes hatred rather than love. His image of the feminine figure is un-stable and inadequate to bear the weight of his adult needs. It os-cillates between the simple peasant girl and the sophisticated Maria. Even Hermine, who most meets his needs is unstable, and sometimes becomes Herman, her masculine counterpart. This accounts for the chaos and frustration of his manhood: when he comes to the threshold of old age he has neither the energy nor the imagination to make the new images required. It is at that point that a transformation begins, with death and resurrection as essential experiences of this renewal.

The most serious defect in Hesse's picture of Haller's ego-self is the absence of an adequate conception of God. Haller of course has to reject the concepts of God given him by his parents and by his Church. But he realises the need for some kind of replacement. The most satisfactory substitute he found was Mozart, but even he is insufficient to meet the total needs of his self image. He gaves him laughter and beauty, but, for the adult, God must give more than this. He must provide all that is implied in the image of Fatherhood. No doubt Hesse was right in implying that another incarnation would be needed for Haller to achieve this discovery. But how nearly the Mozart substitute fills this gap can be seen in this splendid conclusion:

> 'As I reflected, passages of Mozart's Cassations, of Bach's Well-Tempered Clavier came to my mind and it seemed to me that all through this music there was the radiance of this cool starry brightness and the quivering of this clearness of ether. Yes, it was there. In this music there was a feeling as of time frozen into space, and above it there quivered a never-ending and superhuman serenity, an eternal, divine laughter . . . Suddenly I heard this fathomless laughter around me. I heard the immortals laughing.' (ibid, p. 181)

Hesse gives us part of the imperfect ego-self image in man. Two great myths of Greek literature add to our picture and help us in finding a way of recovery and transformation. They are the myth of Narcissus and the myth of Eros and Psyche.

Narcissus

Narcissus was the son of the river-god Cephisus. In his adolescence he rejected the love of the nymph Echo and was punished by falling in love with his own reflection, which he saw in the water of a fountain. In his desire for intimacy with this image he pined away and was saved from death by being changed into a flower. As a narcissus he was gathered by Persephone and carried away to Hades.

Eros and Psyche

Psyche was the personification of the human soul, often depicted as a butterfly. She was loved by Eros who carried her off to a secluded spot where he visited her by night, alone. She was not able to see him and her sisters persuaded her to break her promise not to look on his face. She lit a lamp to see him and he vanished. She spent much of her life looking for him and only towards the end did she find him again: finally they were reunited.

In these two myths we watch the ego trying to make two self-images: one an internal projection of itself and the other a development of the ego by way of division into male and female. We find the same situation with Adam in the Genesis saga. He begins with a self--image. This left him alone, locked up in himself, and God's conclusion was that it was not good for him to be in this state. In the second stage he is enabled to split into male and female forms, and this begins his search for God and his true self. The rest of the Bible is the story of his quest.

Here is the story of man. It is the story of Haller and it is the story of his feminine counterpart, Hermine. Man in adolescence behaves like Narcissus and rejects the images of the self given him by his environment for a self-reflection of his own making. In early manhood he tries to enlarge that image to include his feminine or masculine counterpart.

These images have a life or death of their own. The image of Narcissus, like many of the self-images of Hesse, begins fully alive and then withers. In their living form they often encourage some kind of masturbatory response which seems at some stage or other of adolescence to be almost universal. But it is not a satisfactory response, nor has it permanence. Either it leads to a blocked state of introversion or it destroys the self-image and leaves an emptiness which is a breeding ground for depression. This occurs not only in the first adolescence which Narcissus exemplifies, but in the period before middle age which is the theme of *Steppenwolf*. What it fails to provide is the matrix for receiving the true self, the incarnate Lord.

The myth of Eros and Psyche is more complex and represents a crisis before the ego reaches maturity. It occurs when the narcissistic stage has ended and the ego is presented with the external fragments of the self in its outer environment. Like Adam in the garden of Eden, it has already related to many external objects: the wild animals and the birds of heaven have been considered and found inadequate; the beauty of the garden, its plants and rivers, have been seen and admired. But the self which can satisfy the ego needs to be larger and more complicated to meet the capacity of the human creature for love. It is then that the imagination begins to work and create the internal image of the woman which becomes the centre of creation and a sufficient object for love. This image, as the Genesis story and the myth make quite clear, begins as an internal creation and only later finds outward expression in a human structure. 'God made them male and female' is our Lord's summary of the mystery of man and only later, when the inner images have been clearly made, or, as the psychologist would describe it, the anima is mature, can a man attempt to make an adult relationship with its external counterpart. The Eros-Psyche myth warns us that this projection to an outside being is surrounded with danger and depends for its success on a prolonged period of uncertainty when the ego lives in a situation of darkness without the clear outline of its image counterpart. If clarity is prematurely sought, disaster and an arrested growth may result, as it did with Eros and Psyche and also with Haller. In fact Haller's situation clearly reflects what the Genesis story is saying, for he rushed into the feminine image before he had mastered his relationship with the creatures and the rest of creation, with the result that he was burdened with a half-tamed wolf in his self and left with only fragmented images of the true woman. This disaster can only be remedied by a lifetime's experience of frustrated relationships and the loss of a clear internal image of the Self. Like Psyche, the imperfect fragment of the ego journeys the world in sorrow looking for the lost complementary image. This is the experience of man as he comes through adolescence to manhood, even though he may have the insight of a Dante. The consolation is that, provided he continues his search, the lost fragment can be found and the total ego-self integrated.

There is one last lesson of the myth to note. The discovery of the true self is more than the discovery of the true human counterpart of the ego. Eros was a god and in finding him, Psyche found union with God. So it was with Adam. His making of the feminine image and his union with that image in external form was also union with God, for both of them could now hear 'the sound of God walking in the garden.' (Gen 3:8) The discovery of the true self is more than the finding of the counterpart self to the ego: it is intimacy with God.

THE TRUE SELF

In most of Hesse's books he stated the need for the true self and depicted brilliantly the disaster when this self was not found, but he never succeeded in pointing to the way in which this could be achieved, or created a character in which the true self had been discovered. This was because Hesse could not accept — that the true self in all its stages of creation is primarily the work of God.

Both the losing of the ego-self and the making of the true self is a work of the Holy Spirit. He mortifies and remakes. The undertaking of this work is articulated by St Paul. His old self fell to the ground on the road to Damascus: the new self was built up during the rest of his life by his response to the Spirit. In Galatians he describes the process in terms of a sharing in the crucifixion and resurrection of Christ: 'I have been crucified with Christ: the life I now live is not my life, but the life which Christ lives in me; and my present bodily life is lived by faith in the Son of God, who loved me and gave himself up for me.' (Gal 2:20–1) In this passage he uses again and again the passive verb. It is all something which happened in him, not something he did for himself. And what St Paul says is true of every man. Faith is our attitude to God, who works in us both to will and to do His good pleasure. Hesse was without this faith. Although brought up in the protestant tradition he could not accept it. The result was that he had to think of the making of the true Self in terms of human action, and, with his great knowledge of the essence of the human, he could never create a character with the strength of will needed to perform that task. It was here that Haller was bound to fail. He could fall and then seem to rise, but just as he reached what seemed to be the point of renewal he would fall away. The most Hesse achieved in his characters was the state where the futility of the ego-made self was revealed. He could not move into the resurrection situation of renewal. We are left with Haller embarked on a course which seems very like the oriental theory of reincarnation with all the pieces for remaking his life in his pocket, but until he found contact with the grace of God we can predict yet another round of frustrated failure.

How God helps man in his task of self-renewal cannot be described in terms which fit the experience of every man. His work is always individual and requires a particular response. There is no such thing as the mass production of human selves. Like the works of nature, every new-made self is a new creation with its own particular form. It also requires an individual response.

This response, however, has a general shape which it is possible to relate to every man. It is summed up in the Lord's demand to leave self behind, take up the cross and come with Him. (Mk 8:34)

'Leave self behind'

Leaving self behind assumes that such a self already exists, and it is the making of a self to be left behind which is the first step in the formation of the true self. It involves all that is implied in the myths of Narcissus, of Eros and Psyche and the story of Steppenwolf. Not one self but many have to be made: the adolescent self of Narcissus, the self of Eros and Psyche and the Haller self that still survives as he approaches middle life. This self is made out of the raw materials life provides. Adam made it from the garden of Eden and his companionship with its many forms of life. Narcissus made it from his own reflection in the water. Eros and Psyche sketched its outline in the dark from their relationship with each other. The selves thus made must be alive and have living intimacy. This would seem to involve as part of the creative process emotional and physical relationships. For instance, the Narcissistic image almost without exception leads to the sexual activity of masturbation which can only be condemned when practised with excessive, self conscious repetition. As a growth towards maturity many now regard it as a necessary experience. So with the more mature divided image. Eros and Psyche must have relationships. Often this can be expressed in creative activity where physical sex is neither possible nor necessary. Dante witnesses to this achievement, as do a host of other artists. But one would not rule out some preliminary exploration between the pair, should the relationship require it. In all these ways the ego goes about the creation of its own self and, when this self is made, it inevitably leads to the same frustrations as are described in the classical myths. We see them in Haller in their most intense development because in adolescence and youth he lacked the courage to create his ego-image completely. He made a half relationship with the animal in himself, but it was a monster wolf that emerged. He partly made an ego-image, but the fragments never came together, and his marriage never reached adequate fulfilment. Many others have been much more successful in this process. St Paul achieved a powerful narcissistic image: Dante arrived at a developed Eros-Psyche growth. It is when such a stage of self-development has been reached that the next stage can take place.

This next stage is denial of the self created. This is much more than a state of accepted failure. In any case the ego-self will shrivel, but this denial is a rejection at the stage when it is in full strength. St Paul on the road to Damascus was at this stage. He was in the full growth of a self-made structure: he denied something which showed no signs of failure. With Haller it was different. He never made the deliberate act of self-denial. He allowed his many selves to be destroyed by events. Adolescence, early manhood, the threshold to middle age: all these are moments of immense signifiance in the growth of the true self. They are moments when what has so far been made is rejected. There are many ways in which this can be done. Sacrifice is one means of expression. The offering of an animal in sacrifice, an act familiar in many old religions, is something deeper than the death of a creature. It was the offering of a part of the self which had been made by the worshipper. He had co-operated in the breeding and nurture of what he gave: it was an integral part of himself. This sacrifice was also associated with the supreme act of self-denial in the form of obedience. The worshipper broke his connection with his ego-self by transferring his allegiance to the Self of God. This was the great moment of St Paul's self-denial. 'Tell me, Lord, who you are.' (Acts 9:5) Haller never achieved that precision of denial: his ego selves just faded. So he never achieved more than a partial replacement.

The reception of the true self

It is the replacement of the denied ego-self which is the critical act in the real renewal of the self. This is not setting to work to make another self to replace the one denied. Haller tried to do this and, in spite of the help he was given by Hermine, Pablo and the Immortals, he never achieved more than a temporary success. The way to renewal is not the way of making another, but of receiving a self already made. It is the surrender expressed in the command to 'come with me'. This is to receive a self waiting to be given, the Self of the Son of God who, as St Paul says 'loved me and gave himself up for me'. (Gal 2:21) It is the reception of the image of the risen Christ as the structure of the true self that makes the human biography once the ego-made selves of Narcissus and Eros and Psyche have been discarded.

The Christ we spend all our lives receiving is not a static and distant object. He is present and active. St Paul understood His activity as a perfect self-giving. Christ gives Himself through every part of His creation. He is the cosmic Christ who gives Himself through the universe. He is the Lord who has dominion over all creatures and orders Peter to assimilate them so as to assimilate Himself. 'Rise, Peter, kill and eat.' (Acts 10:13) He is the immanent Christ who is in all men. 'Anything you did not for one of these, however humble, you did not for me.' (Mt 25:45) It is the self-giving, omnipresent Christ we are commanded to receive in order to co-operate in the making of our true self.

This reception of Christ in the emptied human ego, transformed from self-sufficiency to an absolute receptivity, is the work of contemplative intimacy, practised in many ways and always in response to the initiative of Christ and His indwelling Spirit. Against the background of the achievements of the great contemplatives and the failures, like Haller, we can begin to map out our own response. It is physical, emotional and mental. The whole of our being and our faculties are involved.

St Paul speaks of several bodies, the chief being the physical, the psychic and the spiritual. Our Lord as perfect man lives and manifests Himself in all three: outwardly in the physical, inwardly in the psychic and spiritual. The self is expressed partly in the physical and spiritual through the imagination, working in harmony with the Spirit of Christ and rightly described by Blake as the divine imagination. With this instrument we are able in the power of the Spirit to make dwelling places for the Lord, and this is a primary work of contemplative prayer. The raw material of these images is the Christ of the gospels and the sacraments, the Christ of creation, and the cosmic Christ in His glory. A large part of the renewal of the self is the making of these images of the body of Christ and identifying with them. In making such images we shall be involved with our total personhood, male and female, for Christ is the androgen. Like Eros and Psyche the Self is of both sexes, as Haller so clearly understood but failed to assimilate. Again, our imaginative images of Christ will always be imperfect. Every act of contemplation will be a new image, sometimes felt in darkness, sometimes for brief moments seen in glory. Such images, as Haller learnt from Hermine and Pablo, must be as open as possible. This involves the maker in such practices as nudity, movement and the full life of the instincts.

When nudity is mentioned, there is a natural hostility in our present society. Nudism as a cult is suspect. But within the Christian tradition it has an important place. Baptism was a manifestation of the naked body to the congregation and it must have had a traumatic effect on all who took part. The vesting of the priest for the Mass implies the exposure of the body. But far more important is the practice of nudism in contemplative images. The figures made by our imagination should normally be like the Greek *kouroi*, naked. Almost all the unhealthy attraction of pornography would disappear if both male and female images were pictured in this way, and there would certainly be a more effective image of the Christ-self for the contemplative to assimilate. In making these images the materials provided by animals and art should be used.

Living images of the psychic body of Christ form best as we move. Haller was taught this by Hermine. One of her first demands was that he learnt to dance; when he had, his imagination became once more alive. The dance in its many forms is an instrument for this purpose. It awakens the imaginative faculty. So do other movements of the body, such as yoga postures and symbolic gestures, no matter how simple. The stretching out of our Lord's hand was intensely revealing. It was enough to show His hands and His side to convince His disciples of His presence. People whose imaginations are most active speak with their bodies, as do most animals.

Instincts stimulate the imagination in its work of creating images of Christ. Hunger is the basis of the most imaginative act, the Eucharist. The sexual instinct in terms of touch leads to great clarity of image. So it was with Eros and Psyche, who knew each other best in this way. St John understood this when he wrote of his images of Christ:

'It was there from the beginning; we have heard it; we have seen it with our eyes; we have looked upon it, and felt it with our own hands; and it is of this we tell.' (I Jn 1:1)

Here he reveals that his senses were used in making the Christ image. By them the instincts were activated and, when activated, harmonised into the supreme intimacy of love.

The instincts and the emotions are closely related. The emotions follow the instincts and are energised by them. So with our Lord. He communicates with His emotions: He weeps, He loves, He laughs, He is angry and He is inspired with unquenchable hope. All these emotions He communicates to His members through the Spirit. Our images of Him must therefore be alive with all these emotions and our response to them must be correspondingly emotionally alive. Haller was taught this. He was made to laugh and weep: he was initiated into the full experience of the orgasm in all its forms: he began to learn to love.

There are two emotional responses which need detailed consideration, because learning to master them is essential for our contemplative response to the Self image of the Christ. These are emotions which Hermine trained Haller to master: laughter and the orgasm.

Laughter is the first expression of joy. It is a physical release from the solar plexus centre, and is induced both from outside and within ourselves. It is almost a sense in itself for we speak of 'a sense of humour'. The presence of the Spirit of Christ is signified by deep laughter. The psalmist even applies it to inanimate nature, for he writes of the hills laughing. Laughter is also the gift which comes from others. Haller found it in the music of Mozart, and in earlier times the fool had an important service to perform for the community by teaching it to laugh. Every contemplative group must have the means for making laughter and must train its members to be uninhibited in its use. From this laughter joy will spring, that internal joy of the heart which is uttered in the Eucharist and transforms the whole of life into a game played by God with His creatures.

Mastering the emotion of the orgasm is a more difficult matter, for the orgasm has been unfortunately misunderstood and is often associated with something the Victorian rarely achieved and the present-day man and woman are always trying to find in one part of the body. It is worth taking a little trouble to re-state the meaning of the word and the emotional complex it refers to.

Orgasm comes from the Greek word *orgasmos*. This was primarily an agricultural term for the swelling of the soil after rain, the ripening of fruit and the condition of animals when ready for mating. It has in modern times been limited to a particular phase in the sexual act when for a brief period the sexual centre becomes the focus of awareness and attracts to itself the total emotional energy of the body. It is an experience which can be felt both with others and alone. This limited meaning by no means exhausts the full implication of the orgasm, and leaves out much when we apply it as an emotional experience of contemplative prayer.

The sexual centre of the body is not the only centre which is capable of experiencing orgasm. All the centres of the body are capable of the experience and should be trained to have it. The centre at the base of the spine can have the orgasm of perfectly integrated movement. It comes from the dance and from properly executed postures. Roger Bannister referred to it when he spoke of 'switching on the Holy Ghost' in the last few hundred yards of a well-planned mile. There is the orgasm of the solar plexus. This often expresses itself in laughter or fear. There is the orgasm of the heart centre in terms of grief and compassion, of the throat centre in the voice, especially the use of vibrato, of the eye centre in response to beauty and in the head centre in awareness of the divine glory. All of these centres have their orgasmic potential, and it is as they are all used in full harmony that the total orgasm which in the Bible is spoken of as love, *agape*, is experienced and the ego achieves living unity with the Christ-self. Orgasm which is limited to one centre only is inadequate and maimed.

On the other hand, the art of total orgasm is most often learnt by mastering it in separate centres. The orgasm of the lower spine is usually felt first, and one can see it being experienced in young children in the joy of movement. Orgasm in the genital area is experienced in many forms: in a dream experience, in masturbation, and in a variety of inter-personal relationships. With the growth of the personality orgasm in the other centres becomes possible. To limit orgasm to any one centre, or to fail to achieve orgasm in harmony in all the centres is a failure to reach full adult development. The remedy, as in so many other emotional disorders, is to grow. This is one of the most important lessons taught by Hesse in his portrait of Haller. He shows us a man who failed to grow out of adolescence, and out of a maimed adolescence at that. The renewal of the self into the measure of the stature of the fullness of Christ requires a total growth, and the mastery of the fully-developed orgasm is one of its most essential achievements. Only so can the mental faculties be fully opened to receive the mind of Christ. For, in the imagery of the Bible, to have full orgasm is to know each other and in knowing each other to know the Lord.

CELIBACY

The renewal of the self takes place under a variety of conditions. For Haller this happened partly in isolation and partly in community, and this is the pattern for most of us. Man needs time for introspection which involves some degree of inner withdrawal, and equally needs times for receiving the gifts of a well-ordered community life. At this stage of our enquiry we shall limit ourselves to the second of these needs, and examine the conditions and benefits of the celibate life.

The conditions of celibate life

Celibacy has had an honoured place in many ancient traditions. In India and the East generally the celibate or *sunnyasi* has played an important part in the social structure. So it has been in the West, where it is a condition of the religious life and, in many churches, of the priesthood. In the Christian Church celibacy claims the authority and example of our Lord. He made it a special form of life for some when He said:

'That is something which not everyone can accept, but only those for whom God has appointed it. For while some are incapable of marriage because they are born so, or were made so by men, there are others who have themselves renounced marriage for the sake of the kingdom of Heaven.' (Mt 19:12)

And He concluded this teaching with the challenge: 'Let those accept it who can.' (Mt 19:12)

The Prayer Book follows this teaching when it describes celibacy as a divine gift, an honourable alternative to marriage.

St Paul develops this theme further as he names some of the advantages of the celibate life, but he carefully prefaces his remarks with this qualification: 'On the question of celibacy, I have no instruction from the Lord, but I give my judgement as one who by God's mercy is fit to be trusted'.

(I Cor 7:25)

He then gives this account of its advantages:

'I want you to be free from anxious care. The unmarried man cares for the Lord's business. But the married man cares for worldly things; his aim is to please his wife; and he has a divided mind. The unmarried or celibate woman cares for the Lord's business; her aim is to be dedicated to him in body as in spirit; but the married

woman cares for worldly things; her aim is to please her husband.'
(I Cor 7:32–34)

We are not bound to accept St Paul's opinions, but they are worth careful consideration. He makes three points about celibacy which will guide us in our thinking: its vocation, expression and reward.

The celibate vocation

Celibacy is a vocation which is given, like all other vocations, with special gifts. It is not confined to the members of the Christian Church. Buddhism and Hinduism have large numbers of celibate vocations which resemble those found in Christianity.

There are of course large numbers of pseudo-celibates. Haller is an example of one. He tried a distorted celibacy because he had failed in every other way of life. His marriage was a disaster, he failed to master the wolf in his nature, he never achieved any intimacy of a mature and lasting kind with anyone. His attempt at celibacy was a withdrawal which set him on a course towards suicide. This was a perversion of the celibate vocation to which we may assume he was called. Haller stands for all the celibates who have used celibacy as an excuse for withdrawal from life. Celibacy should be the opposite. It is essentially a deepened engagement with life, with the Lord of life Himself.

The vocation to celibacy is God-given and accompanied by physical and emotional signs. Among the physical signs are a balanced body, often with athletic gifts, and a fully developed sexuality. The true celibate is not less than a full man or woman. He is man and woman in fullest harmony, an androgynous being in the highest sense, of almost complete internal independence, capable of living alone without depression or frustration. Humour is the essence of his emotional life, a humour which Haller so markedly lacked and Hermine insisted should be cultivated. Goethe tried to teach him that 'Eternity is a mere moment, just long enough for a joke', but he never grasped the meaning. Mozart laughed and sometimes made Haller smile. Pablo summed up his need when he held up the mirror and showed Haller this way of obliterating the unsatisfactory image:

'You will now extinguish this superfluous reflection, my dear friend. That is all that is necessary. To do so, it will suffice that you greet it, if your mood permits, with a hearty laugh. You are here in a school of humour. You are to learn to laugh. Now, true humour begins when a man ceases to take himself seriously.' (*Steppenwolf*, p. 207)

But that is exactly what Haller had done for so long that he could not break himself of the habit.

The power to laugh, above all to laugh at oneself: that is the essential asset of the true celibate. With that great gift he can welcome his vocation and go forward unafraid. Hesse makes it clear that Haller needed at least another reincarnation before he could do that.

The way of celibacy

The celibate undertakes a great and difficult task. He is doing what Hesse, in another book, called the most distasteful thing of all; he takes the path that leads to himself. (*Demian,* p. 45). The work for which he must at all costs keep himself free is that of unearthing his present self and reconstructing from the ruins of that self his true Self as intended by God. It is a work which in the same book is summed up as the making of the Spirit into flesh, an agony which involves the whole creation, the crucifixion of a Saviour. What Hesse does not say, and this is fundamental, is that it also involves the resurrection and ascension of that Saviour into God. (ibid p. 7). This is an exploration of the deepest intimacy into the old and new selves.

Dante describes the first part of this journey with a wealth of images in the *Divine Comedy* in terms of a descent into the inferno and a pilgrimage through purgatory. It is a confrontation with the old self in fragmentary and distorted images and a growing union with the new Self under the image of the divinely inspired Beatrice. Hesse conveys the same message through Hermine, a rather less adequate symbol. In the early stages of her relationship she resembles Beatrice in that she is almost replaced by others, by Maria and Pablo and the Immortals. In the closing stages she offers Haller herself in ambiguous and changing forms. Sometimes masked, sometimes in the figure of a boy, always changing, always making new demands of intimacy response.

Dante also shows the second part of the celibate's journey in the 'Paradiso' where he achieves the total Self, not merely in terms of union with Beatrice but also in terms of union with God. He learns in this state the full mystery:

'It is inherent in this state
Of blessedness, to keep ourselves within
The divine will, by which our wills with his
Are one.
And in this will is our tranquillity.
It is the mighty ocean, whither tends
Whatever it creates and nature makes.'

('Paradiso', canto iii)

Hesse, realising his limitations, makes no attempt to describe this final achievement. He gives Haller glimpses of it and then teaches that all his attainments must be renounced if he is to go further. So Hermine has to be killed when she is most fully revealed, and Haller is promised, as a reward for his renunciation, greater experiences of understanding. He looks to the future still to be attained in this way:

'I understood it all. I understood Pablo. I understood Mozart, and somewhere behind me I heard his ghastly laughter. I knew that all the hundred thousand pieces of life's game were in my pocket. A glimpse of its meaning had stirred my reason and I was determined to begin the game afresh ... One day I would be a better hand at the game. One day I would learn how to laugh. Pablo was waiting for me and Mozart, too.' (*Steppenwolf,* p. 252–253)

Some of the rewards of celibacy.

The celibate keeps himself free to play the game of life in its most intimate form. It is this freedom to do so which is one of his greatest rewards on this side of death. Unlike the homosexual or the heterosexual he avoids particular relationships. He generalises the object of his love in terms of the whole creation, creation containing and manifesting God. His intimacy is not less that that of others with a more social vocation. He is rewarded with a greater and more inclusive intimacy. He is given what Isaiah writes of in this passage:

'The eunuch must not say,
I am nothing but a barren tree.
For these are the words of the Lord:
The eunuchs who keep my sabbaths,
Who choose to do my will and hold fast to my covenant,
Shall receive from me something better than sons and daughters,
A memorial and a name in my own house and within my walls;
I will give them an everlasting name,
A name imperishable for all time.' (Is 56:3–5)

But to receive this reward the celibate has first to face and renounce his old self, and he must do this alone. Hesse understands this when he describes Haller's life before he met Hermine. It was a life of increasing isolation, of terrifying nearness to the wolf in his nature. It led him to the brink of suicide. Dante realised the same thing at the beginning of the 'Inferno' when he finds himself 'midway this way of life'. confronted by a beautiful mountain, but turned aside by a leopard, a lion and a she-wolf.

This capacity to face the old self naked is indeed one of the rewards of celibacy. The withdrawal from distractions enables the celibate to transcend much that passes for intimacy in social life. He reaches the closest relationship, finds the inescapable companionship with the self he must absolutely deny. It is within the prison of his own being that he has the chance to drain the chalice of self-denial and the opportunity to move into that intimacy offered by St Paul.

'You are all sons of God in union with Christ Jesus. Baptized into union with him, you have all put on Christ as a garment. There is no such thing as Jew and Greek, slave and freeman, male and female; for you are all one person in Christ Jesus.' (Gal. 3:26–28).

Apart from Christ no one has attained this full reward. It has been achieved in fragments by some of the great leaders of mankind: Abraham, Gautama Buddha, Krishna, the Old Testament prophets, the great *rishis* of the Upanishads, Confucius and many of the Christian saints. All these partially revealed within themselves the person of Christ who still works to bring together many nations and ideas and structures into the fullness of His being. The true Christian celibate has the opportunity of becoming a transparency of the divine presence and the advantage of the most effective materials for reaching this goal.

The celibate vocation need not be life-long. In the Buddhist tradition it is accepted as a useful preparation for adult life, and its conditions are used to train youth for manhood. This is an attitude towards celibacy which western religious might well come to regard as normal. There is an equally strong tradition in Hinduism which regards celibacy as a suitable state for the closing years of life. This has also much to recommend it. Western forms of the religious life are increasingly sympathetic to the idea of making celibacy a less permanent state, with machinery to release those who have once embraced it and later wish to enter another state of life. If this attitude becomes generally acceptable the temporary celibate will be free to enter another state of life, not maimed but enriched by his celibate experience. He will certainly have a deepened experience of contemplative intimacy which he can continue to develop in the other states of life to which God may call him.

The freedom of the celibate gives him especially favourable conditions for bringing into harmony within his true Self the total being of the cosmic Christ and of unifying all things within himself. Hesse sees this as a unification of both good and evil, a union which leads to peace, but only through the conflict for which the celibate, through his non-attachment, is especially prepared.

6
Love one another

The inevitable result of internal intimacy with the true Self is external intimacy with that same Self in others. But the converse is equally true. The inevitable result of a failure to achieve internal intimacy with the true Self is an incapacity to love that same Self in others. The first of these conditions is shown in the life of our Lord: the second we can see in the catastrophe of Hesse's Haller.

Our Lord's achieved intimacy is summed up by St Luke when he describes the hidden life at Nazareth and its consequences: 'He advanced in wisdom and in favour with God and men.' (Lk 2:52). The rest of His life was a manifestation and sharing of the glory of God.

Haller's disintegration, on the threshold of his fifties, is expressed in a total incapacity to achieve an effective external relationship. His failure to relate to himself had reached the stage when 'he began to suffocate slowly in the more rarefied atmosphere of remoteness and solitude'. He wanted to be with others, but he had so long lived alone that he could no longer survive any other situation. The world had accepted his decision and now left him alone. From this disaster Hermine tried to rescue him. She used every possible method: she linked him with the immortals like Mozart, with men and women, and finally attempted the most difficult task of all, the task of renewing Haller's image of himself. In this she failed, but not for want of trying. Her mistake was in attempting the renewal in the wrong order. Haller had to be inwardly renewed before he could reach intimacy with the others. However, we can follow him in his journey into the world of others, and we can learn much from his failure.

THE OTHERS

Hermine tried to renew Haller by bringing him into intimacy with others in a planned order. First, with the immortals. Then with men and women. Finally with a family. She failed, but the path she took was sound and applies to all those who would reach full intimacy with others.

The immortals

Like Plato and the mystics of all faiths Hesse makes much of the spiritual leaders who have achieved God. Their achievement is more than personal: it is capable of being shared by all. They open up a way of communion which is a highway for others who seek the kingdom of truth. Hesse includes as immortals a wide range of people from the saints to the poets and musicians. For him Mozart is one of the great immortals, and he writes:

> 'The music of Mozart belongs there and the poetry of your great poets. The saints, too, belong there, who have worked wonders and suffered martyrdom and given a great example to men. But the image of every true act, the strength of every true feeling, belongs to eternity just as much, even though no one knows of it or sees it or records it or hands it down to posterity.' (*Steppenwolf* p. 171)

Haller's growth into communion with the immortals is gradual. He reaches intimacy with only a few, such as Mozart and Goethe and he does not attain God through them. Even Bach can do no more than draw veils aside and invite him to enter, but at least they show him a glimpse of the kingdom and part of its glory.

The immortals are needed to lead mankind to full contemplative intimacy. They include the angels, and the noble living and dead of all traditions. Slowly Christians are beginning to realise this and to open their eyes and ears to what God is saying through the poets and musicians and artists of all religions. It is a slow process, for there are many inhibitions to break down and a great fear that the acceptance of other traditions brings the danger of denying one's own. This is not so, but suspicions die slowly, especially among the Christians who are eager for some kind of martyrdom. It is in the East where this way of intimacy is most clearly understood and expressed in what may be called the *guru-chela* relationship.

The late great exploring Benedictine, Père Le Saux, has written with deep understanding of this relationship in his book *Guru and*

Disciple. There he sums up the function of the guru in this way:

'Beyond the experience of things and places, of watching and participating in rites, of reading or meditating on the scriptures, or of attending lectures, there is the experience of meeting with men in whose hearts the Invisible has revealed himself and through whom his light shines in perfect purity – the mystery of the guru.'
                                        (Henri Le Saux O.S.B., *Guru and Disciple,* p. 28)

He goes on to follow the Hindu tradition that when the disciple is ready the guru will automatically appear. He sees the function of the true guru as the making of spiritual experiences arise in the heart of the *chela;* or disciple.

Haller used not one but many *gurus,* some of them most unlikely masters. Pablo, for instance, was a dance band leader with little apparent theological insight, but for Haller he opened the doors of the kingdom. This must echo the experience of many of us. Often the guru is a man who does not share the spiritual background of his *chela,* a man of little education. He is like King Lear in his relationship with Kent. Shakespeare described the meeting with the deepest understanding.

Lear.	Whom wouldst thou serve?
Kent.	You.
Lear.	Dost thou know me, fellow?
Kent.	No, sir; but you have that in your countenance which I would fain call master.
Lear.	What's that?
Kent.	Authority.

                                                                   (Act I, sc. 4)

Authority: that is the secret of the relationship between the guru and the disciple.

Most of those who achieve contemplative intimacy with others do so through the ministry of many *gurus.* The first are parents. Then come teachers. Then friends. As the disciple grows more mature he finds his *guru* through reading the great works of the past and making contact with musicians and artists. Patanjali is insistent that one of the ways to spiritual maturity is meditation on the lives and teachings of the great leaders of the past. For the Christian the Christ of the gospels and His tradition is the source of contact with the greatest of all the immortals: He is the supreme *guru.*

Using Christ as the *guru* involves making acts of *anamnēsis.* This is a technical spiritual exercise which is carried out under the influence of the Holy Spirit. It includes the making of an internal image out of materials supplied by the gospels and the symbols of the Church: and making a relationship with the image in terms of emotional and mental contact. From this develops the capacity to identify and assimilate with the Christ within the image and through that union His life is shared. It is much more than an intellectual exercise. It is more than discursive meditation, which is as far as most sermons can take us. It is meditation transformed into contemplation, as described by St Ignatius when he makes this important comment in his preface to the Exercises:

'Why did the Son of God become man? To speak to our senses, to move us, to instruct us, by the great spectacles of the manger, of Thabor, and of Calvary; by this wonderful sight to fix our imaginations, to attach our hearts.'
(*The Spiritual Exercises of St Ignatius,* p. xv.)

For Christians Christ is the chief *guru*. All others point to Him and in Him find fulfilment. There can be no question of rivalry or competition. In His own right and by His fruits He stands supreme. All others constellate around Him, confirm and illustrate His greatness. To Him all eventually come who are to attain contemplative intimacy with God. Haller did not achieve this because he stopped short of Christ. Christ alone leads to the intimacy He describes in the parable of the vine:

'I am the vine, and you the branches. He who dwells in me, as I dwell in him, bears much fruit; for apart from me you can do nothing.'

(Jn 15:5)

It is important to remember that Christ and the immortals come to us through the imperfections and distortions of human instruments. This Hesse teaches us in that strange interview between Mozart and Haller, when Haller watches Mozart assembling a wireless set which spat out 'bronchial slime and chewed rubber'. But behind the slime and rubber there was sure enough something 'like an old master beneath a layer of dirt, the noble outline of that divine music'. The inadequate instrument did not totally distort the divine music'. Haller as he listened was able to 'distinguish the majestic structure and the deep wide breadth and the full broad bowing of the strings.' Mozart explained laughingly:

'Please, no pathos, my friend. Anyway, did you observe the ritardando? An inspiration, eh? Yes, and now, you impatient man, let
the sense of the ritardando touch you. Do you hear the basses?
They stride like gods. And let this inspiration of old Handel
penetrate your restless heart and give it peace. Just listen, you poor
creature, listen without either pathos or mockery, while far behind
the veil of this hopelessly idiotic and ridiculous apparatus the form
of this divine music passes by. . . . When you listen to radio you are
a witness of the everlasting war between idea and appearance,
between time and eternity, between the human and the divine . . .
and exactly as it strips this music of its sensuous beauty, spoils and
scratches and beslimes it and yet cannot altogether destroy its spirit,
just so does life, the so-called reality, deal with the sublime pic-
ture-play of the world and make a hurly-burly of it.' (*Steppenwolf,*
p. 246–247)

Even the greatest of all the immortals, Christ Himself, allows His
gospel to be written by men whose eyes and ears and pens distort its
truth with their own imperfect vision. But this does not destroy the essence of the truth, nor hinder us from making anamnēsis of His
presence. And what is true of the greatest immortals is also true of the
lesser ones as well. Mozart's rebuke, that this is no cause for pathos or
regret, is timely in these days when so many are shaken in their faith
by the work of historical criticism on the gospels. The very imperfections sharpen our own senses and give us a share in the imaginative
adventure of penetrating beyond the shadows of the reproduction to
the full light of the original.

Creation

Haller reached the climax of his disorders on the verge of suicide.
His progressive withdrawal from life, as Hesse remarked, made him
unsociable to a degree he had never experienced in any other man. His
unsociability was not merely a withdrawal from human companionship: it was a withdrawal from all life into the desert of his
ego-self. This frightful description of his daily routine sums up the
depth of his isolation:

'The day has gone by just as days go by. I had killed it in accordance with my primitive and withdrawn way of life. I had worked
for an hour or two and perused the pages of old books. I had had
pains for two hours, as elderly people do. I had taken a powder and
been very glad when the pains consented to disappear. I had lain in
a hot bath and absorbed its kindly warmth. . . . I had done my

breathing exercises, but found it convenient to omit the thought exercises. I had been for an hour's walk and seen the loveliest feathery cloud patterns pencilled against the sky.' (ibid, p. 33)

At this stage we find him almost totally withdrawn, but not quite. He could still respond to the beauty of nature. The 'loveliest feathery cloud patterns' reveals a man who could still recognise the voice of nature. It was on this one living branch of his being that Hermine was to build. She led him out of his appalling loneliness into a renewed intimacy with life, but she never completed the journey of leading him through life to God.

Hermine began her work when the last thread of Haller's social life had been broken. She took the initiative and asked him to wipe his glasses. With instinctive wisdom, she decided to lead him back by first renewing his senses. From there she went on and compelled him to learn to dance.

These actions led Haller back to a renewed contact with nature. And as he went out to meet nature so she came to meet him. He began to realise that he was not living in a hostile world, but in a world which came out to love him and was ready to amplify every gesture he made of friendship.

This is a reassuring discovery. Even though man may reject life with suicidal intentions, life never rejects him. Its friendly vibrations play continually around the heart and call out for a response. God to the Indian seeking Him is not a theological proposition or a dogmatic statement appealing to the mind: He is the essence of joy, *ānanda,* and claims the heart. Shakespeare understood this and shows it working in *King Lear.* As he approaches total disintegration, nature surrounds him with increasing intensity. The lightning flickers, the thunder roars and shakes him out of despair into action.

'Blow winds, and crack your cheeks. Rage! Blow!
You cataracts and hurricanoes, spout
Till you have drench'd our steeples, drown'd the cocks
You sulphurous and thought-executing fires.'
(act III, sc. 2)

Here are intimacy and shared violence enough to shake Lear into action. Then follows a renewal of his compassion. He recognises the needs of his fool for the first time as they enter the hovel.

'Poor fool and knave, I have one part in my heart
That's sorry yet for thee.'
(act III, sc. 2)

From that moment his healing is assured.

Life comes out to man and will not be refused. Man is healed as he comes out to meet this many-featured nurse. Nature gives us happiness and sorrow, even life and death with joyful indifference. The man who would be healed must learn to live with her in all her moods.

By ordering Haller to wipe his glasses Hermine took him out of his myopic state and opened him to the full light of day. In this light he was able once more to look well at nature. She went further and, by introducing him to the greatest artists, the musicians and the poets, gave him new spectacles to look again with clearer gaze at the marvellous creation he had rejected. In the early stages of renewal in life the help of others who have already penetrated its mysteries comes to guide us. This was understood by the builders of a cathedral such as Chartres, where the glory of life is intensified and interpreted to help those who share it to go out and look for themselves. The Church has done some of her best work by using her artists in this way. The mere simplification of life, which is now expressed by vernacular translations and reformed liturgies cannot do this unless the inherent glory and truth are preserved. Contemporary forms are essential, but they must be inspired contemporary forms which will send men back to the source of life in nature.

The admiration of nature is one part of the way to contemplative intimacy with her, but it is not the whole way. Nature insists on co-operation. The artist must look and see but then he must reproduce. He finds union with nature as he remakes her through his art. Renoir saw clearly when he remained a workman and rejected the precious and esoteric attitude towards art. All who work with nature are artists, workmen who use her gifts to create for themselves. It is through their creations and the interchange they involve that man reaches a full and loving intimacy with the natural models he must use.

Haller had looked well at nature, but he had never worked with her in any creative action. Hermine touched the nerve of his recovery when she led him to make his response in a most unexpected way: he must learn to dance. She herself led him to master the simpler forms. He had to use another teacher for the more complicated movements and then through them he came to relate to Hermine and the rest of the outside world.

The dance is an art form which has enabled man to connect most spontaneously and effectively with his environment. In unsophisticated conditions we find social life built around the dance. This was true in Britain, where the country dance was an essential of community life. It is still in Indian villages, and it is the life-blood of Africa.

It is a great tragedy that healing movement has been almost excluded from the life of the Church and its worship. It is an equal tragedy that in the more sophisticated western world the simple dance forms have been replaced by the ballet and the modern dance rhythms, which are often debased. This means that in the West a large number of people are deprived of that intimacy with the Spirit in nature which could lead to healing intimacy with God. There are signs that this loss is being recognised and that steps are being taken to replace it. There is a growing interest in oriental dance forms, particularly in the Chinese T'ai Chi Ch'uan, and efforts are being made to restore the country dance tradition in our country.

In the Church the last vestiges of the dance were extinguished by the recent simplification of the ceremonies of High Mass. New forms of the dance could enrich the new ceremonies.

But this would have to be done skilfully. Where the dance is used without careful training in religious matters it is easily degraded to hysteria.

In using the dance for religious purposes there are certain sound principles to follow:

i. Good dance movements and appropriate music go together.

ii. Good dance movements always come from sound traditions. These traditions have evolved over a long period and have been tested in the only satisfactory way, by long use.

iii. New dance forms will certainly emerge as the dance revives, but they should not be used for religious purposes until they have been tested by use. Spontaneous movements in religious matters usually result in a small group imposing themselves on a large congregation; this is contrary to the working of the body of Christ where every member has a vocation and ministry.

What is true of dance movement is also true of music. Roberto Assaglioli writes wisely about both the good and the bad results of certain kinds of music. Good music may be a powerful means of therapy: bad music may lead to disintegration. He goes on to analyse the principal elements of music in terms of rhythm, tone, melody, harmony and timbre and their effect on human beings. Good music, with these elements well balanced, leads not only to physical relaxation but to emotional renewal. He writes:

'There is a kind of music, both instrumental and vocal, of a strong and virile nature, which arouses the will and incites to action. Such music has stimulated innumerable individuals to noble deeds, to heroic self-sacrifice for an ideal. Against all negative and depressive emotions, such as despondency, pessimism, bitterness, and even hate, music of a gay, vivacious and sparkling character, and also music that expresses true humour, acts as a true counterpoise. It cheers and gladdens, smoothing the wrinkled foreheads and softening into smiles the hard line of tightly closed lips. Such effects are produced by many compositions of Haydn, Mozart and Rossini.' (Roberto Assaglioli, M.D., *Psychosynthesis,* p. 247.)

How inadequate is so much Church music to produce this effect, and how inadequate so many church organs to communicate the energy of the Spirit and guide us to contemplative intimacy.

Both the dance and music require technical mastery. No art is simple and spontaneous. Renoir may have liked to appear a workman, but he was a skilled workman who took a lifetime to master the techniques of his craft. Every movement which leads to contemplative intimacy presents techniques which have to be mastered. The eastern tradition insists that sexual intercourse presents this challenge, and that many of the frustrations both within and outside of marriage arise from failure to master these skills. It is equally true of all dance movements, of the Yoga *āsanas* and with most manual crafts such as pottery, woodwork, gardening and housework. To use movement for developing contemplative intimacy means incorporating what Dr Assagioli found essential in music: rhythm, tone, melody, harmony and timbre.

Near Poona there is a wonderful Buddhist Temple, and each day at noon a group of men stop their normal work and perform an intricate drum rhythm which makes the earth shake and the whole temple vibrate with the energy of life. To be present at that ceremony is to carry an unforgettable experience of the way in which music and movement can renew creation with a pulsating beat of life. When this is seen, it seems as if for the first time one reaches a living intimacy with nature and finds in that environment a door leading to the presence of God Himself. This door is always open to those who have mastered the rhythms of dance and music, and it can be shared by those privileged to listen and receive them.

RELATIONSHIPS

We have already seen that internal intimacy with the self involves a series of relationships within the instinctive and physical nature, the emotional and psychical nature, the androgynous wholeness of male and female and finally union with God Himself in the human nature of Christ. This internal intimacy has to be projected in a series of external intimacies with the created world, with mankind and with God in His kingdom. Such an interchange between inner and outer intimacy is essential to balanced growth and to the full circulation of love. Hesse understood this. He marks the moment of change in Haller's process of healing when he meets Hermine: from then onwards he has to project his disturbed inner relationships and have them healed. The most vital of these projections brings him into direct contact with mankind. He has to project his inner sicknesses on to mankind. We can look at these with reference not only to Haller but to mankind.

The Bible insists that mankind is a mixture of male and female. (*see* Gen 1:27) This Hesse emphasises in his analysis of Haller. He goes further and writes of 'the illusion of the unity of the personality' and insists that the 'self is made up of a bundle of selves': he defines the essence of the ego in this way:

'Every ego, so far from being a unity is in the highest degree a manifold world, a constellated heaven, a chaos of forms, of states and stages of inheritances and potentialities'. (*Steppenwolf*, p. 7)

He goes on to conclude that in representing the ego the most effective art form is the drama. Yet true as this is we may still follow the Bible division as a general description of the ego, and treat it as a duality of male and female. When externalised, this leads to two potential forms of intimacy: the homosexual and the heterosexual.

We must first reconsider the words available to describe these relationships. Although we are free to use all words not all of them are desirable because of the many unfortunate associations they gather around them through unwise use. This is especially true of the words homosexual and heterosexual. Both have now such a limited range of meanings, many of them not to our purpose, that it will be best to substitute others whilst not losing the special forms of intimacy reserved for these words. We shall use the word 'friendship' for homosexual intimacy and the New Testament word 'fellowship' for other kinds of intimacy. In this way the unfortunate overtones connected with the other words will be avoided.

Friendship

The fierce opposition in the West to any form of homosexual relationship has done much to dwarf the meaning given to friendship. This relationship has often been limited to pre-adolescent intimacy, and been suspect when allowed to continue into adult life. Yet the Lord gave the dignity of friendship as His highest gift to His disciples before His crucifixion.

'There is no greater love than this, that a man should lay down his life for his friends. You are my friends if you do what I command you'.

(Jn 15:13)

It is right for any community to defend itself against the destructive social activities of those who exploit homosexuality. This needs to be done with any other selfish activity which ignores the rest of mankind, but when wise precautions have been taken, then the demands of individual freedom must be considered. We have already moved in this direction with the revision of some of the laws intended to give this protection, but much more needs to be done, and we can only hope that all involved in the debate on this revision will consider it against the widest possible background, the background of total intimacy and not merely with regard to the necessary control of certain limited activities and the protection of the young. This is a pastoral, moral and spiritual problem of great importance and it has far-reaching implications.

Before handling friendship in its complete forms it must be emphasised that the sexual relationship almost exclusively referred to in the word 'homosexual' is a distorted limitation of human intimacy. There are many other centres of human intimacy besides the sexual which are more complete and effective in bringing people into union. These are physical, mental and emotional, fully legitimate and often in need of wise development.

Hesse recognises all these forms and shows Haller passing through them, with an enlargement of his personality as he does so. He avoids the mistake of prefacing Haller's exploration with a series of prohibitions. He is open to all experiences in his search for friendship. He starts at a stage of permissiveness, and gradually grows out of many forms of relationship which at the beginning he needed for full growth. Like an artist he finds the limits of his potential for relationships through these preliminary explorations, and for him these limits are his law, written, as St Paul would put it, in the heart. There is no other law which can lead to mature intimacy or real friendship. This freedom, of course, opens the way to all kinds of dangerous aberrations, but the law of love requires it.

In his recent book *Yoga and God,* Déchanet writes about naturalism and yoga and encourages the development of what he calls 'Christian naturalism'. He stresses the need for Christians especially to see nature as 'a kind of sacramental, a medium, an ambience, in which one encounters God.' He is well aware of the danger of pure

naturalism without the deeper insights of the Christian faith and
relationship within the body of Christ, but yet he writes:

'Once all vestiges of Manichaeanism have been brushed aside,
Christian naturalism is a return to the same ideas of the original
witnesses to Christ, based on belief in the redemption of the human
body and of nature through the incarnation of the Word.' (ibid,
p. 19)

Among the practices he recommends under the heading of Christian naturalism is some use of nudity as a way of physical hygiene and
relationship, and he illustrates this from his own experiences in Africa.
Others have had equally convincing experiences in India and other
countries.

Even among the most manicheistically dominated cultures forms of
nudity are common. Young children are accustomed to the naked
body. The tragedy is that this healthful practice is so often stopped at
puberty when it would be of the greatest value. For it is then that concealment leads to what has been described as the phallic fantasy, an
undue emphasis on certain organs of the body and a failure to keep
them in balance with the whole.

In the West nudity can only be practised in esoteric and rather self--
conscious groups. It is also too closely connected with psy-
cho-therapeutical treatment to be treated as a normal expression of
friendship. But in spite of this misuse nudity is a legitimate expression of Christian naturalism, and a normal preliminary to Christian intimacy.

This was recognised in the early baptismal rites of the Church when
the candidate was presented naked to the congregation, immersed and
then led out of the water to be clothed with the chrism garment. This
still survives in the rubric for baptism, where the minister is ordered, in
the case of a young child, to 'dip it in the water discreetly and warily',
and in the case of a person of riper years is ordered either 'to dip
him in the water or pour water on him'. In both cases this presumes
a degree of nudity in the presence of the congregation. The vesting
of the priest or bishop for the eucharist again assumes a public
exposure of the body, even though not to the point of nudity. God
himself took the human body at the incarnation and made it a temple
of His manifestation.

The naked body is a marvellous and complete self-expression, as
the creators of the Greek *kouroi* so well understood. When uncovered,
it speaks with the simplicity of the child, the questing longing of the
adolescent, the discovery of old age. It is a sheath revealing something

so much more wonderful than itself, the psychic and spiritual bodies described by St Paul.

When human beings have recovered their familiarity with the naked body it becomes a powerful instrument leading to the intimacy of friendship. It speaks of the total mystery of God and creation for it is a microcosm of the universe. Through it all the human emotions are made visible and the mind becomes able to speak with the full language of eurhythmic disclosure so well understood by Rudolf Steiner.

The Bible summarises the essence of this intimacy through the naked body when it describes the relationship between Adam and Eve in Eden:

> 'Now they were both naked, the man and his wife, but they had no feeling of shame towards one another.' (Gen 2:25)

Through their naked confrontation there were none of the sniggers of pornography, none of the ingrown narcissism of the introvert: rather a release from sterile loneliness into the friendship of life. Under these conditions they heard the voice of God in the garden and lost it when they grew ashamed of their nakedness.

Christians have so much to learn and so much to give through their bodies. The compassion they are to show the world can only be seen when their hands and sides are uncovered to reveal their wounds. Joy can only be truly shared when the full glory of youth and age are seen. It is distorted when the body is covered with the man-made stitched fig-leaves of present-day fashions.

Out of the intimacy of nudity grows a form of sexual intimacy which the Bible describes in its fullest meaning as 'Adam knew his wife, Eve, and she conceived.' (Gen 4.1)

Today, under the influence of the media, the significance of sexual intimacy is both outrageously exaggerated and limited. It is presented as the deepest form of intimacy and as an end with no further sequel of growth. This is not the oriental attitude, from which the Bible attitude springs. In that tradition the sexual centre of consciousness is no more than one of the vital centres of the body. Union at these centres leads to deep and growing intimacy which does not end with the brief orgasm of sexual intercourse. Beyond these centres are the higher intellectual centres of imagination and reason and insight where even deeper relationships are possible. All these centres of consciousness are exercised in friendship, and God as the creator of them is found in each. Any one centre operating alone, or with an unbalanced emphasis, obstructs the full flow of intimacy and disturbs the harmony of friendship. Intimacy is a flow of energy through all the centres leading to fulfilment in God. This is the essence of the allegory of the *kundalini* which, under the symbol of a serpent, ascends through all the centres, opening their full communicative energy and leading to God.

We can watch the distortion and the attempt to correct this process in the life of Haller. He came to the crisis of his life because his sexual centre had not been opened or rightly used. He failed in the marriage relationship, and in preliminary relationships as well. His attempts at celibacy, instead of opening him to the wider intimacies of friendship, imprisoned him still more completely in himself. Hermine tried to release him from this, but she did not fully succeed. She forced him to face his sexuality and to use it.

Haller's physical explorations were mistaken and never completed, but at least they were begun and no matter how inadequate they led him some of the way toward wholeness. There was his marriage, dismissed in his confession to Hermine with the curt statement: 'I haven't a wife any longer. We are divorced.' (*Steppenwolf*, p. 106) There were his adolescent adventures with Rosa, Irmgard, Anna and many others. Then the more mature relationship with Maria, through which he achieved full sexual experience and, finally, the attempt to find real intimacy with Hermine, which was left unfinished. As we share Haller's retrospect, we can see how much of his tragedy came from incomplete sexuality and how necessary it was for his total balance that this should be healed. Haller in this stands for us all. He had to face the sexual side of his nature and bring it into union with God in order to be fully healed. How this is to be done has never been fully discovered. It is one of the urgent tasks of the Church, of both its ordinary members and its theologians, to research into this problem and to present a solution for the world. It is the Church which must do this, helped by the psychologists, for she alone has the depth of experience to make it possible. We may be thankful that in these days many Christians are alert to this need and are taking thoughtful steps to meet it. A width of sympathy and compassion, an absence of prejudice and an awareness of the amount of distortion in our tradition which has come to us through Manichaean and Augustinian influences will be needed.

As the Church approaches her task it will be well to keep in mind that those who cry out most loudly for help are often their own worst enemies. This was true of Haller. It is true of many of our most vocal homosexuals. The way in which they advertise their cause in newspapers and by propaganda leads to unnecessary alienation; and the disloyalty and treachery they often display towards each other must be eradicated if they are to be treated with the compassion they claim.

There has also been a negative and prohibitive approach in much of the traditional moral teaching of the Church: an attempt to fence off large areas of exploration in physical relationships with savage prohibitions. Homosexuality has been condemned too absolutely: the legalistic approach to marriage in an attempt to preserve it at all costs ignores the fact that human beings are involved and that love cannot be enforced by law. Fortunately many religious have already moved away from a rigoristic attitude to their vows and have opened a path to a more straightforward and guilt-free system of dispensation. There is still a long way to go, but the Church is leading in the right direction. It cannot be said too often with the authority of the Lord Himself that love is the end of the law and that love cannot be created by anything but the Spirit of God working in the surrendered wills of men.

Anna in her simplicity saw this when she located God in the middle of everything, even of sex. She saw Him there, not as a critical observer but as the supreme loving Father who gives the love we are called to share. This love, great as it is, must be learnt under certain preliminary safeguards, but when they have been mastered then we can enter on the freedom of love defined by St Augustine: *ama et fac quod vis*. This free love is much more than the sexual experience, the few brief moments of the orgasm in the sexual centre. It is the opening of the whole being to continuous and complete intimacy in contemplative fullness.

The Christian Church has noble examples of a fulfilled sexuality in her tradition. There is the 'Song of Songs'. There are the lives of David and Jonathan, the relationship of our Lord and St John, who achieved that mysterious intimacy which is described as being in the heart of Jesus. The lives of the saints abound with examples of such intimacy. Scott writes of it just before it was sealed by death:

'We could have got through if we had neglected our sick. I do not regret this journey. Had we lived, I should have had a tale to tell of the hardihood, endurance and courage of my companions which would have stirred the heart of every Englishman. These rough notes and our dead bodies must tell the tale.'

(Scott's Last Expedition)

This approach lifts friendship beyond mere homosexual relationships with either sex. It includes a wide range of physical intimacy which needs a great deal of open-minded exploration, but, however satisfying, this is at best no more than an incident on a much longer way, leading often through shared suffering, as with Captain Scott and his party, with shared joy, as with David and Jonathan, with the complete intimacy of loving faith, as with our Lord and St John. This is not to under-estimate the importance of the physical relationships. The incarnation seals them with an essential emphasis, but they are not exclusive. They lead on to other experiences, and it is when they become ends in themselves that friendship withers and the contemplative goal is lost. The remedy for this failure is not to reject the physical intimacy: it is to develop it and make it more complete. The sexual contact should be corrected by widening the physical union through shared manual work, shared postures, the dance and other arts. Haller was guided to this wider relationship by Pablo and Mozart: as he responded his intimacy grew more complete. On the Ross Sea ice barrier this fulfilled intimacy was achieved by a group of men who had passed through all the degrees of physical relationship. Their friendship is summed up in this final description of their death. It is the model of what is involved in every completed friendship.

'Bill especially had died very quietly with his hands folded over his chest. Birdie also quietly. Scott died later, his arm flung across Wilson.'

Friendship is much more about emotional and mental intimacy than physical. David and Jonathan, and our Lord, show this. Jonathan risked his life for his friend and died in his defence and David spoke the depth of a friendship which included every part of his being:

'O Jonathan, laid low in death.
I grieve for you, Jonathan my brother;
dear and delightful you were to me;
your love for me was wonderful,
surpassing the love of woman.' (II Sam 1:26)

The fourth gospel is a marvellous saga of St. John's total love for our Lord.

As one studies the growth of friendship between these men one is struck by the gradualness and the completeness of the process. This is especially true of David and Jonathan, the classic example of fully developed homosexual love. In them intimacy began with a complete surrender symbolised by the exchange of clothing. Jonathan stripped off the cloak he was wearing and then gave David his sword, his bow and his belt. Even Saul was able to see the depth of this surrender: Jonathan 'had given his heart to David and had grown to love him as himself'. (I Sam 18:1) From that beginning they passed through the whole range of emotional intimacy, reaching an understanding of mind with mind and finding in their love the presence of God Himself.

The emotional side of friendship grows through shared experiences. These include all the main emotions: fear, joy, grief and hope. From this comes a mutual emotional growth so that each is able to balance the emotional range of the other. So often friendship breaks at the point where there is not sufficient emotional strength in one partner to match the needs of the other. This may well lie behind the tragedy of Othello and Desdemona. It happened frequently in Haller's friendships. Even at the end of his pilgrimage he still had far to go before he could respond adequately to Hermine.

It is the sharing of emotions which develops the power to achieve friendship. Our Lord chose His disciples that they might be with Him and in the measure of their capacities they shared the events of His life, including His death, resurrection and ascension. Such sharing led to their growth in emotional response. It needs often to be said that terrible as war is it creates friendships of a depth that can compare with its destructive powers. Under war conditions fear and grief, joy and hope can be shared in their deepest forms. With war no longer a likely possibility on the grand scale, one of the most urgent needs of this generation is to discover alternative ways of providing the same conditions of emotional growth. Shared expeditions are one possibility, but much more satisfactory are explorations into contemplative intimacy in small, carefully chosen groups. We have to discover a way of reproducing the conditions of *Pilgrim's Progress,* but with a higher purpose than that of saving our souls. This is the urgent task of religious communities, and the real justification for their continued existence.

Physical and emotional friendship is maimed and incomplete without 'the marriage of true minds.' The classic achievement of this in a corporate form was achieved by the early Church, which earned this description of its life and work: 'the whole body of believers was united in heart and soul.' (Acts 4:32) St John's gospel shows how this was achieved between the beloved disciple and his Lord.

This mental intimacy comes in many ways: in conversation, in reading, and above all through corporate meditation around a shared theme. It is no chance that those who became most intimate with the mind of Christ shared the transfiguration and the Gethsemane prayer. These contemplative conditions train the mind to become more receptive to others and are the foundation of the deepest friendship. When Haller was most absorbed in the music of Bach and Mozart he most nearly became one with them. It was the shared goal of reaching the South Pole that kept the members of Scott's expedition together: without it they could not have reached that unity of purpose which made them of one heart and mind.

In the adventure of exploring this depth of intimacy mistakes are bound to be made: its early stages will expose those who attempt it to criticism and misunderstanding. This is a risk that has to be taken in every worthwhile exploration. The real question is whether the achievement of the goal makes these risks worthwhile: those who have achieved it witness to the greatness of their reward. The suffering through which they reach it is cathartic rather than destructive. The sorrow is the raw material of their joy.

Fellowship

This word is often used to translate the Greek word *koivōnia*, which St John expounds in his first epistle as the deepest of all corporate forms of unity. He sums it up in the inclusive statement: 'You and we together may share in a common life (*koinōnia*), that life which we share with the Father and His Son Jesus Christ.' (I John 1:3)

This is contemplative intimacy in its most complete form, a union with God and mankind.

Before attempting to analyse this life and the way to it we may note the reticence of the Bible about so many of its details. It is the work of the Holy Spirit and the Spirit blows where He wills. The fellowship with each other in God takes many forms and must not be limited nor fenced by unnecessary laws. It is a tragedy that in the Church form of this life so much legal structuring has been attempted. It is an equal tragedy that in its more personal forms a like mistake has been made.

There is one law, the law of love, and it expresses itself in innumerable ways. This is true of fellowship in all its forms; in the relationships between the sexes, in home and family life, in the intercourse between the soul and God in contemplative prayer. Disastrous consequences have followed attempts to define and codify the expressions of love. We must all love in the form appropriate to the present moment, or fail in our quest for the fellowship described by St. John. St Augustine's teaching on loving freedom applies. Perhaps the first stage to this form of love is to break down many of the regulations that have tried to limit it to expressions which cannot contain it, and, to claim our freedom to love now as the Spirit leads.

Yet, while we must admit this, there can be no fellowship without some structure, and it is of this structure we must now think.

Haller tried many fellowship structures and failed in them all. His marriage broke up, he turned his back on his Church and he never achieved a permanent community relationship. It is not difficult to find the weakness which led to the failure: he had no place for the divine Self and substituted for it what Hesse called a contempt, which was not world-contempt but self-contempt.

The centre then of all community structures, of all fellowship is God. This is the message of St John and the Christian Church and it is seen in all fellowships, whether national or religious: in primitive conditions – the Indian village, for instance, where the temple is one of the essential centres near which the *panchayat* meets and where the divine presence manifests and rules. No other centre is conceivable, even in these days when so much of the divine presence has been taken over by various forms of bureaucracy. And this divine centre is the essence of the three main forms of fellowship, the home, the Church and the community.

The smallest and most fundamental fellowship structure is the family. This begins as a relationship between the man and wife and God. It is the smallest type of fellowship and often the most effective and the most beautiful. Each social organisation has certain tested conditions for the building of this fellowship which can be summarised as: a relationship between the husband and wife, mutually sustaining, usually envisaged as permanent, though not necessarily life-long; duties relating to sexual intercourse and to the growth of sympathy and understanding between the two partners; obligations for the care and nurture and education of any children. These conditions are based on the great instinctive needs of human nature and cannot be basically changed so long as human beings continue as they are. The home is not at risk now any more than it has ever been. What is happening is that some details of these conditions seem to require modification or development. These relate primarily to what is called the indissolubility of marriage and to the relationship within the marriage between the partners and God.

It is well to point out that marriage in the strict sense has never been indissoluble. There has always been the separation of death and, in many traditions, other reasons for dissolution have been recognised: for instance, where there is a total breakdown of sympathy, or where one partner has deserted. In the western tradition the conditions for dissolving a broken marriage are receiving wise reconsideration and it may well be that some of the wisdom learnt in the handling of breakdowns in the religious life and the granting of dispensations in these cases may eventually be applied to the handling of this side of the marriage problem.

More important and urgent is the need to teach the married partners how to integrate themselves with the divine centre of their home. This is a long-term goal and requires a re-thinking of what is called religious education. It is no longer possible to introduce God in terms of an infallible teaching system which claims absolute obedience, for the simple reason that such a teaching does not exist. What does exist is the recognition that we have moved into a situation of pluriform theology and that what has to be learnt is a way of using the theology of others to make our own. In practical terms this means teaching people to pray contemplatively, especially under the conditions provided in the Christian home. This is where the Christian family has a vital function of exploration and communication to contribute. Its members have to master the elements of this type of prayer and then to share what they have found in sound theological form with others. This will lead to the work of finding God in all the relationships of married life: physically, in the sexual life; emotionally, in the harmonising of different emotional tensions and mentally, in the bringing of the mind into union with the mind of Christ. There are already many techniques waiting to be tried, such as the pushing-hands relationship of the Chinese tradition and the shared posture movements of yoga. But none of these can be magisterially communicated: they have to be selected and mastered by each individual. Out of such experiment will grow a theology which is not primarily concerned with the intellectual understanding of God, but with the contemplative intimacy with Him which is the end of all sound theological enquiry. When marriage is accepted as involving this search it will become a more satisfying way of life and may have more chance of surviving the testing period after the children have left home. This might well become a period of theological advance greater than any other, and the time of greatest creative insight.

It is in the Church that the most serious instability exists. Unlike the family the Church is not built on unchanging instincts, but on intellectual insights which change with growth. The insights which led to the formation of a strongly structured Church and tried to make it an outpost of the kingdom of heaven have in these days shared the breakdown which has already overtaken the parallel political structures. In the last fifty years more imperial structures have collapsed than at any other period of history. This need not leave us in despair. The political collapse of empires has been followed by encouraging revolutions into new forms and most would say that the new is better and much more full of hope.

The past forms of the Church which have broken down are concerned with structure and theology. In structure they relate to the concept of a kingdom of this world: in theology to the concept of an absolute and unchanging truth.

The Church after the Edict of Constantine became part of an already existing structure and in the years that followed rapidly took on the shape of the empire in which she found herself a leading partner. This imperial structure expressed itself in the monarchical ministry and the separation of the Church from the world. It found its counterpart in the idea of an absolute emperor and the concept of the empire as the source of civilisation for a heathen world waiting to be civilised. These absolute concepts have now disappeared both in Church and state. No longer can the Church claim an imperial monopoly of truth, of grace, or of the kingdom. It has now been accepted that the logos enlightens man, that the Spirit, like the wind blows everywhere and that the kingdom of Christ is greater than any form of the Church likely to be conceived by man.

So the Church must share in a restructuring with no more than the barest outline to work from. These outlines are the possession of the Holy Spirit, the tradition contained in the Bible and the creeds, and the objective presence of the creation which God has both made and sustains. Out of this all members of the Church, not just the ministry or the theologians, have to build a fellowship which will make possible a contemplative union with God.

A step in this direction has been made in the report by the Doctrine Commission of the Church of England, *Christian Believing*. This is a valuable contribution, not so much in terms of new material as in terms of new methods. The old position of an absolute formulation of faith to which the orthodox must unwaveringly adhere is replaced by an attitude to theology formulated by Bernard Lonergan in his book *Method in Theology*. In this work he adopted an open attitude to the theologies of other religions and was content with a series of theologies rather than a single orthodox standard. He also, like the members of the Doctrine Commission, was concerned with the act of believing rather than the statement of the faith believed. Of course the change of approach has troubled those who were looking for a re-affirmation of the traditional formularies of faith, but for those who wait for the Church to approach her faith as a road to understanding, a way to contemplative intimacy, this is a trumpet-call many will rejoice to hear.

Already there are signs that the Church is returning to what Karl Barth saw as her essential structure when he wrote:

'In this matter (of the apostolic succession) there is only one true succession, and even on the part of the Church it is the succession of service. If the community is really to find itself and to act in line with Jesus Christ and His apostles, there is only one attitude, and that is the attitude of subjection and obedience.'

(Church Dogmatics, vol. IV, part 1, p. 720)

Our Lord claimed to be among us as one who serves, and as the Church is deprived of her marks of imperial glory in the modern world, so she grows alive in service. Again, Karl Barth helps us by pointing out what that service should be. It does not take the form of institutions, but of witness to Jesus Christ living as the Lord of His body, and this involves a life in conformity with 'the earthly-historical form of His existence.' It demands that every member must take part in the process which reproduces Christ in their daily lives.

Out of this demand is growing a variety of new community structures with many modifications of the old. The established religious communities in all parts of the Church are remaking their fellowship forms. This is happening as they shrink in size, surrender their institutions and buildings and are obliged to give up their dependency on endowments. The result is a renewed type of fellowship, based on the traditional models, but with adjustments to enable them to share in the life of the world. New forms of community life are growing up to meet new needs: the communities are seeking ways not of separating from the world but of integrating more closely with it.

Religious communities are especially engaged in re-interpreting the three evangelical counsels of poverty, chastity and obedience. Poverty becomes more clearly an expression of simplicity and smallness; chastity, of intimacy in terms which are wider than anything provided for in the marriage relationship; obedience is not a blind adherence to certain written laws and orders, but a delicate technique of listening to the voice of God speaking in innumerable ways. We have been recalled to the derivation of obedience from the Latin word *audire,* to hear, and this brings a flood of light to bear on what was once little more than a kind of military relationship between God and one's superiors. It is now being interpreted as the loving intimacy between a Father and his children, with much greater demands on their insight and response to His will.

The relationship between religious communities, the Church and the world is under critical scrutiny. The idea of detachment and enclosure is beginning to be thought out again. The fellowship in religious life is not a withdrawal so much as a going forth to a deeper intimacy than is possible in any other community life. Religious are people who make themselves available to a greater extent than any other part of the community. They make themselves available both to God and to their fellows. This may well mean smaller communities more widely dispersed. It will certainly mean a simpler way to the hearts of people in terms of contemplative union. There is a great discovery waiting to be made.

Other types of community fellowship will certainly develop in freedom from the traditions of the older religious communities. They should be for many purposes, some not directly religious. For instance, there are already communities for sharing the dance, poetry and drama, and these are a legitimate form of fellowship within the concept of St John's teaching. Housing societies are another type. Each need will generate its own community structure. This will make demands of sympathy on the traditional communities as they welcome this growth but see many novices who might have found their home with them drained off to other fellowships. In spite of the long unbroken history of the traditional communities, fellowship is a present and living work of the Spirit and is always new.

Some basic fellowship principles

True fellowships cannot be legalised: their essence is to be free. When the Cluny hand of uniformity laid its laws on the Benedictine monasteries, a great many of them died. Their resurrection came when they asserted their independence from central control. Every member of any fellowship must always be alive to this danger and resist it to the point of martyrdom. We must be free. Yet within this freedom there is a structure, because we find our freedom in serving the Lord, and He is not a capricious master. We have to discover His way of life and then rejoice to live in harmony with it. In other words we have to study the working of His Spirit. This working expresses itself in certain clear rules of relationship; a use of the body and emotions to make contact; and a growing illumination of the mind in loving understanding.

Haller's isolation reached a climax when he attended a funeral in which the ceremonial had become absolutely dead. It is true that the clergyman addressed the mourners as 'dear fellow-Christians' but there was no fellowship among them. They were all separated and embarrassed and wishing for nothing else but a swift ending to the uncomfortable and unreal function. This was a crucial moment, when Haller witnessed the death of the religious tradition. It was followed by another experience and death. He met a young professor who invited him to spend the evening at his home. Haller went and during the evening was nauseated by the etiquette of civilised society, and insulted his host. This finally severed his tenuous connection with others and opened up the abyss of his own schizophrenia. He summed up his experience in these words:

> 'For it was at once clear to me that this disagreeable evening had much more significance for me than for the indignant professor. For me it was a final failure and flight. It was my leave-taking from the respectable, moral and learned world, and a complete triumph for the Steppenwolf. I was sent flying and beaten from the field. . . . I had taken leave of the world in which I had once found a home, the world of convention and culture. . . .' (*Steppenwolf*, p. 99–100)

Haller, in rejecting the manners of civilised society, had cut himself off from his tenuous relationship with others. His rejection made even the most elementary intimacy impossible. It was from this predicament that Hermine rescued him, and she did it by forcing him to return to an observance of a code of good manners.

Good manners are much more than mere regulations to control human relationships: they are principles relating to the life of God with His people, a kind of natural law which leads to preliminary intimacy and without which intimacy cannot even begin.

On a code of good manners fellowship is founded. This code will vary in different places, but it exists wherever people have achieved a social life. In primitive societies it is often more clearly articulated than in more sophisticated ones. This is true in India, where there is a custom to meet every social situation. Part of a sound education is the teaching and mastery of this code. It is by no means a legal burden. It is a way of freedom which makes possible all the other more complicated relationships of contemplative intimacy. It is the foundation of the moral life. Haller found the animal nature can only be mastered by this law and nature thereby set free for other activities.

Another principle of fellowship is the use of all the faculties in achieving it: body, mind and spirit, or in present-day language, the body, the heart and the ego. So often attempts are made to limit fellowship to part of the whole humanity so that it is reached in mental agreement or in emotional approval and no notice is taken of that harmonious physical relationship which is the basis of everything else. Hermine did not make this mistake. She brought the body into her relationship with Haller from the first moment of their meeting. He was persuaded to eat, to drink and to use his body in the movement of the dance. From that point Hermine led him to fellowship with his other faculties. He never reached that ego identity with his true self but he went a long way in that direction. It is in this order, too, that the human faculties in the attainment of fellowship should be used. The body first; then the heart; and finally that ego union with others and eventually with God. It is a mistake, as our Lord so clearly taught, to by-pass the needs of the body. First He healed those brought to Him and later He touched their hearts and opened their eyes and showed Himself. St John describes the whole orderly process in his account of the healing of the man born blind in the ninth and tenth chapters of his gospel. The climax of fellowship is reached when the man exclaims: 'Lord, I believe', and bowed before Him. (Jn 9:38) This principle needs to be observed in the practice of ecumenism. So much of the effort towards this end is doomed to failure or the shallowest achievement because it begins with schemes compiled by a few negotiators working in isolation from the main body of the Church and appeals almost exclusively to the reasonable faculties and leaves out the body and emotions. An outstanding example of the failure to achieve a purpose through misunderstanding the working of human nature occurred at the end of the war when anti-fraternisation orders were issued to the troops occupying Germany. They broke down almost immediately for the obvious reason that human beings living in the closest physical and emotional contact could not resist the forces tending to fellowship under these conditions. The orders were never obeyed and eventually they were ignored. Once people are brought into close physical contact and given the chance to relate heart to heart they grow together.

There are many ways of practising this principle and the more spontaneously they grow the better. Almost every shared activity is suitable: the dance, the Pushing Hands of the T'ai Chi Ch'uan, drama and recreation of every kind. There is room for much exploration. It will lead to fellowship of contemplative proportions.

We have already noticed that theology has entered an area of greater freedom, and this will increasingly reflect itself in the expression of fellowship. This freedom is the right to hold different opinions within a generally accepted tradition, and the right to explore within an agreed ambience of symbols. Dr John Macquarrie has developed this method of doing and expressing theology and shows how much greater freedom is available when the language of theology is enlarged:

'Symbols, so far from being mere empty ciphers, have Being "present-and-manifest" in them. . . . They are not just ideas floating in our minds but are the concrete ways in which Being (God) accomplishes its self-giving and self-manifestation. . . . Symbolic language is not just a poetic language of images, but does throw light on actual structures. The typical language of symbolic theology is a mixed one in which both images and concepts play

their part. We should remember Paul Tillich's good advice: "One should never say, Only a symbol, but one should say, Not less than a symbol." So we should be far from despising symbols, for they have an indispensable part to play in our knowing, providing the only way in which we can attain insight into and talk about Being'.
(John Macquarrie *Principles of Christian Theology*, pp. 162–163)

And since symbols are essentially the raw material of contemplative prayer, this approach to theology opens up the way to that more complete use of the mental faculties which is provided by contemplation. It is this mental activity to which the new theological freedom invites us and, as we respond, we find our deepest fellowship in some form of this prayer, shared where two or three are gathered with the Lord as the living and controlling centre and His Spirit in the midst.

Martin Seymour-Smith, in his exhaustive treatment of present-day sex and society, analyses the various forms of fellowship into categories which correspond to sexual needs: women, masculine sexuality, deviance in terms of homosexuality and bisexuality, and the virtuists and sexists who try to impose a partially exclusive veto on the contents of human community life. He is a realist in recognising and frankly describing these ingredients of the community, and he eventually comes down against those who would aim at a limited fellowship of compatible parts. For this we may be grateful. Any attempt to reduce fellowship to less than the widest range of human beings is bound to lead to something starved and incomplete. We need to insist on the greatest variety of parts in every fellowship and to challenge the life of the fellowship to discover a way to hold these parts in balance without trying to convert them to other more easily acceptable forms. But this is no more than the negative side of the task. There is a positive side of much greater significance.

The positive need in every fellowship is to provide an environment where the parts can reach their full stature of intimacy not only with each other but with God. This is a demand for the widest expression of love. Hesse puts it forward, in *Steppenwolf,* under the symbol of the Magic Theatre. Here every kind of human being is met and each performs a service to Haller in the remaking of himself. He needed them all, the good and the bad, the effective and the failures. It is the recognition of this fact which is so clearly put before us in the Bible with its panorama of human life greater than any other presented to man in either real life or imaginative literature. And it is in this extent of fellowship that each part has a chance to find his ultimate union with God. We must resist the attempt to make the fellowship exclusive. It remains to insist with equal emphasis that the presence of all

the parts is integral to the whole and that everyone in that fellowship
has the right to be there and to use his place in that environment to
become whole. This is to assert that the Church is not the home of
saints only, but equally of sinners, and that the intimacy between them
all is the way to God.

7
Divinisation

Père Le Saux, who spent most of his life in India and immersed himself in Hindu spirituality whilst keeping a firm grasp on the Christian tradition, wrote prophetically when he predicted the need for Christian theologians to face the meeting between the Christian faith and the advaitic experience:

> 'Christians may boldly assert that the encounter between Christian faith and advaitic experience will on the one hand be an agonizing process of mutual integration as each appropriates the truth of the other – the 'dark night' of the mystical tradition – but that, on the other, it will finally lead to the most glorious resurrection of both in the innermost depths of the Spirit.'
>
> (Abhishiktananda *Saccidananda,* p. 49)

GOD AND MAN

Le Saux saw many points of agreement between the Vedanta teaching of a total immersion in God and the Christian doctrine of union, but he omitted to say that Christian theologians had faced the issue, already, at the time of Eutyches and the Monophysite controversy. As a result of that dispute the Church formulated her teaching at the Council of Chalcedon (451), defining the union of God with man in terms of two natures, divine and human, united in the one divine person of Christ. This teaching was put into liturgical form in the Athanasian Canticle, which has since been the orthodox answer to the advaitic teaching of Vedanta Hinduism. Contact with present-day advaitic teaching would modify the concepts with which Christian theologians today would have to deal, but a translation of the Chalcedonian solution into present-day language and ideas would equally present the Hindu theologians with new insights. Abhishiktananda may well prove to have prophesied correctly, and after a period of discussion and suspense the impact of these seeming contradictions may well bring an increase of light to both sides.

We are not concerned with this side of the question. What we are concerned with is the fact that the deepest form of intimacy, union between God and man, has been experienced in the two great traditions of Christianity and Hinduism. In the interpretation given by both traditions to this experience we shall find much to enlighten ourselves.

The Vedantic approach emphasises the overwhelming nature of the divine in the act of intimacy. One could almost compare it to the relationship between the praying mantis and her mate. In its early stages there is a distinction between the two partners: the human and the divine preserve their identity. But, as with the praying mantis, in intensifying the relationship the identity of the one is absorbed in the other. When the process is complete only one partner remains: the divine absorbs and we might say annihilates the human.

The Christian approach emphasises with equal force the depth of intimacy between God and man. It has the advantage of a perfect model in the incarnation of Christ and it is by carefully analysing this mystery we reach the conclusion that in the divine-human intimacy there is no annhilation of the human partner: rather the identity of the human partner is increased by the relationship. There is no absorption in terms of destruction: as with Christ, the human nature, is raised to the very throne of God to sit there and reign with Him. There is in the process a real divinisation of man, not in terms of a loss of his humanity but in terms of an addition to this humanity by 'the taking of the manhood into God.'

The Hindu interpretation will keep before us the dangers of over-emphasising the divine part of the equation: the Christian interpretation will supply the outline for our further development of the mystery in terms of the human nature which is divinised, the divine initiative and the human response.

The transfiguration of man

In order to avoid any misunderstanding about the survival of human nature in its union with the divine we shall use the symbol of transfiguration rather than the word divinisation to describe the process. This provides us with an unambiguous word and a model of the process.

The human nature to be transfigured is what the Bible calls the flesh. That is the total material that makes man. It was shared both by the Lord and the disciples with whom He ascended the mountain. There is no need to emphasise the fact that this nature in that form is in Christian tradition heavily associated with sin. We may content ourselves with the observation that it is capable of growth, *'capax Dei'* as St Thomas Aquinas described it. We need not heavily underline that sin gravely hinders and distorts this potentiality: it is enough to recognize that it exists as the essence of every man. What we need to do is to describe in greater detail the essential ingredients of this nature.

Human nature confronts us as a number of ego-bodies. By this we mean that there are a vast number of individualities, or egos, within a shared humanity. This is the picture of human nature we see as Peter and James and John ascend the mountain with Jesus. They are all men but they are distinct as Peter, James and John, and what is more our Lord treats them as authentically individual and not as just a group of disciples. This is a recognition of an essential fact of human nature which can be ignored only at immense risk both to the individual and to whoever tries to obliterate the fact of our separate ego structures. This is the fatal mistake of all attempts at totalitarian government. When individuals are treated as a single mass to be manipulated by the devices of mass media, then the essential mark of human nature is destroyed: the result is not obedient or revolutionary human beings but monsters of frightening destructive power. History has many examples of the disasters which follow this gross misunderstanding.

Man is an ego-body, and side by side with his individual being there is the shared human nature. This human nature is essentially a complex of physical and psychical powers at varying degrees of development and understanding. Before trying to describe this body in greater detail we must consider the ego in greater depth. We shall first examine the teaching of Freud on this subject. He has had immense influence on theological thought and from his work many valuable insights can be obtained.

Freud called the ego the 'reality principle', an organisation of consciousness relating to the 'id', or unconscious, and the external world. It exists in varying degrees of consciousness and can relate to different parts of the conscious and unconscious. It can also identify with different centres in the body. For instance, Freud divided human growth in terms of places in the body where the ego was especially conscious: in childhood, the oral and anal centres; in adolescence, the genital and emotional centres in terms of phallic and Oedipal consciousness. Another fact he noted about the ego was that from the age of three or four the ego splits and creates the superego which operates as a controlling force over the functioning of the ego, often with disastrous results in later life.

There is much in the Freudian description of the ego which corresponds to experience. His idea of it as a power of consciousness is vital. It corresponds to the Bible teaching of the essence of the ego as a gift from God. 'Then the Lord God formed a man from the dust of the ground and breathed into his nostrils the breath of life. Thus man became a living creature.' (Gen 2:7) It also recognises that the ego has a creative capacity which is shown to us in Adam, but this is not in its true form a power of independent creation. It is a work of co-operation with the God who makes, using the receptive ego as His instrument. Freud also saw that the ego could usurp this capacity and attempt to create in its own power, and that from this misuse of its creative faculty came the disaster of the ego-self usurping the place of God as the true self of the ego.

Freud was mostly concerned with the ego in some state of sickness which it had reached through failure to develop fully or by introversion on itself. He never reached the full contemplative understanding of the ego which is found in both western and eastern contemplative traditions. This understanding sees the ego as essentially the seer, the *drashta* of the Yoga tradition, who sees God as its true object and then reproduces by the power of God the image of what it sees. In other words the ego has the capacity to reflect living images of God.

Many egos in one body is a possible definition of human nature, and one that is illustrated in the transfiguration mystery, only here the extra phrase needs to be added: many egos in one body and that the body of Christ. 'There was nobody to be seen but Jesus alone with themselves' (Mk 9:8) is a masterly summary of humanity transfigured with the ego operating in its full consciousness.

The ego in its early stages of growth attempts to individualise the one body, especially in the western tradition. In the East this is not so complete. A sign of the maturing of the ego is the capacity to recognise the one body manifested in many forms. It is with this one body in its process of transfiguration that we are at present concerned. It is the study of a body in the process of growth, limited by its present incomplete development, but with the capacity both for growth and transfiguration.

We are shown this growth in miniature as Christ leads His disciples to the top of the mountain. The shared body grows in union with God and the rest of the members, both the living and the departed. Moses and Elija, Peter James and John are incorporated into the one body. The body grows in glory. It is transfigured by the infusion of the Spirit in the form of the cloud of glory, and becomes master of death and capable of resurrection. It is transfigured through all the stages from flesh to psyche, from psyche to spirit, from the spiritual body to the body of glory. All this growth is telescoped by the evangelist into the short period of eight days, which is a symbol of the re-creation of humanity. It is in reality a process of unknown duration with different parts of the body at different stages of transformation. What is unmistakably clear from this mystery is that the Lord is present in the body at all stages of its growth, from flesh to glory. This is an important principle, sometimes forgotten by ascetics of all traditions, who have suggested that God is more present when the body is more developed. The reality is not that He is more present but that He is more manifest.

Just as the body of humanity is in a state of growth, so are its various faculties: the instincts, the senses, the emotions. Again we find this truth made clear in the transfiguration. The boy at the foot of the mountain is damaged in both his instincts and emotions: the senses of the disciples are raised in their ascent to see hidden things. There is a radiant joy over the whole mystery as it moves to its climax and the emotions of fear and anger are transfigured. All this happens under the control of the divine presence. In the climax we see the faculties of the body in their restored glory, instruments through which the material creation makes contact with God, instruments through which God communicates with His creation and preserves and leads it to perfection. These faculties, like the body itself, have a capacity for infinite growth and as they grow so they more perfectly share in the life of God.

The humanisation of God

Divinisation, when applied to human nature, is dangerous enough: humanisation when applied to the divine nature is even more dangerous. This danger has been faced by previous generations, and an attempt to avert it has been made in the words applied to the process of incarnation: 'not by conversion of the Godhead into flesh: but by taking of the Manhood into God'. This is a general caution, but it is enough to prevent us from making the error of thinking of the transaction as an absorption of the divine nature into humanity.

This error is not always avoided in the East, where the avatar of Krishna so often assumes a purely human form and leaves his divinity behind. It is also a possible interpretation of the advaitic solution, where the Godhead ceases to have any relationship with a humanity which has ceased to have a separate existence.

The Catholic expression of the mystery avoids description. It does not explain the process. It is content to place a veto on the possibility of God ceasing to be God by the process of incarnation. Equally it vetoes the possibility of manhood ceasing to be humanity by being taken into God. We are thus left free to probe into the mystery of the relationship between man and God, protected against fundamental error; this exploration is a challenge for the Church in all generations. The tragedy is that the Church, in trying to avoid error, has often been afraid to explore truth. There is an urgent need to re-state the mystery, not merely in verbal terms, but in terms of a contemplative intimacy which must always be the most satisfactory expression. We can take a part in this exploration by considering the nature of the inner life of the Godhead and the share of that life which the humanisation through the incarnation brought about.

Macquarrie uses the phrase 'Holy Being' to describe the nature and life of God, and this is satisfactory so far as it goes. But the Bible revelation and particularly the revelation of the life of God given by our Lord takes us further. He reveals a relationship between different centres of consciousness, called Father, Son and Spirit. These names are technically symbols and should be interpreted far beyond their literal meaning. The Father symbolises creative love, the Son receptive love and the Spirit communicating love. We may then rightly add to the phrase 'Holy Being' the word 'loving' and this gives us as a description of the inner life of God the phrase 'Holy and Loving Being'. It is this inadequate description which nevertheless enables us to penetrate deeply enough into the life of the Godhead to begin to understand how a process of humanisation in this Holy and Loving Being can take place. But first we must go one step further and think of the relationship of the three Persons within the Godhead.

When we think of the word nature, applied to both God and man, there is a tendency to think in terms of something static, something permanent and unchanging. This may be justified in terms of complete knowledge, but that we are without, and so our knowledge of the nature both of God and ourselves is in a state of emergent growth. John Macquarrie argues convincingly for this interpretation of nature as 'being emerging, coming into light.' (*Principles of Christian Theology*, p. 274) When this is accepted, we have a less static view of the divine and human natures, one which fits more convincingly into our present-day modes of thought. God is always being revealed and the revelation is never complete. The Spirit who leads into all truth continually proceeds both from the divine nature in terms of revelation and from the human nature in terms of reception. There is no end to the process.

It is within these natures that there is a continuous relationship. In the divine nature it is a relationship between three perfect egos in one loving and holy being: in the human nature it is a relationship between an infinity of imperfect egos in one growing, received being. The divine and human natures are linked by the connecting link of the divine ego, the Son, who brings them into a giving-receiving relationship with the Being and Life of God. This relationship makes no internal change in the life and being of God, but it continually changes the life and being of man, who is thereby brought into a growing intimacy with God and enabled to grow in power to respond to the demands of that intimacy. Before considering this demand we must examine more carefully the life and being of the Son both in the Godhead and in the Manhood He has assumed.

The traditional doctrine of the relationship of the Son to the Father and the Holy Spirit in the Godhead is summed up in certain key words which need reinterpretation and even replacement in every age. But this does not mean that the truth they enshrine changes: rather, it grows in clarity as each generation contemplates and shares the mystery.

The words are:

Father	(*patēr pantokrator*)
Son	(*huios monogenēs*)
Holy Spirit	(*pneuma hágion*)
Godhead	(*ousia*)
Source of Godhead	(*monarchia*)
Coinherence	(*perichōresis*)
Person	(*prŏsōpon-hypóstasis*)

Out of these words is built up the verbal description of the being and life of the Godhead. Briefly this doctrine in terms of Being states:

i. There is one, uncreated, loving and holy Being which is called God.

ii. Within this Being there are three centres of consciousness: the Father who is the originating principle, the Son who is the receptive principle and the Holy Spirit who is the loving relationship between them. These three centres are perfect consciousnesses. Each receives and communicates the other. They perfectly interpenetrate each other.

iii. The loving, holy Being of the Godhead communicates itself outwardly in a continuous act of creation which is tuned to the receptivity of the creature. In this act of creation the Son and the Holy Spirit take active parts: the Son communicates Himself and the Spirit energises the creature He makes, whilst the creature flows back in sacrificial giving to the Father through the Son and Holy Spirit.

This is the mystery in present-day words, but there are other and more effective ways of presenting it. There is the way of the eucharist and the way of baptism.

In the eucharist the three-fold being of God is presented dynamically in terms of the congregation and the acts performed. The congregation and the building and sacrament represent the creation in its relationship to the Godhead. They are His temple. The priest represents the presence and activity of the Son and Holy Spirit. The Father is the source from which all proceeds and to which all is given. There is a continuous flow of life from Him to the other Persons of the Trinity and through them to creation. This model of the humanisation of God is more explicit than any doctrinal definition.

In the sacrament of baptism there is another model of equal efficiency. Here creation is represented in its most chaotic form, water. On this non-being the Loving and Holy Being of God operates in terms of communication of the three Persons and out of this contact emerges another member of the body of Christ. Again the life of the Trinity is vividly presented in the threefold baptismal formula by which the presence of the Godhead in its inner life is revealed and man's participation in it made clear.

The inner life of God makes contact with our humanity possible: the incarnation doctrine of the Church is an attempt to express it in words. This expression is of necessity inadequate, and needs to be re-expressed in every generation. The tragedy is that the Church has for so long been content to repeat a splendid formulation unaltered since the time of the Chalcedonian definition of the fifth century.

The Chalcedonian definition speaks of Christ, the incarnational bridge, in these words:

'One and the same Christ, Son, Lord, Only-begotten, recognized in two natures, without confusion, without change, without division, without separation; the distinction of natures being in no way annulled by the union, but rather the characteristics of each nature being preserved and coming together to form one person (*prosōpon*) and subsistence (*hypostasis*), not as parted or separated into two persons, but one and the same Son and the Only-begotten God the Word, Lord Jesus Christ.'

In this definition we are again faced with certain key technical words: nature (*physis*), person (*prosōpon*) and subsistence (*hypostasis*). They all need a new understanding if they are going to say today what they intended in 451 A.D.

For instance, from the word 'physis' is derived the science of physics which was once described as 'the science treating of properties of matter and energy or of action of different forms of energy on matter in general.' Modern physics would now deny any basic separation between matter and energy: both matter and energy are the same fundamental energy at different levels of intensity. When we apply it to theology we find Dr Macquarrie describing it in much the same way as 'the process of arising, of emerging from the hidden'. In other words it is a state of becoming rather than a static and unchanged material condition. So the divine and human natures which are united in Christ are perfect and underived Being and imperfect and derived being. One produces the other. There can be no confusion between the being which is derived and the Being which is communicated. But there must be a relationship of dependence and continuous giving.

When this meaning is applied to human nature it is clear that the attempt to treat the process of union between divine and human being in historical terms is inadequate. The process is always going on. Human nature is always emerging as it receives divine Being, and divine Being is always in a state of loving giving. This fact is expressed in the doctrine of the Trinity in terms of the eternal begetting of the Son by the Father and the eternal procession of the Spirit from each. There is no beginning and no end. In the same way, the incarnation is more of a dynamic and eternal relationship than a final and completed state. This may well be what the symbol of the virgin birth is most intended to preserve when it places the moment of incarnation outside the categories of the natural procreative model.

'*Prosōpon*' is the word used to describe the divine ego in its relationship to the human being. While remaining unchanged in its divine perfection it unites with the imperfect human ego, and by this union enables it to become fulfilled. This fulfilled human ego is then the complete consciousness in terms of a capacity fulfilled by union with a perfect object. Put in another way, the human ego is completed by union with the divine self.

'*Hypostasis*' describes the divine ego of the Son, complete in its consciousness within the divine Being, receiving that Being through the gift of the Father and sacrificing that Being through the Holy Spirit both within the Being of God and within the being of creation.

Here we may note that the Holy Spirit plays an essential part in the loving life of God and in the loving life of God in creation. It is a disaster that, owing to the Christological controversies during the time of the councils, and to concentration on the mystery of the incarnation, the work of the Holy Spirit in relation both to the life of God and His presence in man was not given its balanced place. The result has been to make of the incarnation too precise a historical event in time, and the continuity of the mystery through the Holy Spirit has been obscured. The incarnation was not merely a once and for all event through the Virgin Mary. It is a continuous event through the working of the Spirit, and takes place each time the Spirit is confronted with the permissive 'Behold the handmaid of the Lord. Be it unto me according to thy word'. An exclusive concentration on the historical incarnation, whilst necessary as a preliminary, seriously obscures the continuation of the mystery in the members of the body of Christ.

Dogmatic definition is one way of proclaiming the mystery of God in man: another method, the method of the Bible, is to use symbols. We find this method most effectively used in St John's gospel. He summarises his teaching under seven statements beginning with the phrase I Am. The statements are:

I am the loaf of life. (Jn 6:35)
I am the light of the world. (Jn 8:12)
I am the door of the sheepfold. (Jn 10:7)
I am the good shepherd. (Jn 10:14)
I am the resurrection and I am the life. (Jn 11.25)
I am the vine. (Jn 15:5)
I am the way; I am the truth and I am the life. (Jn 14:6)

These symbolic sayings enormously increase our insight into the mystery of the divine presence in creation. They also enlarge our insight into the extent of human nature. It is not a small thing: it is as large as creation, and the Lord indwells and is united to every part.

In an article entitled 'Model and Symbol' Harry Williams has brought deep insights into the mystery of the incarnation. He sees Jesus as the supreme symbol of both the Godhead and the manhood. This he describes as follows:

'Jesus symbolises the presence of the universal and eternal God in a human race composed of particular individual men and women. Jesus can do this because he is presented to us as an individual aware of and hence in the particularities of his life fully articulating his unity/identity with God. He is therefore a symbol of mankind's unity/identity with God because he is a partaker of its reality and power.'

('Theology', p. 17, Jan. 1976)

He goes on to insist that the symbol must be rightly used. Jesus as symbol must not be confused with the reality He symbolises. For our civilisation 'the particular symbol which is Jesus may have ... an overwhelming power of meaning which, so far as we are concerned, excludes all other unrelated symbols'. For our cultural group the symbol which is Jesus is exclusive but this 'is not at all the same thing as to claim that the reality conveyed by the symbol which speaks overwhelmingly to us may not be conveyed with equal power by a different symbol from those belonging to a different culture.' (ibid, p. 18) We may take this valuable insight further if we interpret Jesus as symbol in the way article twenty-five defines sacraments as 'certain sure witnesses and effectual signs of grace, and of God's good will towards us, by the which he doth work invisibly in us, and doth not only quicken, but also strengthen and confirm our faith in him'. In other words, Jesus is the greatest of all sacraments, with all other symbols and signs relating to God depending upon Him.

When we approach the gospel-Christ in this symbolic way we find that it is a contemplative instrument supplying us with a wealth of symbolic material through which the divinity and humanity of God are revealed and presented for our participation. These symbols lead us to share in the insight of St Paul in Ephesians:

'I kneel in prayer to the Father, from whom every family in heaven and on earth takes its name, that out of the treasure of his glory he may grant you strength and power through his Spirit in your inner being, that through faith Christ may dwell in your hearts in love. With deep roots and firm foundations, may you be strong to grasp, with all God's people, what is the breadth and length and height and depth of the love of Christ, and to know it, though it is beyond knowledge. So may you attain to the fullness of being, the fullness of God himself.' (Eph 3:16–21)

Here is an exposition of Jesus as the supreme symbol which echoes the insight of Harry Williams and takes us still further through this symbol into the very presence of God.

Christ is the symbol which reveals God and Man. In this revelation there is another symbol. It is the symbol of Our Lady, who is given a special prominence in St John's gospel. She is shown as integrally one with our Lord: the Mother and the Bride of the Lamb. Through her in Christ is manifested that mystery of the Godhead which is so clearly recognised in the East as shakti and so often obscured in the West: it is the mystery which Julian of Norwich so aptly describes as the

motherhood of God and develops in chapters 58 to 63 of her
Revelations of Divine Love. This quotation summarises her teaching:

'I saw the blessed Trinity working. I saw that there were these three
attributes: fatherhood, motherhood and lordship – all in one God.
In the almighty Father we have been sustained and blessed with
regard to our created natural being from before all time. By the skill
and wisdom of the Second Person we are sustained and restored,
and saved with regard to our sensual nature, for he is our Mother,
Brother and Saviour. In our good Lord the Holy Spirit we have,
after life and hardship is over, that reward and rest which surpasses
for ever any and everything we could possibly desire – such is his
abounding grace and magnificent courtesy.' (ibid, p. 58).

The motherhood in God is symbolised in Jesus and Mary, that great
dual symbol of androgynous significance which reveals the divine
nature and the secret of our own humanity, too.

The humanisation of God involves, as the mysteries of Christ in the
gospels show, the taking of human flesh in all its forms. It is the flesh
of the infant, the child, the adolescent, the man, in all its limitations
and potentialities. It is the flesh in sickness and health, in sin and in
virtue. It is the flesh in the earthly body, the psychic body, the spiritual
body and the body of glory. It involves the conditions of Bethlehem,
Nazareth, Calvary, the tomb, hell, the resurrection and the ascension.
In each state the Lord is united to our human nature, and through this
union He is renewing the whole manhood in its male and female
forms, 'making a single new humanity in himself, thereby making
peace.' (Eph 2:16) It also involves the conditions of Our Lady symbolised in the mysteries of her conception, annunciation, visitation,
purification, in the temple with the Lord at the age of twelve, standing
at the Cross and sharing in the resurrection and the ascension as the
Bride of the Lamb. So the divinised humanity, male and female reveals
through all the stages of its descent and ascent the indwelling glory of
God.

LIFE IN THE DIVINE-HUMANITY

Harry Williams writes:

'Jesus symbolises the presence of the universal and eternal God in a
human race composed of particular individual men and women.'
('Theology', p. 17, Jan. 1976)

Jesus not only expresses the oneness of man and God: He creates and evokes it in others. We must now consider that evocation in ourselves, but in order to begin with an objective study we shall first watch the life in the divine-humanity as expressed in the mastery of Dante, a supreme exponent of the mystery.

Dante

The achievement of Dante is rooted in the imagination. He is able to use this faculty to such effect that he can project all the experiences of human life, the dark and the light, all the supernatural experiences which normally wait the illumination of death, and that he has a range of symbols capable of making the invisible God visible in our humanity. Through imagination he paints the disaster of our present predicament. He can go down into hell and find God there. He can climb up into heaven and find him there also. He can look into his heart and find the divine glory there, and in the face of Beatrice and in the poetry of Virgil. Blake once wrote: 'If the fool would persist in his folly he would become wise'. Dante is one of those who persisted, with the result that he gave us a picture of life in the divine-humanity which has never been excelled.

The world Dante desired was one in which the good of intellect was restored, where the division of humanity was healed and where a state of living in God was realised. He sought life in the divine-humanity and, through a massive imaginative creation, he found and expressed it.

Dante saw the rift in humanity arising from a dislocation of love. This he traces to a failure to unify the male and female in one creature. It was part of his discovery and imaginative achievement to find the unifying agent in his imaginative creation of the figure of Beatrice.

Dante did not fail in his married life. Married in 1297 to Gemma di Manetto Donati, he remained faithful to her until his death. They had three children: Jacopo, Pietro and Antonia. These shared part of his exile. But this form of love, adequate in its own degree, he saw was not the whole. The other form was expressed in the image of Beatrice, whom he first glimpsed when he was nine and Beatrice was eight. The second crucial meeting was when he was eighteen, in the year 1283. These were the two physical meetings, for Beatrice died on the eighth of June 1290, already married to someone else. But the necessary fertilisation of the imagination had taken place. From these two physical experiences Dante drew the material needed for his supreme imaginative structure of love. He confined his attention to this structure, for it was in this that Dante found and described the secret of unifying love.

Charles Williams in his book *Religion and Love in Dante* sees Beatrice as made by Dante's imagination the vehicle of love in all its forms. She was for him the contemporary symbol of all that is contained in the gospel image of the Virgin Mary. Her function was similar: she was for Dante the vehicle of love, bringing not only herself as the perfect female counterpart to himself, but enshrining the Lord. As Charles Williams puts it, she contained both eros and agape. She lifted Dante out of the failures and compromises of middle age and raised him through the experiences of the dark night, purgation and union with God to the Divine City in Paradise. She stimulated Dante to love and contemplate God with such clarity that he came to see 'how man is in-Godded'. Through her he sees 'the circle which is Christ painted with the image of man'. She is the sacrament of the indwelling Lord, for he sees her revealing the divine presence through the sacred smile of her Lord.

But great as is the function performed by the image of Beatrice, she is not alone. In the early stages of Dante's pilgrimage he is guided by Virgil, who symbolises the masculine side of the divine humanity. He performs a vital task in leading Dante through the 'Inferno' to the beginnings of the 'Paradiso'. The divine humanity is male and female. In his infatuation for Beatrice Dante does not forget this.

Williams concludes from his study of love in Dante that the way of falling in love was for him and ourselves a way of sanctity for he writes:

> 'This is not to make us heavy and solemn; Eros need not for ever be on his knees to Agape; he has a right to his delights; they are part of the Way. The division is not between the Eros of the flesh and the Agape of the soul; it is between the moment of love which sinks into hell and the moment which rises to the in-Godding.' (ibid, p. 40)

Dante had both experiences, and they are open to us all. Love without God is hell in whatever form it is expressed. Love with God is an in--Godding, whatever the technique used. This is the foundation truth of all morality and of all sex. It leads to that contemplative awareness we may rightly call the vision of God and is given in every event of life which offers us a loving participation in God.

This way of sanctity is a restoration of what Dante describes as the lost good of intellect. He is told of this loss as the way to Hell at the entrance to the 'Inferno' when Virgil says:

> 'We've reached the place I told thee to expect,
> Where thou shouldest see the miserable race,

Those who have lost the good of intellect.' ('Inferno', canto III: 15–18)

What this good of intellect is in negative terms is the theme of the Inferno: it is the loss of the vision of God. In its positive recovery we are shown it in the events of the 'Purgatorio' and the 'Paradiso', where Dante slowly recovers the capacity to contemplate God and to find loving union with Him. The good of intellect or we might say of consciousness is the possession of God, not only as an object of vision but as the goal of love.

God as the object of vision Dante stammeringly describes as a state of bedazzled mind, of amazement in which the ego stands 'fixed in wonder, motionless and intent'. It is a growing state where wonder is ever kindled and the gaze never satisfied. It demands the ever-open mind which is ready to receive increasing light and sustain the strain of an unlimited growth of understanding.

God is also the energy of love which Dante experienced as a transforming relationship in which his will was caught up into the life of God.

'High phantasy lost power and here broke off;
Yet, as a wheel moves smoothly, free from jars,
My will and my desire were turned by love,
The love that moves the sun and other stars.' (Paradiso', canto XXXIII)

For Dante the Being of God is more than the sum-total of all creation, though all created being finds its perfection in the divine being. The being of God is uncreated, perfect act, first cause, and above all the source and preservation of all derived being. Because the Being of God is eternally creative it must be continually manifesting, and, since love is the most manifesting of all acts, the Being of God manifests itself in perfect acts of creative and manifesting love. These are focused in human nature in the Lord Christ, but He is also the centre of all creation and therefore the source from which flows the love that moves not only the human mind but also the sun and other stars.

Northrop Frye, in writing of Blake, puts this mystery in the clearest form and we may use what he says to sum up the essence of Dante's insight into the true divinity of man.

'God is God-Man, the Jesus in whose eternal and infinite risen body we find our own being after we have outgrown the imaginative infancy which the orthodox conception of the Fatherhood of God implies for us. The final revelation of Christianity is, therefore, not that Jesus is God, but that God is Jesus.' (*Fearful Symmetry,* p. 53)

When we link this up with what we have already considered about Jesus as the supreme symbol of the divine-human mystery we can see how He provides the essential imaginative material out of which the human imagination can make the controlling image of God-Man needed to reach the good of intellect which we are all in process of finding. For this Jesus is not confined to the Jesus of Nazareth and the gospels: He is the cosmic Christ of St Paul's captivity epistles, the beloved of the 'Song of Songs', the bridegroom in the book of Revelation, indissolubly united with the human Bride who brings the divine into union with creation. He is, in Dante's imagery, the circle within the square, the divine centre of the city.

Dante saw that the union of the divine and human natures in Christ was no lifeless, static relationship, but one of endless growth. In it the fallen creation is being continually taken into union with the divine nature to share the life of God. This is an activity summed up in the matter-of-fact words of Father Benson: 'Christ's coming into the world takes it into himself, bit-by bit.' (*Retreats,* 1872) The union between the divine and human natures is a state of growing intercourse.

For Dante this mystery was essentially realised in the imagination. It involved a constant replacement of images. Old images made from inadequate materials had to be replaced by new images derived from a universe in process of being renewed. He described this centred in the cosmic Christ with himself involved as a member of that Christ, part of His body and sharing in the divine Person, the true self of all mankind. The smile on the lips of Beatrice as it expanded to irradiate all mankind and the angels symbolised for him this growth of imaginative response which moves through the whole universe.

The human intellect as it shares in this good in the cosmic Christ in Dante's vision was taking part in a good of infinite proportions and never-completed growth. But this was its joy, not its frustration. As it contemplates the divine in its humanity, so the creative imagination grows, making new images of greater perfection through which more perfectly to contemplate and reveal God. Some of the images given us by Dante in the *Comedy* are the measure of his stupendous response, and their structure helps us to grow in our own way towards a similar imaginative response to the divine-humanity we also share.

We cannot hope to do more than underline some of the outstanding processes of Dante's creative imagination as he responded to his insights into the divine-humanity and shared the divinisation to which it leads. We can do no more than extract some of his imaginative principles and apply them to ourselves.

The first striking fact about Dante's imaginative activity is the material he uses. Poet as he was, he is not independent of outside sources. He does not spin his images like a spider out of his own fantasy. He uses for the most part external, contemporary and concrete events and experiences. Virgil is no nameless daemon, but a historical figure whose mind and works Dante had mastered. Beatrice is a real person whom Dante had met physically and absorbed into his heart. Many of the characters of the *Comedy* are Dante's contemporaries, and he handles the actual facts of their lives. Above all, Dante surrenders the working of his imagination to the control of a master--mind, St Thomas Aquinas, whose theological thought in the *Summa* gave him a mental pattern to sustain his own.

Patanjali in his classic *Yoga Sutras* teaches that the imagination requires for its creative activity three kinds of materials: a sense perception of an object (*pratyaksha*), a sound process of reasoning (*anumāna*) and a living tradition (*āgama*). (*Yoga Sutras,* 1:7) All these materials Dante had and used with brilliant imaginative force.

Dante, like Blake, proved that imagination is stimulated by the imitation of models, just as the musician attains imaginative freedom by the mastery of scales. This practice is essential in the preliminary stages of an art and can be superseded by inspiration when it has been mastered. Dante also operated within strict poetic forms, but this limitation did not hinder his freedom. Freedom came to him through the mastery of his forms.

Symbols were the essence of Dante's creative imagination, with one particular symbol of divinised man. In using this symbol he was within a great tradition which had already been taken into the Church as the controlling symbol of the spiritual imagination. It appears with overwhelming force in the Old Testament in the vision of Ezekiel and in the New in the vision of the glorified Christ in the Revelation.

Ezekiel uses this symbol to draw together the threads of his complicated storm images. In a series of disconnected fragmentary images he disorders the mind and emotions and then, when the reader is in a state of painful perplexity, he brings them together with this single master stroke.

'Above the vault over their heads there appeared, as it were, a sapphire in the shape of a throne, and high above all, upon the throne, a form in human likeness.' (Ezek 1:26)

St John the Divine uses the same technique.

'When I turned I saw seven standing lamps of gold, and among the
lamps one like a son of man, robed down to his feet.' (Rev 1:12–13)

Blake explains this focusing of the images of the creative imagination in the human form as the making of 'the human form divine', and
sees it as the climax of the work of imagination as it seeks for the
supreme symbol of the divine-humanity: the divine-humanity which
eventually takes the form of Jesus manifested as the essence of all
human forms, from the prisoner waiting to be visited to the king upon
his throne preparing to reward his faithful servants.

Dante's imagination works in the same way: he makes this symbol
out of the creation, the human forms of Virgil and Beatrice, the world
in chaos in the 'Inferno' and being restored and glorified in the
'Purgatorio' and the 'Paradiso'. Always this symbol emerges in
greater clarity and glory as he climbs the spiral leading to the vision of
God.

The Dante symbol of divinised man has a divine centre in
Trinitarian form. He describes it thus:

'Eternal light, that in Thyself alone
Dwelling, alone dost know Thyself, and smile
On Thy self-love, so knowing and so known.' ('Paradiso', canto
XXXII)

But within the eternal light shines the human form in all its manifold
glory. He writes:

'The sphering thus begot, perceptible
In Thee like mirrored light, now to my view –
When I had looked on it a little while –

Seemed in itself, and in its own self-hue,
Limmed with our image, for which cause mine eyes
Were altogether drawn and held thereto.' ('Paradiso', cant.
XXXIII)

This human image was of intense variety and richness, centring all
creation in the image of the rose, uniting the male and female in
perfect androgynous harmony, an image of transparent glory capable
of taking him into itself and transforming him into its loving glory.
Dante describes it as a centre 'enclosing everything the will has ever
sought'. We find the same concept in Blake when he writes: 'Man is
all imagination. God is Man and exists in us and we in him'. And the

climax of the divinised humanity is love: a perfect integration of man in his sexual duality, a perfect union with the whole of creation, a loving and joyful communion with God. All this is summed up in Dante's creative image of the divine-humanity, which is the heart of his poetic achievement.

Ourselves

In Dante we can see the process of the divinisation of a great artist gifted with amazing power to describe the process, and from his description we learn much about ourselves. For we belong to the same body and, though less articulate, share in the experiences of the artist as we grow towards the same goal. For us too it is primarily an affair of imagination, of certain dominant symbols and the images formed from them. It is also a growth which waits fulfilment in conditions beyond death.

Although God has united our humanity to Himself, our participation in the divine nature is not automatic. God recognises our freedom in this part of our life as in everything else. He does not compel, though He offers us the choice and makes it possible. We have to co-operate all the time if the divinisation of ourselves is to take place, and this co-operation is above all a work of creative imagination.

Mankind shares the destiny outlined in the life and work of Dante: the opportunity to reproduce from the innumerable resources of creation, reason and tradition image after image of the divine-humanity as manifested in Christ and His saints. This imaginative achievement is not the work of unaided nature. It is the work of the Spirit, infused into the receptive heart. Without this inspiration, man is like Dante in the middle of the wood, lost and powerless.

The inspired work of the Spirit operates through many instruments. For Dante it worked through Virgil, angelic messengers, Beatrice, the theology of St Thomas Aquinas, the infusion of light and a host of other experiences. With everyman He works through the growth of intimacies with others, through the experiences of life as we pass through its different phases and come to the critical menopause. At each critical period, man has to make an inner image of the completed experience, interpreted in the light of the past and, under the influence of that image, he passes on to the next phase of his growth. His pilgrimage, like that of Dante, is towards an increasing divinisation of the self as he moves through the worlds of nature, of men and into the kingdom. It is a journey which begins with the physical, sensitive experiences of life and culminates in an image of that life animated by love.

Dante makes his image of nature as a poet, though he is also aware of the scientific approach. He begins with nature as she is, incomplete and distorted and then he makes an image of her renewed in the transparent glory of the 'Paradiso'. The Bible follows the same path with an image of the fall of nature, culminating in the new heaven and earth of the Revelation. Above all, Dante makes an image of nature as the temple of God, watched over by Him continually.

'There gaze enamoured on the Master's art,
Whence never He removes the eye of Him,
Such is the love He bears it in His heart.' ('Paradiso', canto X)

This contemplative intimacy with nature is the path of man. It is a way of both rejection and affirmation. Nature in one form has to be rejected. The ugliness, the distortions have to be seen and renounced. But the renewed form of which man is in part the creator is accepted.

The rejection of fallen nature culminates in the glad acceptance of death. Dante, like all the great poets, never attempted to ignore death. He did not treat it as an event to be postponed as long as possible and grudgingly accepted. St Francis welcomed it as 'sister death', an instrument for the fulfilment of God's purpose. Our intimacy with renewed nature begins with a death which includes above all the death of the old ego-self in preparation for the reception of the new Self in God.

Renewed nature is partly the work of the creative imagination, inspired by the Spirit. It is an inner structure made through intercourse with the risen and ascended Lord out of the fragments of fallen nature. It grows with the growth of the creature. Dante symbolises this in its perfection in the image of the celestial rose, which expresses the glorified and divinised humanity. Man's growth and nature's renewal are different parts of one mystery.

Divinised nature, like divinised humanity, is alive with the presence of God. God is at the centre of the garden of Eden and God is the centre of the celestial rose. He is there to be found and enjoyed. The climax of intimacy with this nature is not perfect sight or perfect knowledge, though these are stages on the way: it is contemplative love. Dante proclaims this at the end of his pilgrimage in terms of union with the love that moves the sun and the other stars.

Nature and all her creatures, when renewed, are to be loved, and through this love man comes to his full stature. Wordsworth discovered this secret, and traced it in 'The Prelude', where he shows the renewal and transformation of his imagination through intercourse with the nature he irradiated with the power of memory and illuminated with 'the light that never was on land or sea'. This is the task of man, no matter how little developed his poetic faculty. This task requires the great creative effort of making an image of renewed nature by interiorising the fragmented materials of objective nature. This is a life-work, which Wordsworth shows moving to completion on Snowdon when he sees, through his restored imagination the glory of God. (*The Prelude,* bk. 13) It was the climax of a journey through nature in many forms: the beauty and mystery of youth; the period when his passionate nature was haunted by the cataract and its glory; the time of stillness when these emotions were chastened and subdued; finally the joy and harmony of communion with the God of nature as his ego found the divine presence in divinised mankind.

Such living intimacy with divinised nature is the quest of mankind. It is the end of contemplation, and we can reach it from the lowest form of work to the highest act of imaginative creation. The gardener and farmer have the opportunity as well as the poet and the man of prayer. Refusal to grow in this natural intimacy is the beginning of that disordered imagination from which Wordsworth was saved. Freud used to remind his patients that they must learn to love, or face an illness. This is the choice of us all. The artistic approach to nature is one way. It has been taken and proved by an innumerable army of poets, painters and musicians. Contemplative prayer is another. In this the body is treated as a potential garden of Eden, and renewed through physical movement and stillness from a Gethsemane to a resurrection Garden. This way has been taken by the saints of all traditions and is an ever-open door leading into God. Each of us must look well at the images of nature he makes in his heart, and chose the one that leads him to God.

Out of the materials of nature Dante made his 'Inferno', his 'Purgatorio' and his 'Paradiso'. We must make our own reproductions from similar materials of these places. And we must use them either as ways to loving intimacy or to loneliness and failure. Nature is herself impartial and gives what is asked. She is ambiguous, like the tree of the knowledge of good and evil in the garden. Our creative and loving image of her offers us either a paradise of affirmation or a hell of rejection. Literature is full of the examples of men who have taken and proved this way. Izaak Walton's *Compleat Angler* is one of the most unselfconscious records of these achievements of contemplative intimacy. He knows the ways of rivers and of fish, and they lead him into the presence of God. Thomas Traherne came to the Lord through a similar intimacy with His creation.

The crown of nature is God, and we come to the deepest intimacy with God through the images we make of our divinised manhood. For Christians the model is the gospel portraits of Christ, understood not as the imperfect works of a historian, but as the imaginative image of great poets. On this material we have to use our own creative imagination to make an image, not of the past historical Christ, but of the cosmic Christ of the present.

The crown of nature is man, and we come to the deepest intimacy with the divine-human nature in God as we make images of the divinised manhood. In I Corinthians 15 St Paul speaks of this nature in four complementary forms: the flesh, which is its most primitive material, shared equally by birds, fishes, animals and men; the psychic form, which is a creation of the imagination; the spiritual body, which is created by the Spirit using the events of death and resurrection; and finally the glorious body achieved by Christ and His Saints. It is in Christ that human nature has been fully divinised. We follow Him in various degrees.

Christ is the prototype of the completely divinised human nature. This is not an achievement of the past. It is present and made available to the members of His body. In Him each phase of human nature exists in perfection. In Him the body of flesh, the psychic body, the spiritual and the body of glory are present and made available to each believer as he grows up into the measure of the stature of the fullness of Christ.

The work of the Christian in sharing in the divinised nature of Christ is to make images as perfect as he can of each of the forms of the manhood of Christ, and to use them to enter into union with Him. These images will be expendable as we grow out of them. St Paul at one stage discards the image he has used of Christ in the flesh, and replaces it by another more adequate. This is a process which can be painful, and which all growing Christians must experience. But Christ is present in the most imperfect images we make of Him, and in using them for contemplative intimacy we grow and pass through them to make others. Dante found Christ in the 'Inferno':

'I saw One come in majesty and awe,
And on His head were crowns of victory.' ('Inferno', canto IV)

This presence is affirmed in the creed: He descended into hell. This asserts the presence of Christ in His divinised humanity, in the harlot as well as the saint, in the sick as well as in the whole, in the nightmare vision as well as in the imagination transfigured by the cloud of glory. The difference is not in His presence but in His manifestation. The true forms of the imagination reveal Him so that He appears with increasing clarity, as Dante is renewed in his journey through the 'Purgatorio' and the 'Paradiso'.

The materials out of which we make the images of the divinised humanity of Christ can be as rich as those used by Dante. He had the male and female forms in Virgil and Beatrice. We also need both, for the true image is androgynous. He used the supernatural in the figures of saints and angels, the immortals, as Hesse would describe them. We also need them. He incorporated nature in all her forms and with all her creatures. Nothing less than this variety is sufficient for our own work.

It is not enough to make an image of the outer structure of the divinised humanity. This is a framework. The image is of humanity alive, and this leads on to images of the emotional life and the deification of that life in God.

Dante finds the climax of the emotions in the smile of Beatrice. For him this smile was a sign of the presence of Christ upon whom the Father smiles in the life of the Godhead. It is not the exuberance of a laugh. It is deeper than happiness. It is akin to the eastern conception of joy as one of the highest forms of contemplation summed up in a smile. Our Lord traces its growth from sorrow which is transformed into joy. (St John 16:21) This climax comes from the full use of all the emotions until they become harmonised into a simple joy. Our created images will gradually take this form, but only through a creative travail like that which attends the birth of a child. The contemplative does not escape the pain; he uses it as the road to his joy.

Deification, or *theosis,* is a teaching which is given special prominence in the Orthodox Church. Kallistos Ware in his book on that Church writes:

'This talk of deification and union, of the transfiguration of the body and of cosmic redemption, may sound very remote from the experience of ordinary Christians; but anyone who draws such a conclusion has entirely misunderstood the Orthodox conception of theosis.'
(Timothy Ware, *The Orthodox Church,* p. 240)

He then goes on to elaborate the ways in which ordinary Christians may share in this experience.

We may also think of the deification of humanity not as a 'confusion of substance or nature' but as a unity of action. In other words, deification means, among many other things, being given a capacity to share in the work of God, to be His fellow-workers. The ways of our deification are: first, to follow the example of our Saviour Christ and be made like Him in life, death and resurrection. This means reproducing by the power of the Spirit the incarnate mysteries of the Lord and of Our Lady as they are set before us each year in the liturgy. Then, it means acting like God in terms of forgiveness, ministry and above all love. We become what we do and it is in working with God that our nature is interpenetrated with His nature and we become one with Him, remembering always that our deification, as the Church and the Bible so often insist, is not achieved by us ourselves, but because we have been made God's children by adoption and grace.

All this corresponds very nearly to what Kallistos Ware says is needed of the ordinary Christian when he lists the following duties: go to Church, receive the sacraments regularly, pray to God 'in spirit and in truth', read the gospels, follow the commandments. It is the theme of all the great spiritual traditions: we see it shining through these verses of the *Bhagavad Gita*:

> 'Give me your whole heart,
> Love and adore me,
> Worship me always,
> Bow to me only,
> And you will find me:
> This is my promise
> Who love you dearly.' (section XVIII)

8
Ecstasy

Poulain defines ecstasy in these words:

> 'Supernatural ecstasy is a state that, not only at the outset, but during its whole existence contains two elements: the first, which is interior and invisible, is a very intense attention to some religious subject; the second, which is corporeal and visible, is the alienation of the sensible faculties.' (*The Graces of Interior Prayer*, p. 243)

In other words he distinguishes between two kinds of ecstasy, a natural and a supernatural, a preliminary and a mature. John Donne in his great poem 'The Ecstasy' brings them both together and bridges the gap between the natural and supernatural forms:

> 'Our hands were firmly cemented
> With a fast balm which thence did spring;
> Our eye-beams twisted and did thread
> Our eyes upon one double string;
> So to intergraft our hands, as yet
> Was all the means to make us one,
> And pictures in our eyes to get
> Was all our propagation.'

Donne's poem describes with masterly insight a state of ecstasy achieved by two persons. They pass through all the stages which lead to that supernatural state defined by Poulain, where human nature finds fulfilment in a living and loving union with God. It begins on the pregnant bank with two human bodies, an affair of physical relationship. Then it passes on to a union of souls in emotional and mental harmony and reaches a climax in a spiritual awareness of God with the mind perfectly unperplexed and illuminated by the divine presence. It is an ascent through the physical, the mental and the spiritual. It is an ascent changelessly directed towards a single object, an ascent energised by a mutually shared energy. All these stages of the journey are landmarks on the road to contemplative ecstasy, and we shall try to describe them helped by the masterly description of Donne's poem. We begin by examining the energy which makes this journey possible.

Philip Sherrard has recently published a valuable series of essays on the theme of sexual love entitled 'Christianity and Eros', in which he pleads for the abolition of the traditional distinction between *eros* and *agape*. He traces the source of both kinds of love to the Holy Spirit, and therefore denies that there can be any fundamental difference between them. Of *eros* or what is commonly called sexual love, he writes in this way:

> 'In a sexualized sacramental love there is no such distinction. It is transcended and eliminated and there is but a single participation of the man and the woman and the divine in each other.'

He then goes on to trace the energy behind the state of orgasm in all its forms to one source:

> 'This sacramental form of sexual love is not simply a human emotion or impulse or even a created cosmic or elemental force. Still less is it to be identified with a bodily or psychosomatic energy. It is rooted in the divine life itself.' (Philip Sherrard, *Christianity and Eros*, pp. 2–3)

This is a very important truth, with wide implications. It identifies the energy which produces the orgasm with the energy that leads to divine ecstasy. Both are from the one divine source. It is the Holy Spirit who inspires the experience of orgasm in all its many forms. Eros and agape are the work of the one divine Spirit.

When this is recognised, every form of ecstasy has a sacred meaning. This has always been recognised in India where the *lingam* is the symbol of the divine presence, and sexual intercourse is as much a relationship with God as the most profound contemplative prayer. Philip Sherrard laments that in so much western Christianity this insight has been lost. Sexual orgasm is often treated as a regrettable necessity and limited to the procreation of children: spiritual ecstasy is regarded as something quite different, as inspired by another force.

Donne, in his poem, does not make this grave error. He sees all love as coming from God and in his understanding of love certainly includes the sexual orgasm. But he does not limit ecstasy to sexual intercourse. He sees the loving energy of God bringing ecstasy to the other centres of consciousness. God energises the genital centre, but equally He energises the centre controlling movement and the dance, the centres of emotion and of understanding. All have their right to ecstasy, to the experience of orgasm. The Spirit must not be limited to one place: the Spirit of the Lord fills the whole world and works to raise all life to an ecstasy in God.

ORGANS OF ECSTASY

The body

Ecstasy is first of all an affair of the body. It is not limited to one part of the body, but to the body in all its parts. This Donne emphasises when he names the parts of the body as he describes its ecstasy. The hands were firmly cemented, the eye-beams were twisted together, the affections and faculties controlled by sense were all employed. There was a perfect stillness and integration of the bodies of both partners: they became obedient sharers in the total ecstasy.

Donald Goergen in his recent book 'The Sexual Celibate' handles in great detail the various ways in which the body may be used in sexuality. He shows tactility, genitality and the affective elements in the body all making important contributions to the state of ecstasy, but he sees them working in harmony and never alone. The sense of touch stimulates one range of faculties, the genital area another. And then there is a whole range of affective experiences which contribute to the full orgasm. The body is much more like an orchestra than a solo instrument. The arousal to ecstasy is the result of a skilful blending of many parts. The full experience of the way in which these parts are raised to ecstasy can only be reached by courageous exploration by each individual or by small, selected groups. To achieve physical ecstasy through movement it is essential to select from the rich dance tradition and to persevere with regular and deepening repetition until the body is raised to that stillness which is the climax of ecstatic movement.

Ecstasy in the genital area often is given the limited description of 'orgasm', but this describes the beginning of a rhythmic movement which is intended to be prolonged in ecstatic contemplation between the two partners. Donne insists on this development of ecstasy in the genital area. His lines hint at an experience which surpasses words.

The task of raising this form of physical ecstasy to its full development requires as much training and mastery. It is what the poets have insisted, an art of love, to be mastered with the same perseverance as other arts. It should be said emphatically that orgasm in the genital area without the accompaniment of some degree of contemplation is doomed to failure and frustration. This is a lesson which the Church would be far better engaged in practising and teaching than in trying to limit the scope of genital sexuality and devising conditions which often make its full expression impossible.

From these ways of ecstasy flow all that affective life which deepens and completes the ecstatic experience. This requires the full purgation of the senses and their development in a harmonious and complete activity. It is the process described by St John of the Cross as the dark night of sense, a night which is but the introduction to a dawn in which man 'attains to living the sweet and delectable life of love with God.' Ecstasy is not the absence of grief, joy, hope and fear: it is their full integration in love, and to achieve this there must be a full life of the senses: sight, touch, smell, hearing, tasting, with common sense to blend them together. In this all the arts play a vital part, music, painting and above all poetry. It is by exposing all the senses to their influence that an ecstatic intensity is reached. A great deal of our Christian energy should be concentrated on developing these arts. If the presentation of art or an act of liturgy raises man to taste the experience of ecstasy, it is justified, no matter what expense is involved. It would seem that this is the opinion of the Lord Himself who expends so much on the daily presentation of His own cosmic drama.

The Heart

Donne writes of ecstasy that 'it leads love to grow all mind'. It comes to a climax in a union of hearts. 'This ecstasy,' he says, 'doth unperplex'. It leads to an insight so complete that 'it tells us what we love'. In ecstasy the heart comes to its full growth, using all its latent faculties under the stimulation of love, and heightening both the memory and imagination.

Wordsworth defined poetry as 'emotion recollected in tranquillity' and he often describes states of ecstatic awareness inspired by recollection. 'Tintern Abbey' is largely devoted to this theme, and the remembrance of the daffodils will raise him to dance in joy with them. But this is not the result of unaided memory. It is memory working with imagination that leads to this mental ecstasy. Memory provides the raw materials for the imaginative structure: the imagination working under the inspiration of love makes it. It is this image presented to the mind that raises it to ecstasy. In other words, memory and imagination provide the object for contemplative ecstasy.

For Christians the object of ecstasy is the cosmic and glorified Christ. This is the message of the New Testament, where we can watch the image of the Christ gradually forming out of many symbols: the child of Bethlehem, the Son of Man, the crucified Saviour, the risen Lord, the ascended King. It is the work of great contemplatives who spent their lives contemplating these symbols and making the image which is finally given to us in all its perplexing glory in the Revelation. There we are shown a Christ who is the centre of creation, who is man in glory, who is the Son of God. He combines male and female in androgynous harmony: He is on the throne of heaven and served by angels. The image is a marvellous achievement of the creative imagination, an image to inspire, but not to replace, the image which must be made by every man who would reach the state of real ecstasy.

One of the tragedies of the Christian tradition is that many Christians have been content to accept images made by others from the materials of a sequence of historically argued events. Jacob Boehme (1575-1624) was scathingly critical of this. He was a German Lutheran, a theosophical author who had many mystical experiences which he recorded in his books. The most popular of them was *The Way to Christ* (1623) from which the following quotation is taken. Boehme dismissed the faith of his day as 'but the history'. He was concerned with making the image of the present Christ within the heart, a work of great labour. 'A man,' he writes, 'must wrestle till the dark centre that is shut up close break open, and the spark lying therein kindle'. When this labour is accepted he affirms that this image of the inner Christ will form. Without it he concludes 'thou hast found nothing but the cradle of the child, that is, the history'. (*The Way to Christ,* pp. 81–83, John M. Watkins, 1964). This may seem harsh, but the present impasse in New Testament criticism and the attempts to reconstruct the historical Christ suggest that it is still very relevant.

Boehme describes the work of making an image of the present Christ as a work of great labour and so it is, but Christ has made it possible by the gift of His Spirit. It is through our co-operation with this Spirit who leads into all truth that we can embark on the contemplative work that leads to the making of this object of ecstasy which is the centre of our loving intimacy with God.

We have already considered the preliminary of this work in terms of intimacy with creation and our fellow men. This preliminary work makes the clay model of the image. If made at all it comes to completion in the middle years of life. Then we are faced with the decision of either leaving it in that form or moving on to the eternal form which comes when the clay model has been cast into enduring material and itself destroyed. This is the experience which St John of the Cross describes in his image of the 'dark night of sense and spirit'. It is an unavoidable work, without which the dark centre of our being cannot be broken up. If it is endured, then we enter through the experiences of death and resurrection, and the image becomes glorified as it shares in the ascension of Christ. Only the image in this ascended glory is sufficient to inspire the ecstasy which we are now considering. This is the lesson of the transfiguration, and of those who write of ecstasy in the New Testament and elsewhere.

The making of this image is gradual and life-long. It is never complete, for Christ grows in fullness. As the image grows so it needs to be expressed and tested. This happens as it is expressed in the physical body and through art forms. It is the duty of the Church to provide, as she has provided in the medieval cathedrals, places where creative work in its highest forms may be shared. This is even more important than theological debate, for it is in creation of this kind that the image grows. And man must engage in creative work if he is to remain healthy in body, mind and spirit.

It is not enough to make an image: the image must be alive, and it is the Spirit who quickens the image. Image makers of this kind of image must themselves be alive with the life of the Spirit. He flows from Christ the prototype image to all the members of the body and is received by them as they breathe in and communicate the Lord, the giver of life. The Spirit is not bound by earthly law. 'The wind blows where it wills and so is everyone who is born from the spirit.' (Jn 3:8) It has been a tragedy to bind Spirit-filled members of Christ with prohibitions and commands. This restriction can be likened to over-formulated art: finally, techniques alone can do no more than produce corpses. Those making an object of ecstasy must guard their freedom.

The Christ image never stands alone. He is the head of a Church and the centre of a city. This means that our own image must contain a model of both structures. There is a constant demand on us to make our utopias. There is a need for every man to construct his own theology. In doing this we must borrow from each other, in the past and in the present. The images we make must always be fluid.

The New Testament gives us many models for our work in making the city. It is a composite structure made up of many parts which reach fulfilment in the vision of the New Jerusalem in Revelation 21. It is a city which comes from God, 'made ready like a bride adorned for her husband'. It is 'clear as crystal', the dwelling place of the sovereign

Lord God. It is alive, and from it flows out the river of water of life. No such city ever existed in physical fact, but it is the most real of images, an ideal which has raised countless Christians to ecstasy.

We cannot hope to make an image of such perfection, but we can stretch our creative imagination in contemplative prayer to do the best it can. Such an image will be made from our best remembered experiences. For one, perhaps, an Indian village at evening with the women preparing the meal and the children playing before sleep, the temple on one side and around the pipal tree the wise men of the village talking. For another, like Sir Thomas More, it is a more complicated and political structure, based on other experiences. All must live with understanding in this world, but all must carry within them an image of the city of the world to come, and through that image be lifted to ecstasy and strengthened to perform their duties here. Such an image sustained and guided the Lord Himself: 'Jesus, who for the sake of the joy that lay ahead of him, endured the cross, making light of its disgrace, and has taken his seat at the right hand of the throne of God.' (Heb 12:2)

The New Testament is a collection of models for the city and equally a collection of models for the Church. It will not provide a complete blue-print, and theologians who attempt to use it in this way are disappointed. For the material is so abundant, and often so contradictory, that every form of the Christian Church and every theology can make a good case for itself when it appeals to New Testament authority. If we are going to do the same, we have to recognise a plurality of both Church structures and Church theology. We may be thankful that Christians of all parties are much more prepared to do this than ever before, but we need to be alert to any subtle attempt under the ambiguous word 'ecumenism' to merge the many parts into a pretended whole and to construct a mere façade of unity.

In constructing the image of the Church the New Testament gives us the great symbol of the bride adorned for her husband, and creates a theology from the symbol of Christ and the energy of the Spirit. It is in using these with imagination that we form an ideal which may eventually reach ecstatic proportions. But once again the images will always be growing and a stage will come when, like St Thomas, we shall dismiss our verbal theology for insight and our Church structure for the worship of the heavenly host. Each image will serve a temporary purpose and, when this has been achieved, another must be formed. It is a terrible thing to find people in old age, like Nicodemus, who have been given the material for new and more satisfactory images but who have refused to use them, and have ended with only the dead body of Jesus to be prepared for burial. The great opportunity of old age is to achieve supreme insights; and to move into the state of ecstasy from the earlier stages of discursive meditation. The old St John on Patmos did this. We prepare for this reward of old age in the middle years by being unafraid of losing the images of the Church and the City made in earlier manhood.

Adjustments

Our Lord when teaching His disciples the way to distinguish between the true and the false gave this brief direction: 'You will recognise them by the fruits they bear.' (Mt 7:16) Poulain gives the following symptoms of ecstasy:

(1) The senses cease to act, or they convey a confused knowledge only.
(2) The limbs become immovable.
(3) The respiration is almost arrested.
(4) The vital heat seems to disappear.

He then goes on to describe certain occasional phenomena which accompany the state of ecstasy:

(1) Levitation; the body rises into the air.
(2) The body is enveloped in a luminous aureole.
(3) It emits a fragrance. (ibid. p. 166–175)

Patanjali in the *Yoga Sutras* describes most of the signs of ecstasy given by Poulain and the western mystics. Here are some of the *siddhis* or signs:

1. Levitation 111.40
2. Radiance. 111.41
3. Smell. 111.37

Patanjali follows his Western brothers in warning against an over-attachment to these extraordinary experiences: he writes: 'By non-attachment to these *siddhis* the seed of bondage is destroyed and *kaivalya* follows.' And this *kaivalya* or freedom he sums up as: 'a balanced purity between the heart and the Lord.' (111.51 and 56)

In the Eastern Orthodox tradition the emphasis falls on what is called 'the uncreated light of God', which was manifested at the transfiguration and shines through the body in ecstatic prayer. There is also a tradition that a special fragrance emanates from the body of holy persons.

From these extreme results of ecstasy, gathered from many

traditions, we may say that the ecstatic is called to make certain physical, mental and spiritual adjustments to new conditions, and that his future growth and health depend upon the success or failure of his response. Our Lord at the transfiguration faced and met similar demands. His example gives us a guide for what is required of ourselves.

First, there must be no undue clinging to these signs; all mystics are agreed with Patanjali that no undue emphasis must be laid on the spiritual symptoms. There is danger in making them more important than they are. Ecstasy and its signs are not the heavenly country: they are transitory glimpses.

Since ecstasy produces changes in the bodily functions some physical adjustments are needed. This is where preliminary mastery of some of the yoga postures and dance movements is of great value for it enables the body to retain its elasticity and health under conditions which would otherwise lead to tension or quietistic dangers. Care should be taken over food and sleep should be natural and prolonged. With this discipline the strength of the body grows and a great many of the so-called physical mortifications can be avoided. There is nothing supernatural in diminishing the health and strength of the body. Our Lord's body after the transfiguration was stronger than before, poised for the physical demands of the passion.

Response to the mental demands of complete ecstasy involves among other things the opening of the higher centres of consciousness. This means reducing the activities of rational and discursive thinking, and resting content with images of light and sound rather than of visual form. It also means learning to make such images, and learning to be content with impressions rather than detailed and constructed thought processes. The ego learns to live in the psychic body and leaves behind many of the thought processes normal in the physical body, when it is stimulated by the senses.

Finally there is the spiritual adjustment to ecstasy. This demands a closer response to the movement of the Spirit, a surrender of the ego to His motivation, an abandonment of the old ways of ego control. This does not imply a mere passivity, for the Spirit is active, and often makes great demands in this state. It is, however, a loss of self-will and a surrender to the will of God. Learning to reach this stage of surrender requires some kind of external help, either in the form of community life or the guidance of a wise director. This is the stage when it is most difficult to distinguish between the various forces operating on the will. The *guru-chela* relationship is essential.

Ecstasy culminates in the intimacy of what is described in western prayer as the spiritual marriage and in the East as the liberation of full consciousness. Before studying this state we shall turn to ecstasy as it is revealed in the life of God.

DIVINE ECSTASY

The Christian doctrine of the Trinity is a theological description of ecstatic love within the being of God. Of course the description is inadequate, since it has to use cold, objective concepts for a loving relationship beyond the scope of words. Nevertheless these dogmatic statements, when used in worship and contemplative prayer, open our understanding to the mystery of the constant and loving ecstasy in the life of God.

One of the essential features of all ecstasy is the mutual going out of two centres of consciousness and their interpenetration. This is conveyed by the two words *'monarchia'* and *'circumincessio'*. *'Monarchia'* describes the Father as the source from which the Son is generated and *circumincession* guards the truth that the Father, the Son and the Holy Spirit mutually interpenetrate each other. Another tradition, which comes from Origen, relating to the 'eternal generation of the Son' by the Father, teaches that the loving movement within the being of God is continuous; not spasmodic, but eternal and unchanging. Finally, there is the eternal going forth of the Holy Spirit within the being of God from the Father and the Son.

John Macquarrie sums up this teaching by applying these adjectives to the concept of being. The Father he calls 'primordial' being; the Son, 'expressive' being; the Holy Spirit, 'unitive' being. (*Principles of Christian Theology*, p. 181–183) This gives us, as far as words can, a picture of the flow of love within the Godhead. It flows from the Father to the Son and is the Holy Spirit. This is as far as dogmatic formulae and words can take us. It is the limit of the Chalcedonian definition.

We can go further when we use the method of the so-called Athanasian Creed. In this document (see appendix) the method is not so much theological definition as worship. 'The Catholic Faith is that we worship one God in Trinity and Trinity in Unity.' This leads us into the regions of contemplative intimacy. The same key words are used as in the Chalcedonian definition: substance (*substantia*) and person (*persona*). There is the same need for reconsidering new words for old truths. But the approach in worship liberates us from mere thought, and leads on to an experience of loving intimacy with God Himself. Through this relationship we grow to share the life story summarised by our Lord: 'I came from the Father and have come into the world.

Now I am leaving the world again and going to the Father.' (Jn 16:28) This is not a single moment, but a continuous movement of love which finds its most complete expression in the Eucharist, where the total mystery of the way to a share in the divine ecstasy is manifested and made available to believers.

In trying to penetrate the mystery of the divine ecstasy there is constant need to remember the inadequacy of mere words. Donne rightly says:

> 'All day the same our postures were,
> And we said nothing all the day.'

Shared ecstasy begins when words have ended. The preliminary to a share in the divine ecstasy is silence.

Whilst Donne says that nothing was said he does not imply there was no communication. There was a communication through images. He writes of pictures in the eyes. It is these pictures given by God and received by us which lead to shared ecstasy.

It is a fair criticism of much of the theology in the Bible and outside that it is over-cerebral and controversial. Theologians have so often implied that God could be only understood through words of their own devising. This is a very different theology from the theology of Christ and of most of the New Testament. Christ's theology is full of living images, symbols and myths, and throbs with emotion. The God He reveals is the living, loving God who is in a state of eternal ecstasy. He is the opposite of the God of the philosophers, whom Blake caricatures so brilliantly in 'the images of Urizen and the God of Job. (see *Blake's Job, A Commentary,* Andrew Wright, p. 35, 'The Lord Answering Job out of the Whirlwind')

In using the images of the divine life we need to remember this tendency to dispense with images in our contemplation of God. The supreme image is the Incarnate Son: man makes fragmentary images of that one image, which shares the inadequacy and the distortion of his senses and creative imagination. Blake insists that if man could make the receptive image perfectly he would see the divine humanity of Christ in glory. As it is, he sees fragments and distorted parts of a whole which he can only at present apprehend through the veil of faith. God's given image in Christ is always perfect: our receptive image shadows the divine humanity and the ecstasy. We see, like Donne and Dante, pictures of this in each other's eyes.

Whilst theologians have so often struggled with words they have remained suspicious of images. Their suspicion of images of God has been based on the risk of limiting the truth and of encouraging anthropomorphic ideas of the invisible Godhead. These are good reasons for being cautious in selecting images, but they are no reason for trying to dispense with images in our contemplation of God. Some are unsuitable, and there is a place for apophatic theology as well as for the Buddhist '*neti, neti*' approach. But the greatest of all contemplative theologians, St John of the Cross, insists on the need for those images which he calls 'the imprinted images' in reaching an insight and a share in the life of God. We cannot grow without a structure of this kind. God did not give the divine image in His Son once: He continuously gives Himself in this way and, by the power of the Spirit, those who turn to this image are allowed to share in the formation of it in their own lives as they pass through the life-experiences which go to its making: birth, death, resurrection and deification in God.

Man receives this image by responding with the creative imagination, inspired by the Spirit. Through this greatest of all faculties he makes an image of the mystery proportionate to his understanding. The New Testament is a gallery of such images, made by a variety of created imaginations, replaced as one becomes no longer able to represent the fullness of received truth. Behind the variety we can glimpse the original prototype, but each has its own features, corresponding to the needs of its maker. Believers have been engaged on the same creative exercise ever since, with varied results. Like the four gospels we must allow each creation to stand, and we must avoid the temptation to harmonise the many into one.

There is a story of a desert Father who lived with an image of the Lord in the form of an ordinary man. He was mocked to tears by some of the wiser brethren. But the mocked fool was wise and through his faithfulness and perseverance to that inadequate image he grew to share the ecstasy of God. He was on the road to wisdom as they mocked, and had only to persevere in order to arrive.

We can learn much from the way our Lord communicates His own image. He uses many symbols, some of which we have already considered. He accepts many titles: Lamb of God, Son of Man, King, Lord, Christ, Son of David. All these and many more open up vistas into the centre of His being. He performs signs to manifest His glory. He lives surrounded by nature and men who are reflectors of Himself. We need the materials which are offered now to make our own image. When we use them all the image of the logos which forms in our heart is the image of the centre of the universe and the throne of God in whom vibrates the divine ecstasy of love.

The state when the heart is without such an image is death and no resurrection is possible without an image to inspire it. The timing for demolishing one image and replacing it by another can only be dictated by the Spirit.

The many images we make require in their making many of the skills of the creative artist. There is the selection of the right material, the discovery of the centre, the animation, the identification between subject and object. All the secrets of life are hidden in the work. It is the supreme exercise in the making and relating of the self. It can be first experienced as a work of art: it comes to fruition as an experience of loving contemplation.

The loving ecstasy of God is an inward mystery, but it also becomes externalised through creation. The Spirit flows out to creation as the giver of life and the life He brings is the life of God. John Macquarrie distinguishes between this life of God and the life thus given in terms of absolute Being and communicated being. It is the difference between the Creator and the creature, both closely related but without confusion of being.

There is a New Testament image which expresses this truth. It is the image of the heavenly throne from which proceeds the river of water of life. This is taken up in the outward signs of the sacraments of baptism and holy communion. It is the life of God given and, because the essence of this life is love, it is life given in terms of love. This love animates the faculties of the divine humanity and stimulates each of its members to a corresponding intimacy both with God and each other.

Christ's body and ourselves as His members are totally energised with this love. It pervades our physical body, senses and emotions and reaches to the very apex of the heart where the ego can only live in health on condition that it has an adequate object for ecstatic love. The body of Christ is totally alive in love: it activates the whole creation with its own love. To this every human being must respond. Sexuality and spirituality are equally to be developed to make a full response.

The divine humanity of Christ already shares the divine ecstasy under the conditions of glorified manhood. How this takes place it is impossible to imagine in detail, but there are images which suggest it. The image of bride and bridegroom; the image of vine and branches; the image of temple and city. These must be used with contemplative concentration if they are to yield up their secrets. It is the unity suggested in the Athanasian Creed by the phrase 'not by confusion of substance but by unity of Person'. The two natures, divine and human, are united in a perfect union of love. From the divine Son the manhood receives all that is needed for a perfect reciprocation of the divine love. The energy of the Spirit enables the humanity to make a full response to the divine love. But this love is mediated to each member of the body in proportion to its power to respond. There is a marvellous gradation of love, so that no member is overwhelmed: each is fully satisfied and there is still an infinity of love to be appropriated. The divine ecstasy of love moves out to be shared in ever-increasing measure.

SPIRITUAL MARRIAGE

Poulain describes this state of contemplative prayer as 'the supreme goal of all mystic unions ... the soul's spiritual marriage with God, the transforming union, the consummated union, deification.' (ibid. p. 283). He goes on to say that this state contains three principal elements:

i. A union that is almost permanent, persisting even amidst exterior occupations.
ii. A transformation of the higher faculties as to their manner of operation.
iii. Generally, a permanent intellectual vision of the Blessed Trinity or of some divine attribute.

This in many ways resembles what is referred to by Patanjali as *asamprājnāta samādhi* (imageless contemplation), identification with the object of contemplation. It is a state of highly developed loving intimacy with God which leads to a transformation of the contemplative. The most remarkable aspect of this transformation lies in the development of the feminine, or *anima*, part of the self by which it becomes capable of reciprocal union with the Lord.

Jung calls the anima 'the woman within' and writes of it as follows:

'The anima is a personification of all feminine psychological tendencies in a man's psyche, such as vague feelings and moods, prophetic hunches, receptiveness to the irrational, capacity for personal love, feeling for nature, and — last but not least — his relation to the unconscious. It is no mere chance that in olden times priestesses (like the Greek Sibyl) were used to fathom the divine will and to make connection with the gods.'   .
(Carl G. Jung, *Man and His Symbols*, p. 186)

This description is valuable because it disposes of a great number of misconceptions of the anima in terms of a merely feminine development in the male psyche which is often expressed in homosexual forms. So far from being an ingredient which unbalances the character it is the source of its mature fulfilment. The fully grown man must have a strong anima element in his character. This is especially true of the contemplative who must take care to develop his anima potentialities to the full if he is going to reach the heights of divine intimacy. We find this development in the character of our Lord and the beloved disciple, St John.

In our Lord the anima and his relationship with it is symbolised by His mother. In St John's gospel this relationship is described at certain critical moments, but these are the uncovering of a union which was continuous. At the marriage feast in Cana we are shown a time when the Lord 'revealed his glory and led his disciples to believe in Him'. (Jn 2:11) It was a moment of profound significance, and His mother is shown taking a decisive part. It was she who instructed the servants to obey Him. And afterwards there is the note of intimacy in the record that 'He went down to Capernaum in company with His mother'. (Jn 2:12). The second critical time was at the cross near which His mother stood. Just before He died our Lord said: 'Mother, there is your son. ... Son, there is your mother.' (Jn 19:27) The intimacy between our Lord in both these cases in terms of an anima relationship is partly lost by the unfortunate translation of the Greek word *gunai* by the word 'mother'. This word stands for something much more significant. It is the word used for 'woman' in the Old Testament, and refers to the eternal feminine, to the universal motherhood which Julian of Norwich recognised in God.

In the book of Revelation the place of the anima in our Lord is even more startlingly expressed in terms of a bride prepared for her husband. This is the description: 'I saw the holy city, new Jerusalem, coming down out of heaven from God, made ready like a bride adorned for her husband.' (Rev 21:2) Here we have an even profounder insight. The mother figure, the anima, has herself reached fulfilment, and finds it in the most intimate union with the Lord.

This anima in the Lord has its counterpart in St John's relationship with the Lord and His mother. As we have seen, he was given the same feminine figure in Mary as the Lord when at the foot of the Cross he was told to see her as his own mother. Later he was to see this anima figure in the Church. It was in union with this anima that John reached the understanding of the Lord which he expressed in his gospel and that union with the Lord which he lived out in a deep union of love.

It is in the figure of Mary that Christians find their true anima growth. The mysteries of her life, expressed in what are called the mysteries of Mary, are the way the Church sets before us the stages of this growth. These mysteries are: the Conception – the Annunciation – the Visitation – the Nativity – the Purification – the Temple at Twelve – the Cross – the Assumption – the Coronation.

In these mysteries are revealed the path of growth of the anima in man, from the discovery of the deep centre of the psyche to its full development in capacity for union with God. The spiritual marriage is possible only when this full growth has been reached; therefore much of the spiritual life must be spent in contemplating these mysteries and reproducing them by the power of the Spirit in the depths of the heart.

Jung teaches that the anima figure in the male psyche and the animus, or male, figure in the female psyche take many forms. These may broadly be divided into negative and positive categories. This we find in the New Testament and in our Lord's experience. There was the anima figure of our Lady and the anima figure of the prostitute, Mary Magdalene. There is the figure of the New Jerusalem and the negative figure, Babylon, the whore. So it is in Dante, where the positive anima, Beatrice, leads him to full integration.

It is important to keep in mind that the anima and animus figures are not static. They are capable of growth and transformation. We find that Our Lady grows from the girl of Nazareth to the Queen of Heaven, that Mary Magdalene is renewed and shares in the Lord's resurrection: there is a growth, too, in Beatrice, from the girl of Dante's youth to the guide who leads him to the heavenly vision.

So it is in the growth of the person. It is external in terms of physical life, passing through the stages of earthly development. It is also internal in terms of the anima-animus growth, where the unconscious grows and changes as the events of life play upon it. A great deal of the secret of contemplative growth is a recognition of this inner life, and the right choice of the anima symbol. For the Christian man this is Our Lady, and the regular meditation upon her mysteries in the power of the Spirit is the most effective way to full anima growth. For the Christian woman the animus figure is our Lord and the way to full animus growth is regular meditation on the mysteries of His life. It may well be that one of the greatest distortions of present-day Christian spiritual teaching and discipline is the error of making our Lord the ideal figure for both men and women, when men for their full development require the anima figure of our Lady. That seems to have been the intention of our Lord who left St John not with the image of Himself, but with the companionship of His mother as the symbol of his own development. And how full and balanced was St John's contemplative intimacy compared with the tumultuous and tortured growth of St Paul whose anima lacked this balance. The problems of homosexuality which are often so acute among both sexes in the

Christian Church could be related to the choice of an unsuitable symbol for contemplative development.

In the spiritual marriage the ego unites with the anima, and within that union finds complete contemplative intimacy with the Lord. This is the process shown in the experience of Dante and described in detail by St John of the Cross in the 'Spiritual Canticle'. In women the ego unites with the animus and finds complete contemplative intimacy with the Lord. This is the process described so vividly by St Teresa in the *Interior Castle*. In both cases the experience passes through preliminary intimacy with objects other than the Lord. Dante first achieves intimacy with Beatrice, the projection of the anima: St John of the Cross with St Teresa, the projection of his anima figure. They then move towards intimacy with the Lord. So with St Teresa. She used St John of the Cross as the projection of her animus image and then moved into intimacy with the Lord both in His glorified humanity and then in His divine nature. The 'Spiritual Canticle' shows this growth towards intimacy.

'*The Spiritual Canticle*' was written by St John of the Cross in the Toledo dungeon where he was imprisoned from 1577 to 1578 during the struggles between the Calced and Discalced Carmelites. He finished the commentary in 1584.

This poem is inspired by the Song of Songs. St John uses many of the images of that great poem, and as skilfully blends natural beauty with spiritual meaning. He achieves a marvellous harmony of created images with the working and being of the uncreated Lord. There is nothing dogmatic or religious in the formal sense in the *Spiritual Canticle,* any more than there is in the Song of Songs. It is a spontaneous work of imagination embellishing the symbols of nature.

St John divides the process of the spiritual marriage into three stages: the preliminary mortification when the soul is disturbed and in a state of unsatisfied desire; a period of tranquility and rest which he calls the betrothal; and then the spiritual marriage, when the soul is transformed into the life of the beloved and shares His secrets. All this St John says in his prologue is done 'by means of figures, comparisons and similitudes which allow something of that which they feel to overflow and utter secret mysteries from the abundance of the Spirit rather than explain these things rationally'. (*The Complete Works of St John of The Cross*, p. 24) We must keep this in mind both in studying the poem and in applying it to our own spiritual life. St John regrets the need for a commentary since 'the sayings of love are best left in their fullness, so that everyone may pluck advantage from them according to his manner and to the measure of his spirit.' (ibid, p. 24) And he frees all from being tied to any particular exposition.

The whole of the early part of St John's life was a preliminary mortification for the state he describes in this poem. He records some of his experiences in his earlier writings, his dark nights of sense and spirit. In the prologue to the 'Spiritual Canticle' he writes of them as things for beginners. The mastery of scholastic theology he showed in these earlier writings he now sees as inadequate. He moves from this theology to what he calls mystical theology 'wherein these verities are not only known but also experienced'. Disowned and persecuted by his community, St John writes the 'Spiritual Canticle' from prison, with his life in fragments and with little hope of restoration. Yet for him none of these experiences was a hindrance to his spiritual life, rather they were the way to its fulfilment. They brought to completion that denial of the ego-self which he always saw as the goal of the negative side of his spiritual growth, and opened the way for the positive development of the inner life.

What we see in St John's life and his writings is a model of the preliminary experiences through which all must pass who reach that degree of contemplative intimacy described in the *Spiritual Canticle*. The details of this mortifying experience vary with different people but the outline is always the same: the rejection of the visual and emotional images which represent distortions of the anima, the process which Patanjali calls the suspension of the images in the heart, so that the ego may be free to unite with the true self. This is a long process, a relentless denial of the ego-self which is both physical, emotional and mental. The so-called life of the world and the internal temptations of the spiritual life, the 'dark nights of sense and spirit' all lead to this death and to the brink of resurrection. There is no way to the spiritual marriage which by-passes these experiences. For Dante the images are the Inferno and the early stages of the Purgatorio: for Bunyan the Slough of Despond and the conflict with Apollyon: for Steppenwolf the verge of suicide.

St John gives us a map of this way, but, more important, he shows that it leads not to mere negation of self but to the outskirts of the discovery of the true self. It is a transforming mortification rather than a mortification of destruction, and the St John in the prison of Toledo is not a broken man but a man on the threshold of his greatest mystical experience. Those called find this true. They deny in order to affirm: they lose in order to find.

What St John finds first of all is a period of tranquil growth, during which he is able to separate himself from obstacles to real intimacy and to begin to create true images with which loving intimacy is possible. Those early relationships we have considered: different forms of ecstasy with nature and creatures, and inadequate self symbols no longer satisfy and these must be discarded. This could lead to the state described in the *Cloud of Unknowing*, when nothing seems left but a great emptiness. But the *Spiritual Canticle* begins from that point and leads on to the growth of a true anima figure in the form of the bride.

In many ways the bride figure of the *Spiritual Canticle* resembles that of the Beloved in the Song of Songs. But there is an originality in St John's creation which makes it his own. He has made a figure more in keeping with his needs. His anima figure is more simple. There is less of the royal dignity and more of the pastoral simplicity about his bride. She is at home with nature and shepherds; she does not consort with kings or with the great of Jerusalem. She is absorbed in love for her spouse.

St John of the Cross made an original figure out of clearly recognisable traditional material. Besides the model of the Beloved in the Song of Songs he undoubtedly used the symbol of Our Lady. These are available for ourselves as we create our own anima figure. But, like St John, we must avoid reproducing mere copies of these originals: ours must be the work of the Spirit co-operating with our own imagination.

We have already considered the value of meditation on Our Lady as revealed in the mysteries of her life. There is another way. The most important fact about Mary is not that she is virgin but that she is holy. And later on, as Georgen writes: 'Mary's virginity is most appropriately understood in this context of chastity, faith, holiness and prayer.' (*The Sexual Celibate* p. 130). He emphasises that the essence of virginity is union with God. All this is important when we use Mary as the model from which to create our own anima figure.

The virginity of Mary in whatever way we interpret it is important but so are many other attributes which the Bible and Church present under the titles of holy, Mother of God, Queen of Heaven, Mother of Mercy. There are also the descriptions of her spiritual state and relationship to God in the phrases: fruitful virginity, full of grace, gate of heaven. All these contribute valuable insights to the imagination in its work of making the image of the anima.

But the most valuable insight of all is given by the Magnificat, in which the inner life of Mary is disclosed: her humility, her exaltation, her relationship to the Lord. Here is set out for us the nature of the truly formed anima and the intimacy required to respond to such inner life. Here is the climax of joy and love and union with mankind and the Lord.

This forms an adequate object for contemplative and loving intimacy. Then remains the making of that relationship of marriage to which St John refers in these verses:

'Let us rejoice, Beloved. And let us go to see ourselves in thy
beauty;
To the mountain or the hill where flows the pure water;
Let us enter further into the thicket.'

The anima figure begins in a state of hiddenness and humility: it
develops in glory like the image of the cosmic Christ. It is with the
anima in the state of glory that the final stage of the spiritual marriage
has to do. With this image the ego grows into identifying union. It is a
way symbolised by Christian marriage, where the bride and
bridegroom become one flesh by the interpenetration of life, and at the
same time find a mutual union with the Lord who indwells them as
Love. St John hints at this union in the *Spiritual Canticle:* he
describes in greater detail what it means in the much shorter but more
intense poem called 'The Living Flame of Love'.

The Living Flame of Love
In this poem St John passes beyond the subjects of the 'Spiritual
Canticle' and describes the union of the transformed anima with the
Lord Himself. This union is with the persons of the Blessed Trinity. It
is a perfect interpenetration of the human and divine natures in love.
He is only too aware that words are unable to express this mystery. 'It
is hard', he writes in the prologue, 'to speak of that which passes in the
depths of the spirit if one have not deep spirituality'. And he goes on to
admit that he has delayed trying to express this mystery until the Lord
has opened his knowledge and given him some fervour. Even now he
is reluctant to speak. The 'Canticle' was about transformation in God:
the 'Living Flame' is about enkindled love in God. Of this St John
writes, using a valuable image which must be given in full:

'When a log of wood has been set upon the fire, it is transformed
into fire and united with it; yet, as the fire grows hotter and the
wood remains upon it a longer time, it glows much more and
becomes more completely enkindled until it gives out sparks of fire
and flame.'
          (*The Complete Works of St John of the Cross,* p. 14.)

Since the fire is God who is eternal love, this union with the flame in a
transformed and indestructible nature brings the ego to share an eternal life of love.

The 'Living Flame' is the name St John gives to God. The short
four-stanza poem is about 'the soul or anima in the intimate com-

munication of union in the love of God'. We shall take from it certain principles of the spiritual marriage:

1. God takes the initiative in this relationship. He 'tenderly wounds the soul in its deepest centre'. This is a vital insight. It is God who penetrates the unconscious, the anima. This is not the work of the ego, but of the Holy Spirit, who takes over the control of the ego and Himself opens the centre of the unconscious. Where this centre is, God alone can discover. It is for the anima, like Mary, to stand ready and permissive for this tender and delectable wound.

2. The spiritual marriage is a death which leads to life. St John writes of it thus:

'In slaying, thou hast changed death into life.'

The ego passes through death and so does the anima or unconscious. This was understood by the masters of eastern prayer. Patanjali trains the body and the soul for this experience. The body he trains by anticipating this death through practising certain postures, especially the death posture, the *shavāsana*. The emotions and the mind are trained by the rejection of distractions and the practice of concentration on selected symbols of God. The ego is disciplined through *prānāyāma* to surrender itself to the rhythms of the Spirit. All these exercises anticipate physical death and lead on to resurrection, to the change St John refers to as death changed into life. This mortification leads to the spiritual marriage and it is in this stage of contemplation that the living flame of God takes over and makes perfect what we could not perfect ourselves. Again there is a comparable teaching in eastern prayer. The final stages of contemplation are the result of the overshadowing of the cloud of glory, the *dharma-megha-samādhi*.

3. The spiritual marriage is a death leading to life in the senses. Their darkness and blindness are filled with strange brightness: they become means of union with the Lord. This is the realisation of what Blake foresaw: the doors of perception being cleansed, the world is seen in its infinity. St John, who was so insistent on the dark night of the senses and the understanding, sees the result not as destruction but as renewal and glory. The senses and the understanding now 'give heat and light together to their Beloved'. They have their place in the glorified body, and they are used in loving intimacy with the Lord.

4. In the spiritual marriage it is the Lord who plays the masculine role in the anima. He awakens in the deep centre of the anima and there breathes forth the Spirit, giving blessing and glory. This gift transforms the whole of the human nature to reciprocate the love of God. This creates a continuous intercourse, a state of perfect ecstasy

between the body, anima, ego and God. What is the essence of the divine ecstasy in God becomes the essence of the human-divine ecstasy between God and man. Beyond this words cannot take us.

9
Procreation

Donne concludes his poem on Ecstasy with the reluctant admission that:

'Love's mysteries in souls do grow,
But yet the body is his book.'

And he goes on to insist that the body shares in the ecstasy and that ecstasy itself leads to renewal of the affections and faculties of sense and must finally imprint its experiences on the body. There is a procreative aspect to ecstasy even in God Himself, who causes creation as an overflow of the divine love within His Being.

INFERTILE CONTEMPLATION

Ecstasy is not complete if it remains barren. The belief that this could be so was the error of Quietism in the 17th century, and it is a danger never far from contemplative prayer. We need to be alert to its symptoms and trained to avoid its snares. This heresy had its roots in the sect called the Brethren of the Free Spirit or Beghards. They spread over Italy, France, Germany and Bohemia in the 13th century and were condemned at the General Council of Vienna in 1311. They taught that the perfect souls need not continue to pray or to do good works, and that they were free from all laws. Eckhart was condemned for certain propositions contaminated with this teaching in 1329. Another kind of this error appeared with the Illuminati in Andalusia in about 1575. They exaggerated the place of mental prayer in the spiritual life, teaching that it was the only duty required from those who would do God's will. In the 17th century the heresy appeared in France and was spread by a book by Molinos. This heresy has never been completely suppressed. It is with us today, and some of the teachings derived from erroneous western adaptations of Buddhism, especially the popular western forms of Zen, contain dangerous Quietistic errors. A clear idea of the main teachings of Quietism will help us to see what they are.

Poulain describes Quietism as 'the error of those who guide themselves by the following maxim: All efforts after perfection consist in suppressing as many of our acts as possible, save in the case of a manifest intervention on God's part. The minimum of personal action thus becomes the ideal of sanctity'. (ibid. p. 487) There is another even more dangerous mistake which stems from a misunderstanding of the very life of God. God is not the Nirvana of the Buddhist, the absence of all action. God is pure act, and this act within His life is love, and outside is the continuous and loving creation of all things. Union with God is participation in this life, which is the ecstasy of love in union with the Trinity and the ecstasy of loving work with God towards the whole of creation. The contemplative, like the tree of our Lord's parable, must bring forth fruit. It is the need for fruit in the con-templative life which Quietism denies.

In a valuable article, 'Creativity in the Arts' ('Cambridge Review', Jan. 1975) J. P. Stern draws attention to some of the Quietistic dangers in the popular forms of Transcendental Meditation. His warnings app-ly to all forms of Quietistic prayer and stress the non-procreative error of Quietism which seems its greatest danger.

He sums up the essence of Christian meditation as close 'to the process of artistic creation' and draws attention to the need of the mind both within and outside of prayer for creative action. He quotes Jung as saying that the oft-attempted imitation of Indian practices and sentiments leads to nothing 'except an artificial stultification of our Western intelligence'. Quietism encourages this denial of mental creativity, especially in the imagination and, in so doing, destroys one of the most important fruits of the mind.

Stern stresses that the object of meditation in the Christian tradition is God, and not the ego self. This means that Christian meditation cannot exist in a vague and formless environment. It requires planned mental activity, which increases as the meditative skill grows. This in-volves the creative activity of the feelings, the understanding and the will. Again, the fruit of contemplative prayer is not idle passivity but an even more energetic and creative use of the human faculties.

He concludes by comparing the creativity of Christian meditation to the activity of the poet, who is not passive in the presence of his object but explores it thoroughly which is 'not a restful activity, today, nor even peaceable.' (ibid, pp. 66–72)

We could put these criticisms in another form. The life of the mind is creative. Its function is to procreate images. Quietistic meditation is largely concerned with anaesthetising the mind to a passive state in which no mental activity takes place. This denies the fruit of contemplative prayer, which is a form of procreation.

SOME FRUITS OF CONTEMPLATIVE PRAYER

One of the important characteristics of God, which our Lord emphasises in His teaching, is the generosity of His rewards. Parable after parable describes Him as a master giving talents and responsibilities, expecting that they will be developed profitably and then giving handsome rewards. St Matthew records the typical parable of the man going abroad and sharing out his capital. The servants are given varied amounts and expected to use them profitably. Those who do are rewarded with the formula: 'You have proved trustworthy in a small way; I will now put you in charge of something big. Come and share your master's delight.' (Mt 25:21) The servant who hesitated and hid his gold in the ground is treated ruthlessly: the gold is taken from him and he is rejected as a lazy rascal. The moral is that Christians are given gifts to use and increase. This applies to all gifts and therefore to the gift of contemplative intimacy. But what are its fruits?

We find these fruits in the lives of the great contemplatives, and it is by studying what they created that we find what we are to bring forth in our own lives. St Teresa gives us ample information for studying these fruits in her life and the life of St Teresa is a main source for the discovery of the important fruits of contemplative prayer.

St Teresa was born in 1515 and educated by Augustinian nuns. She entered the Carmelite monastery of the Incarnation at Avila in 1535. Until 1555 she suffered from much illness. Her recovery began when praying before a statue of Christ. This experience helped her to the formation of what would now be described as a satisfactory animus image and from that date her contemplative prayer developed. The image was first of our Lord in His humanity but later it became what she called an intellectual vision of the cosmic Christ in glory. Her prayer experiences are described in her book *The Interior Castle*, a classic exposition of contemplative prayer. With St John of the Cross she was one of the few contemplatives able to give a scientific description of the entire life of prayer from meditation to the state of the spiritual marriage. St Teresa's contemplative life was particularly rich in examples of those fruits which mark the procreative activity of the genuine master of contemplative prayer. She helps us in describing some of them in detail.

Something dynamic happened to St Teresa's physical body as a result of her entry into contemplative prayer in 1555. From that time many of her former weaknesses disappeared and she became capable of enduring considerable hardship: long journeys and the demands of her religious life as a Carmelite. She later manifested some specifically spiritual capacities such as levitation. She also had the experience of locutions. However she was sufficiently mature not to treat these as of great importance in themselves. Like the *siddhis* described by Patanjali she accepted that these were not essential to her prayer and could be a hindrance if treated with undue emphasis. But she accepted, and we must, that these physical and spiritual powers are signs of something more important: they are symptoms of the procreation of a new body, a body which St Paul describes as passing through psychic and spiritual stages and coming to fruition in a state of glory. This is the primary fruit of all true contemplative prayer. Patanjali refers to this new body when he describes it as of 'beauty, grace, strength and adamantine hardness.' (*Yoga Sutras*, 111. 47). In the Christian tradition the mark of this body in art is the halo. It is a mystery which grows inwardly. Our Lord refers to it as a seed growing secretly and He stresses the need for both death and resurrection for its full development. 'In truth, in very truth I tell you, a grain of wheat remains a solitary grain unless it falls into the ground and dies; but if it dies, it bears a rich harvest.' (Jn 12:24) This new body is the authentic fruit of contemplative intimacy with the Lord.

In her early youth St Teresa had an inadequate animus image. Her father was not able to supply the material she needed, nor was she given it through the Augustinian Sisters in their school. A change came when she saw a new statue of Christ on the Cross, and from then onwards she started making images of the manhood of Christ which gradually developed into communicating symbols: these stimulated her emotionally and intensified her contemplative prayer. Eventually these images became what she described as intellectual visions in which the divine manhood radiated glory. She had grown capable of envisaging the cosmic Christ.

This capacity to create such images is another fruit of contemplative prayer. These images are most powerful when they become satisfactory images of the animus in women and the anima in men. We have considered the importance of such images in the growth of a mature self, and they are one of the most important fruits of contemplation. As they form, so the ego learns to relate to them in a fully emotional and loving union. This leads to that stability of will which is the mark of the true contemplative. St Teresa, both Superior and reformer of the Carmelite order, developed this to a high degree.

If Quietism is not a positive and acceptable fruit of contemplation neither is Pelagianism, a doctrine concerned with self-control in both prayer and activity: the notion that man can control his own destiny is still with us, especially in our Church with its emphasis on social activities and its immersion in political affairs. St Teresa was not committed to either of these errors: this does not mean that she was not concerned with the affairs of God's world. In this world she did what our Lord commended in His parable: she 'brought forth fruit with patience'. (Lk 8:15) Teresa renewed her order, made new foundations, manifested the divine presence in her life and described it in her books. These were all fruits of contemplative prayer. Although she made no attempt to solve the practical, political and economical problems of her world, yet she ministered with great significance to some of its essential needs. She manifested God, and she showed the way to Him in whose presence darkness becomes light and defeat victory.

TOWARDS A CHRISTIAN PSYCHOLOGY

Some of the authentic fruits of contemplative prayer can be valuably applied to present day analytical psychology. Leon Bonaventura, a Christian psychotherapist, in a lecture given to the Guild of Pastoral Psychology in January 1976, shows how much Christians, and the clergy especially, can benefit from the discoveries of analytical psychology. He illustrates from the writings of Tauler how long before analytical psychology so many of its principles had already been discovered by the Christian contemplatives. The real value of his lecture lies in his clear exposition of certain fruits of contemplative prayer and their relationship to the psychological hunger and thirst of so many of his patients.

Leon Bonaventura supplements his study of the sermons of Tauler with that of the writings of the great Spanish mystics, thus providing a sample which underlines the contributions of Christian contemplation to the renewing of mankind. His conclusions can be summarised under the headings of the exposition of the human centre, the symbolism of the life of the centre and the mastery of the shadow of this centre.

The great contemplatives are unanimous that God is the Centre in the heart of man. They speak of the heart as 'a living book' in which the truth of God is written: and they insist that the opening of this centre or the penetration to the Holy of Holies is the goal of man. What is required to complete this journey is an accurate 'self-consciousness' and this is what the great masters of contemplative prayer achieve. They do it by developing and mastering all their faculties and bringing them into harmony with Christ, the Lord of the heart. They also insist that there is fulness of life at this centre, the life of God in the person of the Holy Spirit. All these discoveries are made, not by adherence to a written tradition or to a code of laws, but from the direct experience. They speak of things they know and testify to things they have seen. They witness to the fact that the centre is something more than a place to be believed, it is a place to be explored and experienced. All this corresponds to the experience of St Teresa: through penetration to this centre her whole being was renewed.

In communicating a living experience and manifesting a way the contemplatives have created a rich store of symbolic material in the form of images which describe their way and offer a share in their experience. Of these the image of Christ is the supreme symbol and model of the mystery of the structure and life of the centre. He is surrounded by a host of subsidiary images which illuminate and reveal the unfathomable riches of the self and its environment. The contemplatives have penetrated to the centre: they have returned with a gospel which sufficiently describes what they have found, and guides those who have the courage to follow.

Leon Bonaventura sees these Christian symbols as the counterpart of the archetypes in Jungian psychology. But the Christian images have a far richer content of beauty and joy; they attract the explorer with something of the irresistibility of the invitation of Christ Himself.

The contemplative interprets life as it really is, and this includes both the recognition of sin or, in the language of psychology, 'the shadow' at the centre, and the way this obstacle can be overcome.

Sin, the shadow at the centre, is variously described by Tauler and his fellow contemplatives. Tantler sees it as a result of the assertion of the ego. In symbol after symbol, and in all descriptions of their experience the contemplatives describe the shadow. In giving us this accurate picture of the state of man they bring the sickness into the limits of an accurate diagnosis and prepare a prescription for a complete cure.

It is in giving this prescription, drawn from their own recovery experience, that the greatest gift of contemplatives to mankind is made. It is a simple and profound remedy based on the reassurance that throughout the sickness and all through the cure God is present, communicating His own life to restore His image, and transforming a disaster into the supreme victory.

The essence of the prescription is that the shadow at the centre, the man of sin, is not to be repressed, still less destroyed: it is to be integrated into consciousness and renewed to share in the light already shining at the centre. As Tauler has put it: everything helps the good soul, even sin. Or, in St Teresa's more homely reminder, the great blessing we receive from the world is that it tolerates no imperfection in good people. In other words, we are to use the shadow as a testing instrument, a means of strengthening the spiritual life, converting it from an enemy to an ally in our quest. Tauler puts this with startling paradox: 'Every man has his own individual devil with whom he is constantly engaged in battle and whose action can be as useful to him as his angel's.'

In this is expounded the most hopeful teaching of analytical psychology: the end of analysis is not disintegration, but the achievement of what Jung calls individuation, the glorification of our human nature.

Leon Bonaventura's parallel of the discoveries of the mystics with the discoveries of the analytical psychologists is a reassurance to Christians, to the Christian Church in its present rather defensive position and the clergy especially of their real strength and of the need to rally around the great contemplative tradition which is theirs. The socialising of the gospel, the engagement in politics, premature hopes for ecumenism and the present interest in the esoteric practices of both east and west can be modified: a renewal will be found in the old contemplative tradition of the Church and in the more recent discoveries and teaching of analytical psychology.

Jung with his calvinist background frequently used to say that much of his teaching was a restatement of the deep mystical teaching of the Church, and that he hoped that it would be recognised and accepted by the hard-pressed clergy as an acceptable proclamation of the faith. This has not so far happened and perhaps never will. What we can hope will take place is a renewal of contemplative prayer: if this happens, then we may look for the procreative fruits to follow, both in the world and in the Church: the re-discovery of man's true centre, the restructuring of the real self on the model of Christ, and a creative handling of the shadow self under whose control so large a part of mankind at this time sits in darkness. If such a resurrection takes place then, with King Lear, we may say:

'This feather stirs; she lives. if it be so,

It is a chance that does redeem all sorrows
That I have ever felt.' (*King Lear,* act V, sc. iii)

10
Training Exercises in Contemplative Intimacy

The human body is an instrument for total intimacy with the created universe. This intimacy reaches its climax in intimacy with God, who is perfectly immanent in everything He has made. But the body and the created universe are, in their present state, imperfect and embryonic. Perfect intimacy awaits their renewal and growth. This does not mean that until this renewal and growth have been reached no intimacy is possible. Already the degree of intimacy appropriate to the present stage of renewal and growth is available, and it is in response to this that the following training exercises are designed. They are by no means final or unchanging. They can be modified to meet the needs of each individual and the stages of growth.

There are many possible training exercises for intimacy and each has its own special value. From the many offered a limited pattern will have to be chosen by each individual. Such a choice will depend on his traditions, needs and capacities and, when seriously made, should not be lightly altered. It is persevering practice of a limited pattern of exercises that is one of the secrets of progress in all arts, especially the supreme art of contemplation. This was one of the key teachings of Patanjali, who taught that success in contemplation could only be attained by persistent practice (*abhyāsa*) and an indifference to results. (*Yoga Sutras*, 1. 12)

The created universe offers itself in many ways for contemplative intimacy. We have considered this in terms of: the earth, the creatures, the human self, mankind and the kingdom of heaven. It also offers itself in varying degrees of intimacy, from the intimacy derived from the contact of the senses and emotions to the intimacy derived from the mind and the will. We are not capable of detailed training preparation for all of these degrees of intimacy. Even the preliminary degrees of intimacy are the result of the co-operation of God's Spirit with our own. But this is no excuse for slovenliness or imprecision in preparing to make our own response. The training is precise: there is a place for such aids as a metronome in some parts, and a clock should be used to prevent either unduly shortening or prolonging the exercise. The body, like Exupéry's fox, responds gratefully to regular periods of taming. Further, when these exercises are shared, as is very desirable, such devices protect the participants from the idiosyncrasies of a leader.

St Teresa once wrote: 'The soul's desire can only be assuaged by some other soul which understands it.' This is certainly true in using these exercises. The individual needs a leader, not a master who will dominate, but a leader who will guide and encourage. We can see this need demonstrated in a wider sphere – the need for trained leadership and competent demonstrators is always apparent in the Church and in the state, as it is in every small contemplative prayer group. There are signs that this is being increasingly recognised in contemplative prayer groups, and we may hope that the future training of the clergy will be much more concerned with providing the Church with leaders who can not only talk, but perform the spiritual actions they describe.

Each training exercise which follows has two parts: a negative part concerned with eradicating hindrances to contemplative intimacy; and a positive part concerned with developing the faculties for more complete union. The first part involves what are called mortifying acts which may often involve a creative use of suffering. The practice of these is contrary to much thinking today, but it is well-supported in a variety of traditions. Although it has often not avoided masochistic dangers it is still an essential ingredient in the development of man for the highest degrees of intimacy. The second part relates to the growth of the faculties which comes from wise exercise and is often accompanied by another kind of pain, the growing pains of life which always succeed the wisely used pain of mortification.

Jack Dominian has written of the skill needed to hold these contradictory tensions in balance. The following quotation is from a series of Psychological Essays in Christian Living.

'The risk of self-indulgence in food, drink and sex have reverberated from the pulpits and Christian writing in the sincere belief that, if the body is held in check, the soul will flourish. This view could not be further from the truth. The encounter with God is that of a whole person in which the body plays a central role. Its denial in no way ensures a better relationship with God, and, indeed in the area of sexuality, it has in fact actively impoverished Christian life most severely.'

(Jack Dominian, *Cycles of Affirmation,* p. 54)

In accepting this reinterpretation there is danger of criticism from those who see in freedom the threat of licence and from those who translate the positive emphasis of contemporary asceticism as unlimited permissiveness. But this need not deter us from our course. It is not the asceticism which needs change, so much as those who use it. The energy by which we live is from God, and however much distorted it becomes in passing through the channels by which it reaches us we must not attempt to stop its flow. That would be the mistake of trying to stop life itself. We are called to respond to life and grow.

The exercises by which we train to make this response are arranged under the general headings of the earlier chapters of this book. They are exercises for the development of intimacy with:

The Earth: Creatures: The Self: Mankind: The Kingdom.

THE EARTH

The way of establishing intimacy with the earth is outlined in Genesis:

'Be fruitful and increase, fill the earth and subdue it, rule over the fish in the sea, the birds of heaven, and every living thing that moves upon the earth.' (Gen 1:28)

In other words, man becomes contemplatively intimate with the earth and its creator as he works in it and shares its life. The exercises of this section are concerned with the principles of this work, in the form of both manual labour and art.

The principles of training for contemplative intimacy with the earth are: selection, identification and reproduction. Around these three headings we shall construct some outline exercises leading to the heart of the earth and the divine presence.

Selection

The creation is so rich that some kind of selection is necessary if any deep relationship is to be possible. This means first of all the rejection of large areas which are not suitable for the individual's purpose. The artist Constable did this with great effect. His main work was inspired by the nature he found in Dedham vale. The rest of the world for the purpose of his art he rarely used.

In making our own selection, both in terms of nature and work, we need to be sensitive to our own capabilities. These appear in most people at adolescence: it is one of the main discoveries of this period of life. Youth has its visions as well as its losses as the 'chains of the prison house begin to close'.

A master should be chosen. The artist and the workman who achieve contemplative intimacy never make their own road. They follow a path already made. This was true of our common ancestor, Adam, and it is true of all who have followed him. Constable had his masters in Claude, Poussin, Rubens, Van de Velde, Reynolds, without whose help he could not have mastered the technique of painting in oils. But, having followed them as far as they could take him, he then continued to explore on his own.

In India it would be the other way round: the master must find his pupil. Perhaps the truth lies in between: both must search and there must be a finding. When the master is found he must be obeyed until the pupil is able to find his own way. This must be mutually decided, and there must be no immature clinging to a master who has been surpassed, nor any attempt to dominate a pupil who has grown mature.

Identification

The earth is full of God's glory, and it is by penetrating to the heart of the earth or its centre that this glory is found. It involves a concentrated looking at nature, first in her outward and then in her inward forms.

The practice of looking at the outward form of any created object is called in Yoga asceticism *trātaka*. This is an exercise for clearing the physical vision. It consists of looking at a small object for as long as the attention can stand without blinking. On this object all the senses are focused in turn. This leads to an outward and inward steadiness of vision. It is exactly what Constable teaches in his landscapes. Often the point of concentration is marked by the use of a vivid colour. The eye is invited to dwell on this point: when it moves to the rest of the picture, there is a marked steadiness of gaze.

This is the essence of the concentrated look at outer nature, for which the contemplative may be trained by first using the eyes of the painter and then his own. It is part of our response to the teaching of Dante: 'Look well.'

Looking at the inner forms of nature involves making an image of the outer scene. This is by no means a photograph. It has all the characteristics of the icon, that is of imagination working under the control of the Spirit. This is everywhere clear in the landscapes of Constable and the other great artists. The interior image of the contemplative will inevitably assume human shape; what Blake calls the 'human form divine' will control the image. It is this humanisation of the image which makes it possible to carry out the third part of the exercise, identification.

The contemplative identifies his ego with that which corresponds to its qualities in the image he has made of nature. We watch our Lord doing that frequently in the gospels. 'I am the bread of life', 'I am the true vine'. This requires a deep insight and love. When the process of intimacy is complete, the contemplative can identify with the invisible God within the visible image of His creation. This degree of identification takes a long time to achieve: when it happens, nature has become a mountain of transfiguration for the spectator who sees the divine glory through her outer veils.

Reproduction

Total contemplative intimacy is reached when the contemplative succeeds in reproducing what he sees. The great artist does this.

The reproduction of nature takes many forms: the picture, the poem, the song, the dance, the results of manual work. Each has to find his own style and learn to move in harmony with the Spirit. Contemplation without some creative response is as inadequate as love without a completed relationship. Much prayer dries up and languishes in the dark night when its creative expression is avoided. Man is God's fellow-worker, and he achieves the most complete contemplative intimacy when He works with God. St Benedict understood this, and made his monastery a workshop. The sickness of our present religious houses will be healed when we return to our earlier model and once more take up our tools and make what we have been privileged to see.

THE CREATURES

Training in contemplative intimacy with creatures can best be shown in the form of an example from family biography. At the Anchorhold we gradually came to realise that animals have a vital part to play in training human beings for contemplative intimacy. We found this involved three things: choosing the animal, studying its ways and sharing its life in terms of the instincts and senses. An attempt will be made to describe in outline our experience in the hope that it may be an incentive for others to make their own explorations.

Selection

We gradually formed our animal farm. First came the bees from the Mother House. These were followed by ten hens and a cockerel and recently two goats completed the family. Our choice was not based on sentiment. We had no intention of keeping domestic pets. We chose on the basis that we needed the help of animals in our life, and we chose them because they could make a positive and profitable contribution. This they have always done and continue to do.

Animals selected on these principles start with the right relationship to humans, and make a contribution to contemplative intimacy in their own right and in their own ways.

Study

Studying the ways of animals demands sound knowledge, meditation and the making of accurate images.

There is no alternative to the sound knowledge which can be obtained both from books and from people. We have found the books in the books in the local library and the people in our Sussex countryside, where there are generous bee-keepers and a properly organised system of goat supervision. What they give in terms of a life experience must be assimilated by the slow process of observation and meditation. The psalmist understood this when he described his meditation as a process of 'telling of all Thy marvellous works'. (Ps 9:1) This involved him in making images of the creatures.

Two kinds of images are needed: the outer and the inner.

The outer image is made by long and intense concentration on the creature. This is not merely a concentration on its outside form. It includes its movement and emotional feelings, a sharing of its inner life. It takes long and persevering practice to make such an image; when it is made there is a need to change it frequently to match the changes in the creature.

The inner image is made by the addition of the faculty of imagination to the outer senses. As a result, the creature takes its place in a dimension of creation which includes other parts of nature, and especially man. It leads to the establishment of relationships, and as they form, the creature becomes a lens for revealing both the significance of man and God. Making this image requires the skill of the artist. It is to be seen in the drawings of Edward Wilson at the South Pole. His depicted creatures are always in an interpretative environment which enhances them and the artist. The animal image in this background is able to communicate the full range of its life: it becomes an effective instrument for contemplative intimacy with itself and God.

Intimacy

Creatures are a complex of physical, instinctive and emotional life. They offer themselves without concealment. To get the most out of this openness it is necessary to establish a close relationship with the creature at all levels.

Creatures demand the most intimate contact of all the senses. They give freely of their instincts and senses by avoiding concealment, and the same response is required from their human companions. Verbal communication is of little value: the use of touch, hearing and smell is always effective. Our training leads us to know how to use these senses with the greatest effect. As with the senses, so with the instincts. Creatures respond best to those in whom the instincts are developed and free. Being free themselves, they have much to teach on these matters, but only to those who are humble enough to watch and listen and learn.

The basic emotions are strongly developed in most creatures, as are their methods of expression. In human beings the emotions are often repressed and even when they are expressed, many emotions are fearfully manifested. Here again we must go to school with the creatures. Sorrow and joy, love and anger, find immediate expression in the movement and sound of the creature. We have to put this into the inner image we make of them, and in doing this we shall learn the way to put it into ourselves. Ultimately, we reach the deepest intimacy with the creature along the road of feeling. The skilled rider achieves a relationship of mutual exchange with the creature: the horse uses the rider's mental skill and gives in return his strength, his instincts and emotions. This is the full extent to which the human-creature relationship can lead in terms of intimacy.

THE SELF

In the report of the Doctrine Commission of the Church of England entitled *Christian Believing* there is a valuable chapter on the Christian and the creeds in which the commission emphasises the need for treating the 'Christian life as an adventure into truth'. (p. 40) This, however, does not preclude a firm grasp on the Christian outlines of faith expressed in the creeds. Further, the report disapproves of the attempt to reach easy agreement by opting 'for a radical and simplistic solution by which a decision is taken to rule out one or more of possible competing attitudes' (p. 38) In short, the tension which comes from strongly held convictions must be endured. This is the course we have taken in formulating the following principles about the true self and the adventure of our own exploration into its meaning and expression.

Fundamental principles

1. The origin of the true self is in God. It is manifested in Christ and His kingdom and reproduced in each believer by the work of the Spirit acting upon the materials through which Christ is made known. As the Doctrine Commission insists, this revelation of the self is progressive. (p. 24) It is equally true that its reception by the individual believer is also progressive.

2. The reception of the manifested self is gradual and takes the form of created interior images: the raw materials are of credal symbols energised by the Spirit. The creation of these images is achieved through contemplative prayer and through the growing practice of contemplative intimacy. Just as there is a pluriformity of faith (*Christian Believing*, p. 28) so there must be a pluriformity of images both in the life of each individual and among the different members of the household of faith.

3. In making these images of the true self the following principles must be observed:

i. The Incarnate Christ is an androgynous mystery. In Him there is male and female, brought to a transcendent unity in Himself. (*see* Gal 3:29) And His kingdom includes the whole of creation made new.

ii. The true self is fully alive with the life of the Spirit. This means that every human faculty of instinct, emotion and insight must be allowed its growth to the measure of the stature of the fullness of Christ. Even in the Bible the complete self is not fully described. 'The New Testament itself handed on to the Church a volume of unfinished business.' (ibid p. 30) Part of the exploration into truth is the making of an individual contribution to the completion of that business by the gift of our own discoveries.

Some of the exercises leading to such discoveries must now be considered. They are grouped under the headings of: working with the Spirit, choosing materials and creating images.

The Spirit both mortifies and animates. He mortifies the physical body and develops and energises the psychic and spiritual bodies. This is a process of continuous and glad interchange as the physical body is offered to be transformed into the body of glory. The supreme model of the Spirit's working is the image of Our Lord and Our Lady as presented in the New Testament and the tradition of the Church.

The following exercises of co-operation with the Spirit should last about thirty minutes and be regularly repeated.

i. Choose a suitable, alert posture. There are many to choose from in the yoga āsanas. Once a posture has been found it should be perseveringly used. Sometimes the still posture may be preceded by a period of meditative walking.

ii. Concentrate all the faculties on a symbol. This may be a sound, a colour, a shape, or one of the mysteries of Our Lady.

iii. Break the natural breathing rhythm by centring the breath in the pelvic region lifting the pelvis like a chalice to hold the Spirit energy. Draw in the Spirit through all parts of the body and concentrate it in the pelvic region.

iv. Direct the Spirit energy towards the inner symbol, and surrender to the rhythm of the Spirit which will animate the image. Allow the image to become fully alive with all the virtues and gifts of the Spirit. Build up a full emotional interchange. A perfect example of this is to be found in St Luke's description of the Lord's prayer in Gethsemane. It is centred on the chalice, and with this image He engages in the deepest dialogue and emotional exchange. He is in anguish of spirit, He prays urgently, He communicates with the angel and 'His sweat was like clots of blood falling to the ground'. (Lk 22:42–44). Something of this kind of contemplative intimacy is required from those who would work with the recreative work of the Spirit.

The materials for this work are infinite, nothing less than the whole creation. But they may be roughly divided into two parts, the outward and the inward.

The outward material includes all nature and her creatures, and the state of life in which we find ourselves. Those parts of the natural creation which touch us closely are meeting places with God and the self, and must be contemplated deeply to reveal the secret of His presence.

The inward material is made up of the sense impressions of the outer world from which the imagination makes its images. The traditional image of this process in many traditions is that of a garden, the garden of the soul. In the West many of these sense impressions are drawn from the Bible, the creeds, and the liturgical presentation of our Lord and Our Lady in the mysteries of the Church. Each contemplative selects and arranges this material, and out of it makes the environment of the self, the hidden and watered garden where the Lord is revealed.

The image when the material has been suitably arranged, then the imagination can create under the control of the Spirit an image of the true self in terms of the cosmic Christ and His kingdom. What follows is an attempt to share a life-time's experience of this supreme act of creation.

i. Selection of a single symbol and theme for each contemplation.

ii. External concentration on the symbol followed by the creation of the inward image.

iii. Animation of the image by breathing over it the Holy Spirit.

iv. Discursive relationship with the image by means of repeated meditative phrases. The object is to establish a state of colloquy between the ego and this image of the true self. This involves the establishment of a full emotional relationship. The use of colour, sound, movement and the application of the senses towards the image will deepen this intimacy. It is important to use every kind of intimacy. The 'Song of Songs' and the 'Spiritual Canticle' speak freely of this, and should be taken literally in achieving the greatest possible intimacy with the true self. There can be no detailed rules about this. *Fac quod vis*, provided that love of the true object is the purpose. This is the real adventure of the contemplative, his true exploration.

MANKIND

Before considering intimacy with mankind, it is important to emphasise the total extent of this relationship. It is with all mankind, with what Hesse calls the immortals as well as with our neighbours. It goes beyond that: it includes the angels and archangels and all the company of heaven. God is the centre of a vast concourse of beings and, as He indwells them all and shares with them His glory, so we are involved in sharing that total union.

In another way intimacy with mankind is inclusive. Unlike our intimacy with nature and creatures, where the intimacy concerns some of our faculties, intimacy with mankind involves every human faculty, developed and used to the uttermost. It is an affair of body, mind and spirit. Any attempt to leave out one of these faculties leads to a maimed relationship, a defect in love. This is the root cause of our present social sicknesses. The training exercises for this total intimacy will therefore be arranged under the headings of physical, mental and spiritual relationships.

Before describing these exercises one important point needs to be made. Intimacy with mankind cannot be forced. The most that any pattern of intimacy can supply is a way of removing some of the obstacles to intimacy. That is what law does for the community. It restrains those who would destroy peace, but peace is no more than a preliminary condition for positive development. It is a beginning. So with the exercises: they prepare us for intimacy. True intimacy must always be free and spontaneous. It is the work of the Spirit who blows where He lists. There must be no prohibitions or commands where love is intended.

Physical intimacy

The controlling principle of this intimacy is the sacredness of the human body as a temple of the Spirit. Unless this is recognised, mere training of the body would be dangerous and undesirable. If this is accepted, a true relationship with others will eventually be discovered, whatever mistakes are made.

This relationship starts with some form of nudity and moves through a true use of the body in natural, instinctive and rhythmic intimacy. This cannot be described in detail: the most that will be attempted is to describe some of the principles.

Nudity

The chief instrument used at the Anchorhold for this intimacy is the art model figure which gives a bare structure of the human body in androgynous form. This teaches us the correct way to make an image of the psychic and spiritual body for meditation and to make a full relationship with others and God in them. We supplement this model with the *kouroi*, and *kourai* figures of Greek art.

Other practices of nudity arise from this main principle. We are not concerned with exhibiting the naked human form, which has so often been distorted by wrong usage, but in revealing the basic structures of the psychic body through its centres of consciousness and movement.

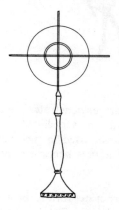

Monstrance for Benediction

A subsidiary instrument of nudity is a monstrance figure, which is reproduced here. This locates the centres of consciousness and emphasises the presence of the Lord within the body. It is essentially a symbol to be used by those who have advanced beyond the preliminaries of contemplative intimacy.

The pushing-hands exercise

This is a Chinese exercise from the T'ai Chi Ch'uan, made up of four basic movements through which two people make the most intimate contact with each other. The basic movements which can only be learnt from a living teacher are:

Press: Roll-Back: Ward-off: Push.

PRESS

ROLL BACK

WARD OFF

PUSH

In this exercise each partner penetrates the centre and energy of the other and shares the divine presence.

Many other games can be used in this way. Once the element of competition is destroyed games become ways to intimacy.

The Dance

The dance, in its corporate forms, is a most effective way of developing intimacy with others. There is a rich store within our own traditions. We use the Skelton sword dance and selections from the

Morris dances. This part of our exploration is still in its preliminary stages, but already it is clear that when the dance is used for intimacy with others and God it becomes more than a meaningless exercise.

Sexuality

Much has already been written about this mode of intimacy: it has been tragically misunderstood and seriously misused throughout the recorded history of mankind. It is an area of intimacy requiring courageous exploration: one of the main opportunities of Christians, and especially of religious, is to make this exploration and to share their discoveries. There is no rigid code of rules. The exploration must be made with reverent and responsible freedom and with God, not self, as the goal.

Sexuality in some form or other is the focal point of all human intimacy. We repress or refuse to use it at our peril. All that can be done here is to assist others in their exploration, and to share certain convictions which have been reached in our own search. These take the form of certain basic principles and an attempt to share the profound teaching of the Indian tradition enshrined in the myth of *kundalini*.

The basic principles are these:

1. Sexual intimacy takes many forms, and must be allowed the widest freedom for exploration. It is certainly not exhausted in the act of procreation. God Himself has already inbuilt important safeguards into our sexuality. We learn as we explore.

2. Sexual intimacy should be attempted only between mature adults who have already mastered the preliminary stages of intimacy.

3. Sexual intimacy is more than a physical relationship, though it is certainly that. It includes all the centres of consciousness, of which the genital area is one. An act of complete sexual intimacy leads to intercourse at all the levels of consciousness and reaches its climax in God. Only when it reaches Him is it fulfilled.

4. Orgasm is a stage in intimacy, but neither the end nor the climax. The orgasm is a brief state of intense physical, mental and emotional concentration: if sexual intimacy ends there it may well lead to frustration and violence.

5. Full sexual intimacy takes place in a state of life appropriate to those who share it. At present there are two recognised states: marriage and celibacy. Both are always in debate as to their structure, and this should be so. Other states may well emerge, and they should be welcomed. If they are unsuitable, this will soon be discovered. The principle is always *solvitur in ambulando*.

The following is an attempt to summarise the basic teaching of the Indian *kundalini* myth. This myth has been shamelessly exploited and misunderstood, but that is no reason for not trying to penetrate to the truth it conveys, and this can best be done by using a sound authority as our guide. For this purpose we have chosen Ernest Wood and his classic exposition of Yoga. (*Yoga*)

The literal meaning of *kundalini* is a coiled snake. It is connected with the word *kunda,* a basin, bowl or pool. Wood defines it as 'a coiled-up potential energy, or curved latency'. (p. 144) He compares it with the Christian idea of the Holy Spirit as 'a spiritual element in the material'. St John's gospel also uses this kind of imagery. The water of Spirit is described as 'an inner spring always welling up for eternal life'. (Jn 4:14) And the man filled with the Spirit is told that: 'Streams of living water shall flow out from within him.' (Jn 7:38) We may perhaps translate the idea of the *kundalini* in terms of the receptive ego under the control of the Spirit.

In the Indian myth the *kundalini* is in a state of latency until aroused. This arousal takes place when spiritual energy from outside is infused. This energy is drawn in by a complicated pelvic method of breathing, which can be dangerously misunderstood and should not be attempted without the direction of an experienced guide. When the *kundalini* is thus roused, it begins a long journey through different stages of consciousness, culminating in loving union with God.

The stages of consciousness through which the energised *kundalini* passes are symbolised by certain centres or *chakras* of energy located in the psychic body and situated at sensitive points on the spine. There are seven such centres, corresponding to different degrees of consciousness:

The *mūlādhāra* centre at the base of the spine. This controls movement.
The *svādishthāna* centre in the genital region, relating to sexuality.
The *manipūra* centre at the navel, controlling the emotions.
The *anāhata* centre at the heart, connected with the imagination.
The *vishuddha* centre of discursive thought.
The *ājnā* centre at the forehead which leads to insight.
The *sahasrāra* centre at the top of the head, which is the meeting place between God and the renewed ego.

It is not difficult to compare this journey towards full consciousness to the Christian way of purgation, illumination and union. Each stage is energised by the same energy as the sexual act, but here the energy is mastered and drawn upwards to develop the ego for complete contemplative intimacy in God. This is the meaning hidden beneath the unusual imagery of the ascent of *kundalini,* and it contains most valuable hints for our own journey.

As with all vital myths, this one has attracted a variety of forms and interpretations and we must be judicious in whatever borrowings we make from it. One of the best safeguards is to compare the teaching contained in this myth with that of other traditions. We have already done this with regard to Christianity. We may briefly do it with the Chinese exposition in the 'T'ai Chi Ch'uan'.

The essence of the 'T'ai Chi Ch'uan' is what is described as the sinking of the mind in the *chi* in the lower part of the abdomen, called the *Tan-tien*. Here life energy is concentrated, then moved in a series of carefully designed movements to various parts of the body. These movements are co-ordinated with the eyes and breathing, which leads to intensified consciousness in various parts of the body, culminating in a state of loving intimacy with the *Tao*. All this is much better expressed in movement rather than words but it is clear that the principles are very closely related to the Indian *kundalini* myth. This comes out most clearly in the Chinese symbol of the Yang-Yin with its integration of the two fishes representing the perfect co-ordination of the male and female elements in the body in God. It is not difficult to recognise in the fishes the snake figure of the *kundalini*.

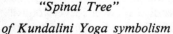

"Spinal Tree"
of Kundalini Yoga symbolism   *Yang-Yin symbol*

Much remains to be done both through careful study and wise experiment to penetrate the hidden depths of intimacy and sexuality contained in the myth of *kundalini* and the 'T'ai Chi Ch'uan'. This may lead to more helpful discoveries than the study of psychiatric case histories or the repetition of past moral principles.

The kingdom of heaven
Intimacy with the Kingdom of heaven is intimacy with the inner life of the triune God and a sharing in His being. This sharing is a part of our being, but the intimacy may be developed by certain exercises, which are the traditional treasure of many of the religious forms of mankind. The recent report *Christian Believing* stresses the variety of writers and teaching in the Bible, but it also insists that the men of the Old and New Testaments shared certain traditions of prayer and worship and above all the 'things concerning Jesus' to guide them to the truth. They put it in this way:

'To help them the men of the Old Testament had certain sacred traditions, their observation of life, and their experience of God Himself through prayer and worship. The men of the New Testament had all these, but also and supremely "the things concerning Jesus." Out of these elements, in the fire of exultation or suffering, their words were forged.' (ibid p. 28)

It is in using these instruments perseveringly and regularly that we are able to make for our use a series of training exercises to prepare us to share in the life of the kingdom. It is sufficient to mention them, leaving each individual and group to find their own particular way:
Liturgical prayer, the sacraments, contemplative prayer, Bible study, the study of church history, music and choral singing, art and manual work.
Perseverance is the key.
Two monks, Aelred and Ivo, sat apart in the glorious surroundings of Rievaulx some eight hundred years ago to ponder the same question which has been the theme of this book. They called their goal 'Spiritual Friendship' (spiritualis amicitia) and began their exploration with this courteous introduction: 'Here we are, you and I, and I hope a third, Christ, is in our midst. There is no one to break in upon our friendly chat (amica colloquia), no man's prattle or noise of any kind will creep into this pleasant solitude. Come now, beloved (carissime), open your heart, and pour into these friendly ears whatsoever you will, and let us accept gratefully the boon of this place, time and leisure.'

(Aelred of Rievaulx, *On Spiritual Friendship*, Cistercian Publications, 1974).

In 1974 coach-loads of religious, the successors of Aelred and Ivo, were in the same place. It was now a heap of ruins and the solitude was broken by what Aelred so much deplored and described as 'man's prattle and noise'. An eager speaker was trying to give a summary of the Cistercian life in the days of Aelred, the staff of a catering firm were busy laying out an elaborate tea, non-religious spectators gazed at this unusual sight. But basically this group was seeking under much the same conditions as Aelred and Ivo the same goal, intimacy with the Lord Christ and with each other. At home in their own communities they too were oppressed and frustrated by what Walter called 'those agents of Pharaoh' to whom Aelred insisted kindness must be shown. Like Aelred they were living in an environment of vocal, meditative and contemplative prayer. They used the same sacraments, read the same Bible, were familiar with the plainsong tradition, practised the arts, a little movement and manual work. But much of their religion had gone dead and they were being encouraged to explore other ways for the renewal of their life. These brave people are still sharing the search of Aelred and have yet to find their answer.

Two years later in the ecumenical centre, at the Château de Bossey in Switzerland, another smaller group of people were meeting to discuss the theme 'Spirituality and Ecumenism'. They were drawn from all over the world: Afro-Asians with their concern for liberation and combat; Chinese who had lost their way in western culture; Americans and Australians; members of almost every branch of the Christian tradition. In this environment the prattle and noise were even greater and the sense of quest even more intense. The crowd from which Aelred withdrew was daily reproduced in the lectures and group discussions. What he wrote in his day was even more true during that demanding fortnight.'All around were talking noisily, one questioning, another arguing – one advancing some point on Sacred Scripture, another information on vices, yet another on virtue'. (*Spiritual Friendship,* p. 51). Like the religious they were seeking intimacy with the Lord and each other under the daunting title of ecumenism, but this ecumenism was in fact no more than Aelred's friendship under another name.

Aelred never found that pleasant solitude and leisure so necessary for growth in spiritual friendship. Before becoming a monk he was at the court of the King of Scots where he acted as High Steward. In 1134 he entered the monastery of Rievaulx. At the age of thirty-two he represented his monastery in Rome on complicated legal business. On his return he became master of the novices. In 1143 he founded the

new abbey of Revesby, returning in 1147 to be abbot of Rievaulx. The
rest of his life until his death on 12 January 1167 was immersed in
monastic affairs and for the last ten years he was dogged by illness.
He never succeeded in escaping the Pharaohs of business. But this did
not frustrate his search for spiritual friendship. Encouraged by the
great St Bernard and by such stalwart companions as Ivo and Walter
he went on, leaving behind the example of his courage and the record
of his discoveries.

Religious, like those who met in the ruins of Aelred's monastery and
ecumenists, like those who discussed recently at the Château de
Bossey and indeed all Christians whose hearts God has touched have
much to learn from Aelred, especially in terms of failure and
perseverance.

The failure we have to accept is our inability to escape from
Pharaoh's agents and find the solitude and leisure needed for our
search. We have to live in the world and share its business. But
Aelred's example reassures us that this need not hinder our growth in
intimacy. Adversity, Shakespeare taught us, can develop friendship
(*As You Like It,* Act II, sc. i), and Aelred shows that these hindrances
need not divert us from our path.

The one thing needed is to persevere. This perseverance was practised by Aelred with a few like-minded companions. It is with similarly
small numbers that we are called to persevere. We can expect always
to be given the two or three companions who ensure the presence of
the third, Christ. It is with these that we perseveringly work, and in
their fellowship may hope to discover an intimacy we too can share
with the world.

Appendix

THE ATHANASIAN CREED

The so-called Athanasian Creed or *'Quicunque Vult'* starts with the advantage of anonymity. It was certainly not the work of St Athanasius, though it expresses his teaching about the incarnation. It originated in Gaul sometime during the 5th century and was written in Latin. Dr Lampe points out that it was neither a baptismal nor a conciliar creed and can be compared to the Te Deum as a theological canticle. In its Trinitarian teaching it was the expression of Augustinian theology. (*see Christian Believing*. p. 61) It was as an act of praise that this creed made its way in the Church and is now used liturgically in the eastern and western Churches, including the Lutheran Church.

There are two parts to this canticle: an exposition of the doctrine of the Trinity and an exposition of the doctrine of the incarnation. Although probably composed before the Council of Chalcedon (451), it expresses in lyrical form the conclusions of that Council and the accepted doctrine of the Church. It is unfortunate that the anathemas usually attached to this kind of document have been included in its form for public use. It is these which have caused the controversy about its recitation in public worship, but there seems no reason why such anathemas should not be omitted when it is used in this way. It is our contention that this canticle compares in its succint form to the *Yoga Sutras* and that it may well be used by Christians as a guide to contemplative prayer. It then becomes a great expression of the divine and human ecstasy, for it has an exquisite poetic and theological form. But it requires that elaboration of interpretation and translation which can best be met by means of a paraphrase. It also requires a method of interpretation which Dante applied to the psalm verse: 'When Israel came out of Egypt, the house of Jacob from a strange people; Judah was his sanctuary and Israel his dominion.' He writes as follows:

'If we express the literal sense alone, the thing signified is the going out of the children of Israel from Egypt in the time of Moses; if the allegorical, our redemption through Christ; if the moral, the conversion of the soul from the grief and misery of sin to a state of grace; if the anagogical, the passage of the sanctified soul from the bondage of the corruption of this world to the liberty of everlasting glory.'
(*see* Charles Williams, *The Figure of Beatrice*, pp. 56–57)

The richness and contemplative value of Dante's poetry depends on the use of these interpretative principles. He used them in his meditation on scripture, and, in doing so, was in harmony with the scholastic tradition he knew from his study of St Thomas Aquinas. He transferred them into his poetry. A similar variety of interpretation may be applied to the Athanasian Creed. It speaks in many ways: of God and His life, of Christ and of man hidden with Him in God.

This creed is nearer poetry and worship than it is to doctrinal definition and theological controversy; therefore by using it in this interpretive way we are being true to its essential purpose. It is a guide to the deepest contemplative intimacy with God.

The literal material of the Athanasian creed is a series of symbols. They are the great symbols of God under the concept of being shared by three centres of consciousness, the Father, the Son and the Spirit. The relationship between God and man is given under the symbol of Christ, who is the renewed manhood raised to union with the divinity through the mysteries of incarnation, crucifixion, resurrection and ascension. These symbols are based on real being and real events: their literal meaning is always under observation and is capable of change to meet new discoveries in science, language and spiritual experience. The exploration in these areas is unending. The need to be flexible is well put in *Christian Believing* in this way:

'Christian life is an adventure into truth, it is the calling of all Christians to deepen their personal faith and understanding to the utmost by being sensitive and receptive both to the lessons of contemporary knowledge and experience and to the wisdom of the tradition.' (Ibid p. 40.)

On the other hand as symbols they can be most effective.
Contemplative prayer uses meanings beyond the literal although

based upon it. The allegorical meaning of the Athanasian Creed opens up the mystery of Christ as He now is, the Cosmic Christ, and shows us the present significances of the Church. Only a growing contemplation of the symbols can open the mind to the full depths of this meaning. It is not one to be reached by discursive reasoning. It requires the use of insight and faith working by love.

The structure of the Athanasian Creed encourages us to use contemplative methods to penetrate its meaning. Like the *koān* of Zen meditation, and the contradictions which Blake saw as essential to the experience of truth, the articles of this creed lead the mind both to doubt, perplexity and faith. It is in a patient waiting for insight under these demanding conditions and in the art of holding both light and darkness in balance that the contemplative reaches union with the truth. This in the view of the Doctrine Commission is the way of Holy Scripture.

'How then could the Bible be anything but a collection of many different insights, most of them passionately propounded, many of them inevitably in tension with one another? That is how, in the Bible, truth is communicated.' (ibid p. 29)

It is certainly the way of the Athanasian Creed and, just as we need the Holy Spirit to interpret and reconcile the contradictions of the Bible, so we need His help in making contemplative use of this Creed.

The paraphrase which follows is a contribution to the making of a form of the Creed which may be used in this way. It is close to the literal meaning of the Latin text but we shall not hesitate to use contemporary language and by means of main and sub-headings encourage the use of the Creed in manageable sections. This is the best way to savour its deepest meanings.

THE FAITH OF ST ATHANASIUS

Preface 1–2
1. Whoever desires to be whole
   Has this work before everything else:
   He must hold fast the Catholic Faith.

2. Whoever fails to preserve this faith,
   Whole and uncorrupted,
   Will undoubtedly be lost.

The Triune God

Three Persons in One God 3–6

3. This is the Catholic Faith:
   We reverence with deepest awe
   One God in Trinity
   And Trinity in Unity.

4. We do not mix together
   The Persons;
   Nor do we divide
   The Divine Being.

5. For the Person of the Father is of one kind:
   The Person of the Son is of another:
   The Person of the Holy Spirit is of another.

6. But the one Divine Nature is equally shared,
   In its glory and majesty,
   By the Father, the Son and the Holy Spirit.

Interpenetration of the three Persons 7–14
(*perichōresis, circumincessio*)

7. Whatever the Father is
   Such is the Son and
   Such is the Holy Spirit.
8. The Father is uncreated,
   The Son is uncreated and
   The Holy Spirit is uncreated.
9. The Father is infinite,
   The Son is infinite and
   The Holy Spirit is infinite.

10. The Father is eternal,
    The Son is eternal and
    The Holy Spirit is eternal.

11. And yet there are not three eternals
    But one eternal.

12. In the same way
    There are not three uncreated,
    Nor three infinites,
    But one uncreated and one infinite.

13. Similarly,

The Father is almighty,
The Son is almighty and
The Holy Spirit is almighty.

14. Nevertheless,
There are not three almighties
But one almighty.

One God: three Persons 15–19
15. So,
God is Father,
God is Son and
God is Holy Spirit.

16. Nevertheless,
Not three Gods
But one God.

17. So,
The Lord is Father,
The Lord is Son and
The Lord is Holy Spirit.

18. Nevertheless,
Not three Lords,
But one Lord.

19. Because just as we are obliged
By Christian truth
To recognise each Person separately
As both God and Lord,
So we are forbidden
By the Catholic Religion
To speak of three Gods or three Lords.

The Relationship of the Persons 20–25
(Monarchia of the Father)

20. The Father is without origin:
He is not made,
He is not created,
He is not generated.

21. The Son is from the Father alone:
He is not made,
He is not created,
He is generated.

22. The Holy Spirit is from the Father and the Son:
    He is not made,
    He is not created,
    He is not generated,
    He comes forth.

23. Therefore,
    There is one Father, not three Fathers;
    One Son, not three Sons;
    One Holy Spirit, not three Holy Spirits.

24. And in this Trinity there is
    Neither before nor after,
    Neither greater nor less.
    But all three Persons are
    Co-eternal with each other and co-equal.

25. So through all things,
    As has been already stated,
    Both the Unity in Trinity and
    The Trinity in Unity
    Must be reverenced
    With deepest awe.

Conclusion 26
26. Whoever desires to be whole
    Must in this way
    Experience the Trinity.

The Incarnation

Preface 27
27. To achieve eternal wholeness it is vital
    That one should also believe faithfully
    The Incarnation of our Lord Jesus Christ.

God and Man 28–31
28. The right faith is:
    That we believe and proclaim
    Our Lord Jesus Christ, the Son of God,
    Is equally both God and Man.

29. He is God, from the Being of the Father,
    Generated before the ages:
    He is Man from the being of the Mother,

Born in this age.

30. He is perfect God,
He is perfect Man,
He is composed of
A rational anima and human flesh.

31. He is equal to the Father
In terms of Divinity;
He is less than the Father
In terms of Humanity.

Two Natures: One Person 32–35
32. Although He is
God and Man,
He is nevertheless not two
But a single Christ.

33. He is one, however,
Not by transformation of Divinity into flesh
But by assumption of Humanity into God.

34. He is completely one,
Not by a mixture of Being
But by unity of Person.

35. For just as
Rational anima and flesh are
A single Man,
So God and Man are
A single Christ.

The Road to Glory 36–41
36. He suffered
For our healing.

37. He descended to the lower regions.
On the third day
He rose again from the dead.

38. He ascended to the heavens.
He sits at the right hand of the Father.

39. From thence He will come
To judge the living and the dead.

40. At His coming

All men will rise
With their bodies
And will give an account of their deeds.

41. Those who have done good
    Will go into life eternal:
    Those who have deliberately done evil
    Will go into eternal fire.

Conclusion 42
42. This is the Catholic Faith.
    Unless a man believes it
    Faithfully and resolutely,
    He will not attain wholeness.

Glossary

There are certain words in this canticle which have many meanings and in the paraphrase we have been content to use the traditional translations in order to avoid unnecessary criticism. In this glossary an attempt has been made to probe the meanings more deeply and to supply a selection of synonyms which the reader may select to meet his own needs.

Person

Greek *hypostasis* = that which settles at the bottom, sediment, ground-work, subject matter, reality, substance, nature, In the 4th century, largely through the work of the Cappadocian Fathers it was identified with the word person, individual reality. St Thomas uses the definition of Boethius for person as 'rationalis naturae individua substantia' an individual being of a rational nature. (*Summa 1. Q. XXIX*)

Latin *persona* = a mask which covered the head and was used in drama and dancing.

Sanskrit *purusha* = consciousness. Defined by Aurobindo as 'an essential being supporting the play of *prakriti*'. It is manifested in mental, physical and psychic forms.

English synonyms = ego-self, personality, ground of being, consciousness.

Substance

Greek *ousia* = property, substance, is-ness, being, state, condition.

Latin *substantia* = that of which a thing consists, the being, essence material

Sanskrit *chitta* = the stuff of consciousness, mind stuff.

English synonyms: the most suitable is being. Other words are ex-

istence, state. In applying this word to God it is necessary to add
the adjectives holy and loving.

Divinity
Greek *theiotes* = divine nature, divinity.
Latin *divinitas* = Godhead, divinity.
Sanskrit *saccidānanda* = being, understanding, joy. This is the Hindu
  equivalent of the Christian doctrine of the Trinity, Father, Son and
  Holy Spirit. It is symbolised in the sculpture known as the *Trimurti,*
  the union of Brahma, Vishnu and Shiva.
English synonyms: divinity, Godhead.

Man
Greek *anthrōpos* = man, man in general, mankind, a generic term for
  the human race.
Latin *homo* = human being, man, human race, mankind.
Sanskrit *ner* = man, male person, the original or eternal man. The
  name of Arjuna.
English synonyms: man, mankind, human race, humanity.

Soul
Greek *psyche* = breath, life, spirit, soul, heart.
Latin *anima* = air, breeze, wind, breath, principle of life, soul, spirit.
Sanskrit *atman* = the soul, mind, spirit.
English synonyms: anima, spirit, soul, life.

Acknowledgements

The publishers and author wish to acknowledge the permission of the following to use copyright material:

The Oxford University Press for *Wilfred Owen* by Jon Stallworthy.

Collins Publishers for *Mister God, this is Anna* by Fynn.

Penguin Books Ltd. for *Steppenwolf* by Herman Hesse

M. B. Yeats, Miss Anne Yeats and the Macmillan Company of London and Basingstoke for *The Collected Poems* of W. B. Yeats.

Bibliography

Abhishiktananda SACCINANDA, ISPCK, 1974
Adamson, Joy BORN FREE, Collins, 1960
Assaglioli, Roberto PSYCHOSYNTHESIS, Hobbs, Dorman and Co,
  1965
Bach, Richard JONATHAN LIVINGSTON SEAGULL,
  Turnstone Press, 1972
Barth, Karl CHRISTIAN DOGMATICS, T and T Clark
  Vol III, 1961
  Vol IV, 1958
Benson, R. M. THE RELIGIOUS VOCATION, A and R Mowbray,
  1939
Blake, William COMPLETE WRITINGS edited by G. Keynes, OUP
  Paperbacks, 1969
Blue, Lionel TO HEAVEN WITH SCRIBES AND PHARISEES,
  Darton, Longman and Todd, 1975
Cherry-Garrard, Apsley THE WORST JOURNEY IN THE
  WORLD, Chatto and Windus, 1952
Church of England Doctrine Commission CHRISTIAN
  BELIEVING, SPCK 1976
Dechanet, Jean YOGA AND GOD, Search Press, 1974
Dominian, Jack CYCLES OF AFFIRMATION, Darton, Longman
  and Todd, 1976
Durrell, Gerald MENAGERIE MANOR, Penguin, 1970
Fullerson, M. C. BY A NEW AND LIVING WAY, Stuart and
  Watkins, 1971
Fynn MISTER GOD, THIS IS ANNA, Collins 1974
Georgen, Donald THE SEXUAL CELIBATE, SPCK, 1976

Hesse, Hermann DAMIAN, Panther, 1974
   STEPPENWOLF, Allen Lane, the Penguin Press 1971
John of the Cross, St COMPLETE WORKS, Anthony Clarke, 1974
Johnson, Samuel SELECTED WRITINGS, Penguin 1968
Julian, Mother REVELATIONS OF DIVINE LOVE, Penguin 1966
Jung, C. G. MAN AND HIS SYMBOLS, Aldous Books, 1975
Kipling, Rudyard KIM, Macmillan Papermac, 1972
Le Saux, H GURU AND DISCIPLE, SPCK, 1974
Lonergan, Bernard METHOD IN THEOLOGY, Darton, Longman
   and Todd, 1972
MacQuarrie, John PRINCIPLES OF CHRISTIAN THEOLOGY,
   SCM, 1974
NEW ENGLISH BIBLE, OUP and CUP, 1970
Poulain, R. P. THE GRACES OF INTERIOR PRAYER, Kegan
   Paul, 1919
Scott, R. F. SCOTT'S LAST EXPEDITION, T and T Clark, 1958
Seymour-Smith, Martin SEX AND SOCIETY, Hodder and
   Stoughton, 1976
Sherrard, Philip CHRISTIANITY AND EROS, SPCK, 1976
Solovyev, Vladimir THE MEANING OF LOVE, SCM, 1950
Sri Aurobindo THE ADVENTURE OF CONSCIOUSNESS, Sat-
   prem, 1973
Stallworthy, Jon WILFRED OWEN, OUP and Chatto and Windus,
   1974
Ware, Timothy THE ORTHODOX CHURCH, Penguin 1964
Williams, Charles RELIGION AND LOVE IN DANTE, Dacre
   Press, undated
Williams, Charles THE FIGURE OF BEATRICE, Faber and Faber,
   1943
Wilson, Edward DIARY OF THE TERRA NOVA EXPEDITION,
   Blandford Press, 1972
Wood, Ernest YOGA, Penguin, 1967